Legacy

Memoirs, Messages for My Beloved Family,
and Commentary for the Times

Michael A. Sable

ISBN: 978-1-0879-6369-3 (hardcover)

Printed in the United States of America

Edited by Diane Stockwell

Designed by Eric Engdahl

Published posthumously on behalf of the author
by Sylvia Sable and Eric Engdahl in 2023

Acknowledgments

Thank you Maria,
For your endless patience with me and for your help providing me with the physical means necessary to complete this work.

Thank you Sylvia,
For opening the doors of technology for me countless times, which inspired me to organize my ideas and to create this book.

Thank you Stephen,
For inspiring me to explore our family lineage through our eldest relatives' stories and photographs; and for providing family history through our own genealogical studies, parts of which I have included here.

Thank you to my parents,
Who stoked my determination to complete this writing through their enthusiasm while sampling the work-in-progress.

Thank you Eric,
For helping me to use the technology and devices which allowed me to store and access the many sections of this work and for putting it into its final form.

Thank you Aunt Jeannie,
For sharing your photos and knowledge of the Sable and Bruzdowski branches of our family tree.

Thank you to everyone who shared your memories, providing me so much material upon request to include in this book.

Most of all, thank you God for giving me time to pull together the efforts of all of those mentioned above, and to create this gift for all of us to enjoy!

Contents

Introduction   vii

Chapter 1
Life Comes At You   1

Chapter 2
My Beloved Wife Maria   13

Chapter 3
Your Wildest Dreams Come True   31

Chapter 4
Living Within the Community   41

    Part 1: On Role Models   41

    Part 2: Giving Back to the Community   46

Chapter 5
My Beloved Family   57

    Part 1: How Special is That?   58

    Part 2: The Invitation   64

    Part 3: Martin Sexton   66

Chapter 6
Parents and Parenting   69

    Part 1: Parents   69

      The Vacation Series   74

      Principles, Life Lessons, and Parenting   99

      The World Travel Series   108

    Part 2: Parenting   123

Chapter 7

Grandparents and Roots 147

Part 1: Santangelo 147

Part 2: Sable 176

Chapter 8

Family Stories 213

The Sables 216

Felese, Demarest, and Haggerty 219

The Farris Clan 226

The Martowitcz Crew 245

Cousins San Angelo 253

The Barankovichs 258

Santangelo Theatre 262

The Gillman and the Garvey 266

Chapter 9

Mike Sable: The Man and His Passions 269

Passion 1: Mike's Family in Photos 269

Passion 2: The Guitarist 287

Passion 3: The Mechanic and His Fast Cars 306

Passion 4: Wilderness Man 321

Passion 5: Chef Mike 351

Chapter 10

Going to School in the 60s and 70s 365

Chapter 11

Commentary for These Times 371

Introduction

Writing this book has felt like fulfilling a premonition. As a young boy I often wondered who would preserve all of the memories and stories our eldest relatives told us? Who would still tell the tales passed down through the generations? Who would fill in the colors of our ancestors' personalities? Who would know our family history and how we all came to live in America?

As a young man I took every opportunity to ask our eldest relatives questions at family gatherings, listening intently to their stories. I figured if it was important enough for them to talk about, well then there must be some value there.

It turns out I have a very good memory, something relatives have verified repeatedly over the years. I've often heard, "I never would have remembered that until you started telling us the story Mike, and then it all came back to me."

To me, legacy means a gift that I leave behind for you.

Included here are stories of the good and the difficult times that we remember, stories that answer questions we've had about the history of our family, stories that bring up great old memories that we would have otherwise forgotten.

Some chapters include predictions of events that might occur after my passing. Some portions of *Legacy* may even offer advice.

Humor will be included, as well as discussion of some of the more sobering social issues of the times. Discussion will also be had regarding ALS, the terminal condition that will soon shorten the time that we have to share together.

Surprisingly there are some blessings that come with experiencing the condition we know as Lou Gehrig's Disease, or ALS—Amyotrophic Lateral Sclerosis.

Since being diagnosed with ALS I've come to the deep realization that I am in fact the luckiest man in the world. Lou Gehrig also stated this in his farewell speech to his fans at Yankee Stadium.

As it was for Lou Gehrig, dealing with ALS has opened my eyes to all of the special people I have come to know and appreciate in my lifetime. People who I now realize have really cared about me.

I have also noted that along with the acronym ALS comes the title CEO! My family and friends seem to just show up and help me with what would normally be considered routine tasks. What's up with that? (I've just got to inject a little bit of humor along the way here!)

Another blessing I've been granted is time to reflect upon my life. Time to truly appreciate the people around me, and revisit the wonderful places I've been to. Time to relive the many experiences I've enjoyed over the past sixty-plus years.

I've lived a long and storied life!

I've learned to count my blessings, and to encourage others to count theirs as well.

I want to offer you all these memories and reflections in this book, *Legacy*. The time that I've spent working on this has brought back many great memories that I now get to enjoy again and share with all of you. What a wonderful gift has been bestowed upon me!

I hope that reading *Legacy* brings you as much joy as writing it has brought me.

It's a blessing for me to have this opportunity to record what I have learned about our family over the years. I hope that it serves us well, as well as our descendants, to study and enjoy these writings in discussion at family gatherings, now and for many years to come!

Mike Sable
October 19, 2021

Chapter 1

Life Comes At You

In late October 2018 I was officially diagnosed with Amyotrophic Lateral Sclerosis (ALS), the condition more commonly known as Lou Gehrig's Disease.

Finally getting the diagnosis had taken nearly ten months of doctor's appointments, tests, and trips to regional hospitals and medical centers specializing in neurological disorders. The condition is terminal. Life expectancy varies widely because ALS manifests differently in each patient. In my case the characteristic decay of neural pathways first became troubling enough to seek medical attention during the winter of 2017-18, when it got very hard for me to breathe.

Rocky Balboa

Here's a little insight into how I have chosen to deal with the ups and downs that life has offered me.

I was flipping channels one night recently and settled on watching the movie *Rocky Balboa,* the sixth installment of the Rocky franchise. Released in 2006, it goes deep into philosophy. I've personally adopted a lot of the philosophy Rocky shares in this movie. Here's some of Rocky's wisdom that seemed to speak directly to me:

"The world ain't all sunshine and rainbows. It's a very mean and nasty place and it will beat you to your knees and keep you there permanently if you let it."

"You, me, or nobody is gonna hit as hard as life. But it ain't how hard you hit; it's about how hard you can get hit and keep moving forward. How much you can take and keep moving forward."

The Most Amazing Day

In October of 2018 I found myself at a cafeteria table at Strong Memorial Hospital in Rochester, New York thoroughly enjoying a grilled cheese sandwich and a bowl of tomato soup. A good portion of my family sat around me. My sisters, my mom, and my son Stephen had met me and my wife Maria for lunch at the hospital to support us. It was truly heartwarming to have such a wonderful and loving family by our side—we are truly blessed! By this time we all understood the testing I was about to undergo would likely result in a diagnosis and, finally, a true glimpse into what road could lie ahead for me.

Strong Memorial Hospital had an electric shock test that would grade the performance of the neural system in strength and acuity. By comparing the results of my neural network's performance with that of the average unaffected person the doctors would be able to identify the nature of my neural disorder and hopefully recommend treatment options.

The test would target the phrenic nerve, which carries the signal stimulating the muscles of the diaphragm which expand the lungs. The shocks that would be administered were intimidating to me, to say the least. A team of neurologists performed the tests with the most sophisticated equipment available while my family anxiously waited for Maria and I to return to the waiting area.

Meanwhile, my daughter Sylvia was in New York City, awaiting word from us. We had already arranged for the test results to be sent to the world-renowned Neurology and Pulmonary Departments at the hospital at Columbia University in New York City, right near Sylvia's home. Maria and I planned to travel to Columbia the next day to consult with Dr. Mark Ginsburg, the best surgeon in the world for care and remediation of these types of breathing disorders. Dr. Ginsburg would have already studied the results of the tests from Strong Memorial, and we were all hoping to plan a route forward.

I could see the expressions on the doctors' faces while they performed the electric shock tests at Strong. I'm sure they tried to conceal it, but I could tell whatever they were seeing was not good. Maria did not say anything at the time, but later she told me she had gotten the same impression. After the team of neurologists studied the test results in private they called us both into the office to give us the news. It was not good—I had ALS.

Maria and I headed out to tell the family. No one was really ready to accept what I was telling them. Maria quietly nodded her head that it was true—the doctors had diagnosed me with ALS. Many questions naturally followed, but the reality was not going to change. Maria and I had already made the arrangements to switch the nature of the appointments at Columbia with Dr. Ginsburg from consultation for remediation to having the Columbia team give us a second opinion on the diagnosis.

Gathered there in our own little corner of the lobby at Strong Memorial, my family offered the most amazing show of love and support I could have ever imagined! They committed to accompanying Maria and I to New York City to meet up with Sylvia, even insisting we'd all stick together for the two additional days of tests and consultation to get a second opinion from the neurologists at Columbia!

We all returned to Keuka for a sleepless night before heading out bright and early the next morning for New York City. Stephen would drive his car with Maria, my mom, and me. My brother Art had also volunteered to join us, and would drive my sisters Julie, Be, and Lisa. That way we had two good drivers who could hold their own in city traffic while simultaneously taking directions from the robot voice emanating from the dashboard. We had all agreed to keep our brother Andy out of the loop, at least for the next few days. He was out of town receiving critical training for his new job flying corporate jets for Corning Incorporated, and he would have insisted on joining us if he had known, jeopardizing his job. So we collectively decided it would be best to just not tell him anything yet. (He's still mad at us over that! Get over it, Andy. We love you and we're all so proud of you.)

We arrived in New York City later in the morning and went straight to the hospital where the first of our appointments were scheduled. Finding parking was almost impossible. Round and round the blocks we went—we got one hell of a tour of that part of the city that morning! Once finally parked, as we made our way to the hospital I was amazed by both the sheer numbers of people walking along the sidewalks and the rapid pace of their collective stride.

It was like a snake of never-ending upright humans winding its way up the block, and not one of them was speaking. Head up, mouth shut, carry on!

Once inside the hospital not much changed in terms of overcrowding and the fast pace, except now we had a roof over our heads. That hospital was a very busy place, but we managed to find our way to the appointments and tests without any issues. We left the hospital late in the afternoon and drove back over the George Washington Bridge and into New Jersey.

We arrived at the hotel in Fort Lee where we had reservations for the night, and then the games began. The process of finding and securing our rooms at this joint was unlike anything we'd ever experienced before. The scene that unfolded was like a farce, which while initially frustrating, also provided some comic relief from the stress of driving in the city and the overall experiences of the day thus far. We just needed a moment to take it all in, and then it was funny.

We entered what appeared to be the office for our check-in only to find an empty desk, without a soul in sight. Ringing the bell on the front desk and calling out for assistance didn't seem to rouse anyone. We finally got the attention of two sleepy looking individuals coming out of the back room, who it seemed weren't accustomed to checking in hotel guests with "reservations."

Yes, it appeared that this particular establishment regularly checked in guests who showed up unannounced, but rarely anyone with reservations. And the typical clientele apparently didn't bother to check out when they left either. That may have explained why the desk had no record of which rooms were occupied, which had been vacated and required making up, and which rooms were ready to accept guests.

The desk clerks kept wordlessly exchanging looks, and each time we were issued keys to a room they'd nod their heads yes, or shake their heads no, or throw up their hands in an "I don't know" gesture! My best guess? It seemed the desk clerks were running their own little side hustle in the hotel by daylight, renting rooms by the hour for guests with no interest in sleeping. Not one of them knew the status of any given room at any given moment.

As we arrived at our rooms the fiasco continued. Some rooms hadn't been cleaned, so we headed back to the front desk for another round with the clueless clerks. Behind some doors we found rooms that were supposed to have two beds but there'd only be one, or vice versa. We also opened the door to another room only to find a couple wrestling between the sheets! Later that night we were treated to unexpected guests entering our room with their own key, with a six-pack, a bottle of Jack, and ready to party! They were as happy to see us as we were to see them, especially when we all learned that the entire hotel was sold out for the night. We ended up with one of our rooms with Sylvia in one bed and MJ and Lisa sharing the other! We even moved furniture from room to room to create a special bed out of two chairs to accommodate my disability of not being able to breathe while lying down.

I can only imagine what the next guests thought about that when they entered the room the following day. After getting cleaned up and with the rooms set up the group went out to get dinner. Maria chose to remain behind at the hotel with me.

I was in a bit of a funk. We had seen both the pulmonary surgeon, Dr. Ginsburg, and a neurologist that afternoon. They had both agreed with the doctors at Strong Memorial that in fact I was suffering from ALS. We still had one more appointment the following morning with a pulmonologist, but by then the reality of how much my life was about to change was starting to sink in. It was all hitting me pretty hard.

Maria felt shock and sadness as well. Yet seeing her suffering through all of this was far worse than my wondering what it was going to be like to die from ALS. I was starting to see that my family and Maria were suffering even more from this diagnosis than I was.

Sitting with Maria and sharing a glass of wine together in the hotel room, it suddenly became very clear to me what I needed to do, what I wanted to do, and what I was going to do with the time I had left. It was staring right back at me through the pain in the eyes of the people who loved me.

Two years after I had that sudden awakening in the hotel room with Maria, I came across a quote that sums up exactly where my head was at in that moment:

"You never know how strong you are until being strong is the only choice you have."

And so it would be. There wasn't any choice. There wasn't any sense agonizing over something that we couldn't change. The only way forward for me was going to be just that—moving forward. I had to pick myself back up after the blow I'd just been dealt and move forward with resolute discipline and single-minded determination. Maintaining a calm dignity and keeping a reassuring demeanor while I went about getting my affairs in order, for my Maria and for my children. For my entire family. Setting an example for them to follow when life deals us a terrific blow.

The first test of my new mindset came the very next day as we left New York City for the drive home. I looked back across the Hudson River at the city skyline and I heard this little voice inside me saying, "Take a good long look Mike. You're never going to see that again."

But then a much louder voice yelled back, "NO! NO, MIKE! STOP THAT TRAIN AND GET OFF!" Right then and there I made a promise to myself. I would never allow that type of attitude into my thoughts again. No more "never agains" for this guy. No way!

Several years before, I had already determined that I had lived a long and storied life. A life from which I would depart with no regrets. A life where if I'd missed doing something that I really thought I might have wanted to do, well, that's okay. If I've missed out on things that I might have planned on doing, well, then that's alright too. Because I've been blessed. Blessed to have shared this life with the people I have loved the most.

And as for anything that I may not have gotten to do, I was blessed with having done other things even more extraordinary than I could have ever dreamed about, even in my wildest dreams!

Maria Living with ALS

I laughed so hard I cried the first time I reviewed my reply to an email I was getting ready to send to Marilee, an old friend of mine. She had been emailing me for a few days by that point and had gotten no response. Growing increasingly worried she'd sent me an email with the "Subject" line in all caps:

> MIKE I'M GETTING WORRIED. PLEASE SOMEONE, ANYONE,
> ANSWER ME! I'M GETTING WORRIED. . .

Keep in mind that, at this point nearly a year and a half after my diagnosis, due to the paralysis my typing ability is limited to my right thumb and using my iPhone. In reviewing my response to my friend I realized that I had been rushing my typing, and that my own desperation in trying to finally get this reply to her came through loud and clear. It was obvious in my writing style—all run-on sentences and more than a few run-on paragraphs, so much so it was even funny, and offered an accurate portrayal of a day in my life with ALS. So I cut out a portion of the email and edited it for everyone to enjoy.

Email to Marilee, January 2021

Not to worry! You're not bugging me at all Marilee. Ya gotta laugh if you're in my position right now LOL! Seriously, thank you for your concern and you don't need to worry. I'm still just fine! I have had this gadget in my hand now at least 5 times since yesterday morning with the expressed intent of getting a reply off to you. BUT...

It is pretty difficult for me to complete anything I set out to do anymore, not having any means of fulfilling my most basic needs. Things that we all take for granted. Like even right now. I was just trying to start an email to you about 3 hours ago. Then MARIA, MARIA! Can you please get me my phone and set it up on my left leg for me to write? Then my Mom stopped in for a visit. MARIA, MARIA I need a towel on my lap I'm naked and please take off my ventilator mask so I can talk to my Mom and oh Maria was just about to put a frittata in the oven and then my sisters both stopped in to see if we needed anything oh MARIA, MARIA, oh MARIA. . .My bowels have decided that it is time. NOW. (Remember I took that laxative?) That requires Maria, MARIA, MARIA!, the ventilator needs to be moved to the bathroom and then a sling lift ride to the special chair and a chair ride to the toilet and please put the mask back on I can't breathe and I need the urinal held while I wait and she had just put the frittata in the oven oh yes the frittata and then the lift for clean up afterwards in a special chair and then the ventilator and the mask back on and hanging in a sling for wound care before returning to my living chair put a fresh cover down first and then the food was ready for spoon feeding me and then FaceTime ringing with my daughter on the other end MARIA, MARIA, MARIA! Please put a towel over my naked lap again and take off the ventilator so I can talk and put the mask back on I can't breathe but my nose has an itch and then time for morphine MARIA, MARIA! and then please pick up this gadget and get it positioned correctly for my right thumb to type and everything with Maria helping between her cooking, her own potty trip, and feeding herself and then stoking the woodstove and now I have the ALS acid tears and I can't see well enough to type anymore and the cats are crying they need food MARIA, MARIA! MARIA!!!! and then I opened my email and saw that you were worried about me, Marilee.

You really are a good egg Marilee! Show this to Craig and have a good laugh with me! I'm going to have a drink! Or two! Doctors have no understanding of the proper wine to medication ratio. I could write a book about that! I promise to try later to write you. I do have things that I want to say and yes I'm okay and this damn battery is dead again oh MARIA, MARIA! LOL!

TWYL. MIKE PS.... MORE MORPHINE AND PORT WINE PLEASE MARIA, MARIA? MARIA? MARIA? Are you still here Maria? LOL, GOD BLESS MY MARIA! (ALL THAT WITH ONLY ONE THUMB!)

Going in one more round when you don't think you can—

—that's what makes
all the difference
in your life."

Rocky Balboa

Chapter 2

My Beloved Wife Maria

When Maria and I first started dating one thing we had in common was our marital status—we were both divorced. And we had (and still have) many other things in common:

1. We both have two children, a boy (elder) and a girl (younger).

2. Our four children are from the same generation, ranging in age from thirty-one to thirty-nine.

3. Our four children all graduated from good colleges.

4. Our four children hold good jobs.

5. Neither of us completed college.

6. We both love food, and we love to cook together.

7. We both love wine, and we love to drink it together.

8. We both love gardening together, growing vegetables and landscaping.

9. We both enjoy dining out.

10. We both enjoy boating.

11. We both enjoy camping.

12. We both enjoy traveling and cozy accommodations.

13. We both love our family.

14. We both love and enjoy one another's company.

We, both, enjoy and love children and family. We share the human experience. Together. It's easy to see why we fell in love and got married—we have an awful lot in common!

Back to where I began this chapter. When we began dating . . . Well, I'll go first.

I had been through one heck of a roller coaster ride with my life for the past few years. My children had finished high school and both were attending Cornell University over in Ithaca, New York. I had recently given up my independent mechanical contracting business in favor of the stability of working for a large construction management company.

After only two years with the company I was offered the opportunity in 2008 to join forces with twenty-four of my colleagues to form our own construction management firm specializing in building schools in New York state. The nature of my new job with Campus Construction Management Group meant putting in long hours and staying away from home for months or years to be closer to my work sites. My first project under the banner of our new company was in Olean where I was housed in a hotel for the duration of the project. I was financially better off than I had ever been before. But I was alone, without a mate, and away from any social life I may have had, with two failed marriages behind me. So on the one hand I was in a very good place with my career, but on the other hand feeling quite alone. I had no one to share with.

Now for my Maria. Her son Dave was off on his own living in Charlotte, North Carolina with his wife and daughter, while her daughter Dana was finishing college and living with Maria at home in Olean.

Maria had been through some rough times recently. She'd just lost her mother, who she adored and was very close to, in December of 2009. To make matters worse, her nineteen-year career with a wholesale plumbing and contracting company had suddenly and unexpectedly ended.

Maria was not only heartbroken over losing her mother, she was unemployed and struggling to make ends meet. Her unemployment benefits were about to expire, and there weren't any jobs available in her area where she could expect to make a salary equivalent to what she had been earning.

She had a mortgage to pay, and Maria worried that she had to keep her house. Dana was still attending St. Bonaventure University, and Maria already had a substantial investment at stake, so maintaining ownership of the property was essential.

Maria was also without a life partner with whom she could share her heartbreak and misfortune. She'd lost her interests in gardening and cooking and didn't see any way to change her predicament. Maria was slowly sinking into depression.

And then life changed. Forever. For the both of us!

The Night We Met at AJ's

I remember a song from the classic musical, *West Side Story*, that went something like this: "Maria, Maria, Mariaaaah! I just met a girl named Mariaah!"

Well . . . As the story goes . . .

It was early August, 2010. I was getting really deep into my latest project in the field—my own project for the first time, out in the hills of western New York State.

Field managing a relatively large and very difficult project in my young career, I also had a stake in its success. I was working within our newly created construction management company. Considering this was a $28 million dollar capital project for a new client, which included six schools in the city of Olean, I had a lot on my shoulders, to say the least.

I was on my way back to the hotel suite which was to be my home for the duration of the two-and-a-half year project. I decided to stop at my local watering hole, AJ's Bar, for a cold one, just to settle me down. It had been a rather challenging day for me and my entire team, to put it mildly.

I went in and as I walked by the bar, I was muttering something odd to myself, something like, "I've been inside myself. I've seen tomorrow, and it's going to be okay . . . " Kind of a mantra of sorts.

Then I saw her for the first time. I looked up and couldn't help but notice her. We briefly made eye contact. (Some days later, she told me she had heard me muttering as I passed by her perch at the bar. "Boy, this guy's nuts," she thought.)

Two beers later I saw her bend over the pool table while taking a shot. I figured, I just had to go over and meet this girl. Well, I did go over and meet that girl. Obviously, the story does not end there.

We had a great time shooting pool and talking over a few beers that evening. I walked her to her car behind AJ's Bar and we made plans to get together again for a dinner out.

I watched her drive out of the parking lot that night, turning right and heading down North Twenty-Fourth Street—a dead-end street in that direction. I remember thinking, "She must live down there. Alright. That's a decent neighborhood."

We met out for dinner regularly after that night, probably two or three times a week. Many dinner dates later she had become comfortable enough with me to invite me over to her home to meet her friends for a fall barbecue on her backyard deck. She told me her address: 203 North Twenty-First Street.

At the assigned date and at the assigned time I headed to AJ's Bar, made a right turn just as she had done the first night we met, and proceeded down North Twenty-Fourth Street to the end. There was no house at 203 North Twenty-Fourth Street, just the west end of the soccer field for the local parochial high school. And there wasn't any barbecue going on there either!

My heart literally sank in my chest. "What a way to blow me off. And I was just thinking about how well we seemed to be hitting it off. Now this? It must've been just too good to be true."

Sitting there in my truck with my heart broken, it suddenly occurred to me Maria had told me her address was 203 North Twenty-First Street, not 203 North Twenty-Fourth Street where I was parked! I turned around and quickly made my way over to her house.

We all enjoyed a wonderful barbecue and great company while overlooking the east end of the soccer field from her backyard deck. And the best part was I could tell Maria's friends had given me a thumbs-up!

After dinner was over and her friends had left, I stayed to help Maria clean up. I told her about my mix-up with the address. Why, I asked, had she headed down North Twenty-Fourth Street to go home that night we met at AJ's?

Maria's replied, "Well, you know we both had a few beers that night at AJ's. There was no way I was going back out on the main road through town to get to North Twenty-First Street after having those beers! I just went down North Twenty-Fourth Street and drove across the soccer field and into my driveway!"

Ooooooh Baby! Are we on the same page or what? A woman after my own heart. And so, as the story goes, the rest is history.

The Route 86 Tailgate Incident

There has been a lot of joking over the years about how gullible Maria can be some-times. But truth be told, the funny stories I often tell about Maria have more to do with me loving her innocence than any extra gullibility on her part. I do put her gullibility to the test quite often though. She's a good egg, and she'll laugh right along with me whenever I catch her off guard.

I have to include one classic Maria story for good measure.

The Olean hotel that I called home for the entire first year I knew Maria was replac-ing all of its mattresses in the fall of 2011. I asked what the hotel was doing with the old ones. I knew they were not really very old since it was a relatively new hotel, and the mattresses were in great condition.

I was told they were being sold to a small hotel downtown, and yes, there were ex-tras available to purchase for a relatively small fee.

Being an upstanding member of the populous Steuben County branch of the Sa-ble Family Clan, I knew we all had rooms in need of extra beds. Christmas was just around the corner—I thought about what great gifts these mattresses would make. So I went out and rented a U Haul trailer, one about as large as my entire full size Chevy truck.

A little while later I showed up at Maria's place with the trailer loaded with mat-tresses, soon to be eastbound on Route 86. I was all set to go, heading for the Sable family headquarters out in Steuben County. After filling Maria in on the details of the plan I hit the highway.

For the first few miles or so I regularly checked my rearview mirrors to see how the trailer was hauling. The view of the trailer filled the mirrors with what looked like a very large orange and white box. Then the prankster in me took over.

I picked up my cell phone and called my Maria. She asked how it was going. I paused briefly and said, "I was thinking about you, and l just wanted to call to hear your voice." That kind of tickled her just right. We struck up a conversation that contin-ued on for several minutes. That old Mike Sable charm had kicked in and she had forgotten all about the fact that I was towing the trailer. The deception was going along just perfectly!

Just about when we were ready to end the call, I mentioned there was a large orange and white truck right on my tail, so close that my view out the rear of my truck was completely obstructed. I needed to try and shake him off. She asked me to call her back when it was safe.

I called her back soon after that, telling her I hadn't been able to shake him. That pesky orange and white truck was seemingly glued to my tailgate. Maria wanted to know my location. She was concerned and thought she should call the state police at the Belmont exit and have them pull over the offending vehicle. I told her that I'd try to shake the tailgater again and call her back.

Similar phone exchanges continued over the next fifty miles or so, with my continuing to complain about that pesky orange and white truck, which was *still* tailgating me. l exited the highway. I called her again once I was safely parked in my Pulteney driveway.

I mentioned that the trailer had been a pleasure to tow and that the mattresses had arrived home with me without incident. I think the way I said "without incident" set off an illuminating light of sorts for Maria.

It took quite some time for my Maria to forgive me for that prank. To this day whenever I mention it, she waves a finger at me with a cute little grin on her face!

I Finally Learn What Love Is
(AKA The Underwear Story)

Maria and I had been dating for about a year by this point. We made plans to hit a couple of the stores in Olean that evening to pick up a few odds and ends.

First stop was the local Walmart Superstore. We both needed things that we figured we could get there. Maria is very organized when it comes to shopping, so naturally, we had to make a list.

I told Maria I needed to buy a few packs of underwear and I hadn't been able to find the kind I liked at Walmart recently. It was a very popular brand and she insisted they'd have them. I repeated I was sure that I was right, and we set the wager at $5.00.

We arrived at Walmart and split up, each with our list in hand. Since I knew the underwear I wanted would not be found at that store I didn't even bother looking again and just moved on to the next item on my list. After getting the other items on my list I made my way to the checkout area as agreed and waited for Maria. After a few minutes I spotted her making her way towards me.

She had the biggest smile I'd ever seen as she approached me clutching a few packs of underwear in her hand. I could literally feel the joy coming from her as she thrust the underwear at me, saying, "See! I told you they would have them! They have *everything* at this store!" I admitted she was right, I was wrong, and shaking my head I handed over the five bucks I owed her.

Fast forward to the next day as my crew was getting ready to head home from the office. I don't remember the exact context of the small talk at the time, but our administrative assistant Kathy was asking Mike Church, a colleague at Campus Construction Management, how he would define love? I knew I would be asked next, and I remember struggling to think of how to answer.

Sure enough, the question came to me. Without knowing how to answer exactly, I found myself telling the story about Maria finding me that underwear the evening before at Walmart. Laughing, Kathy asked, "Do I really want to ask what underwear has to do with love?"

It was like a bolt of lightning hit me. "Yes! Exactly!" I replied. "I'll tell you, when Maria held up those packs of underwear with that incredible smile on her face, it made me as happy as I have ever been! I just knew right then what love meant to me. Love, to me, was seeing her happy, making her smile!" (No matter that she was right and I was wrong. That made her smile too!)

Mike Church just looked up at me and said something I will never forget: "Mike, I didn't know you had it in you."

Pilot Coffee

There's a Pilot truck stop at the Kanona exit off of Route 86 near Bath, West New York.

Let's just be clear about that. It's certainly not New York, not Upstate New York, and not Western New York.

Kind of like West Virginia, as opposed to Virginia. We locals consider our particular portion of New York State a separate state altogether. That's why we call it West New York!

Now, back to that Pilot truck stop. There are twelve pumps under the main canopy where motorists can get gas. Inside the main building there's a pretty big convenience store and deli style food service. A Subway restaurant adjoins the main building. There are over twenty filling stations for the tractor trailers in a gated area, with separate entrances and exits to the facility, store, showers, etc. exclusively for the truck drivers.

The Pilot Travel Center name is the biggest player in the truck stop business in this part of the state. They're well known for cleanliness, accessibility, pricing, and of course, great coffee. And there are a lot of these Pilot Travel Centers along the main highways.

Back in those years, around 2010 up through 2017, Maria and I traveled an awful lot up and down those highways. We lived separately—Maria had her home and her job at Dresser-Rand in Olean, and I had my house at Keuka while also living temporarily near my project sites. We did manage to spend our weekends together at least.

Usually we traveled alone to see one another. Sometimes we traveled together depending on what we had planned for the weekend. On that day the wicked prankster inside me emerged once again.

We'd just made a pit stop to grab a coffee and snacks for the ride that day. I was just approaching highway speed, ready to engage the cruise control, when we came up behind a huge shining stainless steel tanker truck and trailer. As we got closer, I looked over at Maria and exclaimed, "Look honey! This tanker truck says PILOT.

BEST COFFEE ON THE INTERSTATE. Can you believe that? And I always thought they made their coffee fresh in each store . . ."

All she did was glance up from her phone briefly and reply, "Wow. I thought they made their coffee fresh too! I wonder if everyone knows that isn't true."

I don't remember how much time had passed but eventually we approached another exit that had a Pilot Travel Center. I got Maria's attention, and pointing my finger towards the Travel Center while sounding a little surprised I simply stated, "Would you look at that?" She looked over just as we were passing by a huge shining stainless steel tanker truck and trailer with the Pilot logo on it emptying a full load of diesel fuel into the underground tanks at the truck filling stations!

My right cheek still smarts a bit whenever I turn to look over at Maria when we travel!

I Ask My Maria to Marry Me

It was Christmas time 2014. Maria's son Dave, his wife Sarah, and their daughters Maddie and Ava (no Clara yet) had made the trip from Charlotte, North Carolina to be with Maria and I for our annual Christmas visit. That year we were gathering in Olean at Maria's house.

It was our traditional holiday visit. Dana and Hags (Brian, her future husband) were there too, as we all enjoyed great food, wine, and watched the children with their gifts. In the evening after dinner we had retired to the living room. Maddie was talking with her grandma in the kitchen while Maria straightened up and packed the leftovers for everyone to take.

During dinner Maria had mentioned that she and I would be heading over to my place at Keuka for the weekend to attend my brother Andy's wedding that Sunday. I heard Maddie from the kitchen ask Maria, "Grandma, when are you and Mike going to get married?"

Well, at least up until that point, I'd been avoiding the subject of marriage. Things were going quite well in our relationship just as it was. At least I thought so. We had touched on the subject of our commitment to one another when we had first begun dating. We had committed to being exclusive and not dating others, and I felt good about that. But now I wondered if that was enough.

Maria and Maddie talking about marriage in the kitchen suddenly got me thinking about how Maria was feeling. We'd been together for a little over four years. Maddie's innocent question for her grandma had me wondering if I should be expecting an ultimatum soon. I was also well aware that marriage had not gone well for me in the past, not once but twice.

I wondered if making any changes to my relationship with Maria might jinx what was cruising along just fine. I certainly didn't want that! Unfortunately, my behavior quickly revealed my discomfort with the subject. To say the least, my reaction was not well thought out, and did not at all reflect what was in my heart.

Once our holiday guests had departed for their ride home to North Carolina, I told Maria how I was feeling. I had overheard her and Maddie talking about us getting married and said I thought she was discussing my brother's wedding with her granddaughter only to force a conversation about our own relationship. I felt like I was being pressured to decide to get married right then and there in front of her family, and I was not happy about that. We parted ways without resolving the issue. Worst of all, we canceled our plans to attend Andy's wedding that weekend as a couple.

I can't put into words how quickly my thoughts and emotions went from feeling angry to actually being sick to my stomach. Had I just ruined my hopes of spending the rest of my life with the one woman who had taught me what love was really all about?

I was truly beside myself. I was angry at myself for my knee-jerk reaction to an innocent question from a wonderful little girl. And I was sick over the possibility that I had ruined what was the best relationship I'd ever had.

After some soul searching, I realized how ridiculous it was that I could have gotten upset over Maddie and Maria talking about what was truly, and certainly through Maddie's eyes, an innocent question about her Grandma's happiness.

And then it hit me like a ton of bricks: What would life be like without having Maria to share it with each and every day? I knew right then that I had to ask this wonderful human being, my Maria, to join my life forever as my wife.

And so it was to be. And so it is today! I love you, my Maria.

Psych?

Psychic Psycho or Psycho Psychic? That is the question. Which is it? Which of these two personas best describes Maria and which best describes me? Let's dig a little bit deeper with another story and see what that tells us.

Now let me say this—Maria and I really have this thing we share, when two people just seem to have a sense of the other person and connect in certain ways. We are somehow aware of the actions, thoughts and feelings of the other person.

The simplest example of this may be when couples finish each other's sentences. But that can easily be explained by each partner's familiarity with the other's speech patterns. That happens with many couples after being together for a few years.

Another example that can sometimes be explained is when partners pick up their phones to call each other at the exact same moment. If there's a routine already in place, like someone always calls when they leave work or when they get home, predictable patterns are at work here, at least to some extent.

But what about when familiarity and patterns are not in play? That really happens with Maria and I, and it's happening more and more often.

And then there are the times when something entirely different is at play. Or more accurately, when someone is playing games . . .

I was on my way home to the house in Olean one day after work, it must have been early October 2012. Maria and I had been together since early August 2010, so a little over two years by then—plenty of time for those psychic moments or intuitions to have begun in a romantic relationship.

I stopped by the wine store as usual for my pinot noir. Sue, the owner, was at the register. We'd developed quite a friendship during my time in Olean. Not only did Sue own the wine store, she had become one of Maria's closest friends at work, at Dresser-Rand in Olean where Maria had recently taken a job. We all knew Maria was getting noticed by the top brass upstairs at Dresser for her experience and knowledge with mechanical drawings. Maria fit in well at Dresser, a high-tech engineering and manufacturing firm. Sue always asked me about Maria when I'd see her at the store.

When I stopped in at the store that evening, Sue had a big smile on her face. She pulled me aside and quietly asked, "Have you heard anything from Maria yet about what happened at work this afternoon?" I replied that I hadn't. She said Maria had been "called upstairs just after lunch." I told her I really had no idea what that meant, but I hoped it was good! But Sue wouldn't leave me hanging—no way! Not Sue.

She said rumor had it Maria had been asked to consider taking a promotion to a significantly higher position in the company. "Don't say anything to anyone else," Sue pleaded in a whisper, and she continued, "Maria knows more details than I do. Ask her about it." Apparently, this was a secret because a management change was underway "upstairs" at the company, and many of the changes hadn't been announced yet.

The prankster in me was about to rear his head again, I could just feel it! I said to Sue, "Please don't say anything to Maria about having spoken with me," and I told her what I was going to do so she could play along . . . Sue agreed.

I arrived at the house with the bottle of wine and Maria greeted me as usual. Nothing out of the ordinary, just our standard chit chat about how things had gone at work that day. The top-secret nature of what Sue had told me had Maria keeping quiet about the changes rumored at work—at least for the moment. Little did she know, Maria was literally walking right into playing her role in the master plan The Prankster had in store!

We were enjoying a glass of wine while discussing our dinner plans when I abruptly interrupted, "I know what I wanted to ask you, honey! I almost forgot all about it. During work today, I was just walking down the hallway at the high school. Maybe around two o'clock? Or a little earlier than that. I think it was just after lunch."

The rising excitement in my voice only added to the drama. "Well, honey, I suddenly got this feeling. A feeling so strong I had to pause and remind myself to ask you about it when I got home! You know, one of those times when we're apart and I kind of feel like something is happening to you? I'm wondering, did someone do something or say anything to you? Like around lunchtime? Maybe something secret? Something you might feel could be a really good thing? That's totally what I was thinking about, what was going on with you right *then*. A little bit after lunchtime today? Was something happening? It was such a strong feeling!"

Maria's jaw dropped, she was speechless! She just stared at me and began shaking her head. Then she began to speak, "I, I . . . I just don't know, I just want, I just . . . How could you possibly know anything about that!?" Still acting surprised, I said with concern, "What happened honey, did something happen to you? Are you alright?"

Maria just kept shaking her head. Finally after a sip of wine she told me the whole story. It was pretty much what Sue had told me earlier. Maria stammered, "I just can't believe it. I mean how could you possibly, I mean, Mike! How could you know that? And even the *time* when . . . it's, it's exactly . . . I mean you, you really are psychic or something."

She was jumping out of her skin by that point. Poor Maria. Was I starting to feel bad? No way! I kept telling myself, Just let it ride, Mike. This will only get even better if you stay cool and just let it play out.

And play out it did. For the next two weeks it just kept getting even better!

This all started on a Thursday night. Two weeks later we both headed to the lake after work on Friday to have dinner Saturday with the family at mom's place. The whole drive over Maria kept telling me about how for the past two weeks she had been talking with Sue, and all of her friends at work, and all over town, telling them all about me and what had happened. She kept telling the story over and over. She was convinced I had some sort of special ability, that I could sense when things were happening to her, and how deeply in touch I was with whatever she was thinking and feeling . . . I mean, this was going even better than The Prankster himself could have dreamed!

Saturday afternoon we sat down with the rest of the family for dinner at the restaurant. Maria told everyone the story, including my mom, which really set it off. Mom was really taken in by the story too, she was just a bubblin' about it! Mom flagged down everyone we knew in the restaurant who passed by our table and insisted that Maria tell them the story. Maria must've repeated the story two or three times as a growing crowd of customers and waitstaff gathered around us.

At this stage of the game, after two whole weeks—and how many people had Maria told this story to?—I was starting to feel a little sorry for Maria. What would happen when the truth came out? How many times would she have to live this down? So . . .

Right there at the table, with the whole family listening, I looked over at Maria next to me. "Maria, honey," I paused as she looked up at me with her loving smile. "Honey, I have to tell you something. You know that day when I came home and told you I had a feeling something was happening to you and, well, remember I brought home that bottle of pinot noir that I had just picked up? From Sue at the store?"

Not to change the subject here, but you know what's been a big money saver for the two of us lately?

Now that my ALS situation has made it possible for me to have access to morphine, we're saving almost $3,500 a year.

You see, we no longer have to make the trips for my annual spinal injections for pain management that I needed after Maria landed that devastating left hook!

Help Wanted

No one could ever replace my Maria! So I thought I would write down some of what Maria does for me to illustrate that.

What if I were to place an ad in the Help Wanted section to find someone to fill the role Maria plays in the drama my life with ALS has become? Do you think anyone would answer the ad? Could anyone answer it? Think again.

HELP WANTED

NEEDED:

Full-time 24/7 Life Assistant

FOR:

Male ALS patient, 62, paralyzed, Keuka Lake area, Pulteney. Patient's diaphragm is paralyzed, affecting breathing so communication is difficult. Patient is attached to a ventilator. Limited speech capacity.

HOURS:

Split time with patient's wife. 84 hours per week.

DUTIES INCLUDE:

- Attend to feeding and or drinking as requested by the patient. (Usually once every two to three hours).

- Assist with administering pain medication, sit with patient until medications have become effective, for approximately twenty minutes every two to four hours.

- Attend to personal hygiene and comfort to alleviate issues associated with excessive production of nasal discharge, saliva, and acidic tears, all common with ALS. These issues usually correlate with drinking fluids, eating, and taking medications.

- Assist with all functions of physical hygiene including bathing, brushing teeth, shaving, etc.

- Toileting assistance is required. Patient is paralyzed but has full function of the sensory neurons. He has bladder and bowel control. A Hoyer lift is used to transport the patient to and from the toilet. His mobile toilet chair tilts back to facilitate hygiene after bowel movements.

- Assistance is required with dressing, disrobing, clothing adjustments for comfort etc.

- Attend to adjustments for comfort throughout the day and night with room temperature and blankets.

- Adjust physical position as needed. Patient requires manual adjustment every hour for comfort and to relieve pressure ulcers in sensitive areas.

- Attend to prevention and treatment of pressure ulcers.

- Apply skin creams, moisturizers, pain and itch neutralizers, etc. as requested. Usually this precedes each body position adjustment.

- Assist patient with the operation and required adjustments to the medical reclining chair where he spends each day and night. Patient cannot be left in a fully reclined position. (Because of paralysis of muscles affecting breathing he is attached to a ventilator 24/7.)

- Move patient between medical chair and hospital bed as needed to relieve pressure and irritation. These moves are done with the Hoyer Lift.

- Assist with placement and removal of the face mask for the Trilogy 200 ventilator that serves as the patient's lungs. This process is ongoing 24/7 for every task requiring access to the mouth, nose, and face.

- Maintenance and operation activities as required for the Trilogy 200 which serves as the patient's lungs. Instruction will be provided by a licensed respiratory technician.

- Daily laundering of all patient care related dressings, towels, protective pads and coverings, bed linens, etc.

- Assist patient with operation of entertainment systems as requested. He is awake more often than not throughout the night.

(Maybe I need to take out a full-page ad!)

Chapter 3

Your Wildest Dreams Come True

Once upon a time
I remember skies
I wonder if you still remember

Once beneath the stars
The universe was ours
I wonder if you think about it

Once upon a time
In your wildest dreams

Justin Hayward

Of Providence, and Personal Projection

I'll start off with one of my favorite quotes:

> God grant me the serenity to accept the things I cannot change,
> the courage to change the things I can, and the wisdom to know
> the difference.

> *Reinhold Niebuhr*

What is actually within our own power to control? I can't even begin to count the number of times I have encountered what I would describe as providence—being in just the right place at just the right time. Being truly *ready,* and able to perform with absolute perfection, when all eyes were focused on me . . . And being able to recognize these moments as they occur, savoring both the *pursuit of perfection and the gratification of the moment,* before, during, and after.

But do these extraordinary moments just happen? Or are they somehow related to the combination of just how *prepared* our bodies are, and just how deeply our own minds are *projecting* these events? Surely these events could be attributed to pure coincidence, to a unique convergence of conditions that allowed them to occur. Or what if what was actually happening at those moments of providence was instead the result of *personal projection.* What if . . . ?

When You Least Expect It

It was early July, 1969. My family lived in the suburbs of New York City in the township of North Edison, New Jersey. I was enjoying the summer break between fourth and fifth grade, playing on my little league baseball team, the Eagles. We were not a very good team that season, having yet to win our first game with only three games left to go. So let's do the math: seven other teams times two games apiece equals fourteen regular season games, minus the three games remaining—hmmm. That means we had 0 wins and 11 losses! On top of that, our defense was not good. We lost many games by double digit numbers!

My grandpa Mike Santangelo introduced me to the game of baseball. Pop said it was "the thinking man's game." More about that later. Anyway, Pop loved baseball! We Sables lived right next to his home in Edison, New Jersey. Just a short train ride from the neighboring Iselin Train Terminal, through the tunnel under the Hudson River, and we'd be in the Bronx in thirty-five minutes or so.

Pop worked in sales in the city for a large freight trucking company that owned box seats right behind home plate in the original Yankee Stadium back in the 60s and 70s. Pop took me to a lot of games after work on weekdays. He gave my dad tickets to take me to a few games too. I quickly became a student of the game as well as a big fan of Mickey Mantle, Joe Peppitone, and Mel Stottlemeyer, to name a few of the better players of the time.

Pop's job had him out on a road trip once a week, sometimes gone for a few days at a time. So we'd go to see a Yankee game together when we could, or he'd be away, or he'd be playing golf with a client. The bottom line is, Pop had never been to see me play in little league.

It was a Saturday, and we normally didn't have games on Saturdays, but that week we had to make up a rained out game. I guess Pop realized I wasn't at home that Saturday and asked Mom where I was. When he found out I had a game he hurried over to the field to see if he could catch a few innings. I had no idea Pop even knew about the game, much less that he was on his way to watch me play!

We were playing the Royals, the team in first place. They were 11-0 (compared with our 0-11), so I figured we were probably in for a lickin'! Besides that I knew Greg Bayard was pitching, a freckle-faced kid who came straight over the top with the hardest fastball in the league! And you could hear him grunt when he released the ball on every single pitch. As hard as he could throw it. Every single pitch!

Since we were having such a tough year anyway, our coach Mr. Kennedy decided to let Chucky Lipsit pitch for us. Chucky had been our team leader from behind the plate that entire season, but he'd been begging for the better part of two seasons now to get to pitch in a game. Chucky was feared by the other teams for throwing out guys trying to steal bases, so we all knew that he had a good arm. I guess Coach Kennedy figured there wouldn't be any harm in giving him a shot. I mean, we were 0-11 anyway.

Well, Chucky sure had a surprise in store for those Royal boys that day. Coming downhill off the mound with every pitch, Chucky had everyone watching the new "Top Dog" of the fastball in our league! And he grunted with every pitch as well, only louder! Yes, Chucky had those Royal boys walking back to the dugout that day, staring at the ground and shaking their heads, many of them without having taken a swing at a pitch!

At the top of the fifth inning the score was tied at 0-0. No one that I knew of in our little league had seen a game go scoreless heading into the final two innings that season. (We played a six inning game in our league back then.) The Royals could not believe the score was tied, much less against the lowly Eagles. Mr. Bayard, their coach, was being pretty rough on them—way too hardcore for a little league coach!

I was set to bat second in the top of the fifth for the Eagles. Our first baseman, Albert Pirocco, was at the plate. I watched from the on-deck circle as he swung the bat— late on the first two pitches, no balls and two strikes.

On the third pitch I was sure I saw Albert start to swing his bat while Greg's front leg was still in the air. He hadn't even released the ball yet! Sure enough, Albert made contact. Foul ball. I thought to myself, maybe I should start my swing earlier too.

Still a count of 0-2. Albert started swinging this time just as Greg's foot hit the dirt. Contact! Fair ball! Line drive over the second baseman into right field, Albert rounded first and returned to the base. Safe. Man on first, no outs.

Listen to how I was thinking through Albert's at bat. It's exactly what Pop was trying to teach me! That's what he meant by "the thinking man's game." And how you play it. You silently talk to yourself, like you're announcing the game. Always aware of the count, the number of outs, what you'll do if this happens and what you'll do if that happens. Ready for every scenario. In the field or at the plate. No mental errors allowed in the game of baseball. Plenty of time between pitches to talk yourself through the plan. That's how you play "the thinking man's game." And then everything turns into slow motion. Or at least my grandpa said so.

I walked quietly out to the plate for my turn at bat. Usually I'd be strutting out there and swinging the bat once or twice. But this time I was thinking—about starting my swing early. I could always hold up on a bad pitch, right? No, Greg didn't throw balls. (He'd have to answer to his dad for that!) No, I had to figure on that one pitch. Straight, hard fastball right down the middle. Focus on that. It's the only pitch he'd ever thrown me. He was betting no one could catch up with it. But Albert Pirocco had.

I took my spot at the plate. I don't think I'd ever even fouled a pitch off from this guy, and he knew it. He had this mix of a grin and a sneer on his face as he stared down at me from the mound. I started my swing just as his foot hit the dirt. I fouled the pitch straight back over the backstop! Strike one. I'd swung under the pitch. Coach Kennedy hollered over from coaching at third base, "Keep your head in there, kiddo!" Keep my head in. YES! Both eyes on the ball. Remember. Not his foot. The ball is in his hand right before he releases it. Lock in on it then. The ball in his hand.

Okaaay . . . Start your swing early . . . His front leg starts to drop. Things switch to slow motion! Switch focus away from his leg position. Focus on his arm coming over the top and look at his hand. I see the ball in his hand, he releases his grip, my level swing comes forward, I stay focused on the ball and follow through with the swing as I feel that solid contact between the ball and the wood of the bat! I start towards first and drop the bat, everything still in slow motion. I raise my head slightly as I speed towards first base. I see a cutoff man running way out into right center field. The ball was well struck, a home run! Over the fence in left or center field, but there isn't any fence here in right field. Run faster! Round second hit the bag, stretch out your stride and glance up at the coach, he's waving me home! Round third, hit the bag, glance at home. The catcher's in position over the plate and sees the ball coming! I'll need to slide, his legs are wide apart, so I slide between them. I hear the ball hit the glove, he starts to fall on me and stretches to tag, my legs cross the plate, I feel the glove tag my head . . . Everything stops and it's quiet. It seems like an eternity, and then I hear the umpire, Big Art, bellow out the call, "SAYEEFE!"

The catcher looked at me and dropped his head. Coach Bayard stood there speechless, his mouth wide open. They couldn't argue with that call. I jumped to my feet and started brushing the dirt off my legs. I saw our guys emptying the third base dugout and Coach Kennedy heading my way. I looked to my left and saw the crowd that had rushed the backstop when they knew there was going to be a close play at the plate.

Standing there in front of the crowd at the backstop fence was my grandfather! A smile beaming from his face. We both reached out and I put my hand to his. He had seen the entire scene from the time I walked out from the dugout to the on-deck circle. He told me later that he had arrived when our team was in the dugout getting ready to come up to bat in the top of the fifth inning.

Providence? Or personal projection? We both found ourselves in exactly the right place, at exactly the right time. And then I experienced the epiphany of understanding what my grandfather had been trying to teach me about "the thinking man's game," and how to play it. For the first time in my life—that I can remember at least—I saw the action of the world unfold around me in slow motion, while I simultaneously possessed the ability to think and perform physically in real time.

We held on through the bottom of the 6th, and we won the only game we were to win that whole season, with a score of 2-0. We finished 1-13. The Royals went on to finish 13-1 and won the league championship. The details of that afternoon have been etched into my mind, my body, and ultimately my soul ever since.

The Analogy

I've been inspired as of late, and even felt driven at times, to use an analogy I've been thinking about for some time now. An analogy I've recently found myself talking about with some of you. It goes like this:

Imagine, if you will, that you and I were suddenly transported to a time before the discovery of electricity, something we all take for granted today. Say, sometime in the 16th century.

Let's also suppose for a moment that we had our smart phones with us when we traveled back in time. No one around us in the 16th century has ever seen, heard, or experienced what a device like this is capable of. How would people who lived back in time react?

People would be suspicious of these devices, suspecting they were some form of trickery or dishonesty, maybe even witchcraft. Some would no doubt be very afraid of such a device, believing it possessed some mystical or supernatural powers. Some might even accuse you and I of heresy and crimes against God and religion! And what effects might such a device have on the family dynamics typical of the time?

Others would fear the effects this strange device could have on trade and the future of the world economy. With such a device in use the traditional methods of exchanging goods and services could be rapidly and drastically altered. What might the effects be on the relationships between the peoples of the planet? What about the effects on the stability of government itself once the citizens realized that their leaders had no means of protecting them against such technology? How might this technology affect the future of mankind?

All of these potential reactions represent the result of the simplest and the most basic limitations of human perception. We cannot see, hear, smell, touch or taste the forces at work that make such technology as our smart phones possible. Just as our five senses can't see radio waves, hear microwaves, smell electricity running through a wire, touch light, or taste the conductivity between elements on a microchip, neither can we commonly detect certain energies, magnetism, radiation, ultrasound, infrared and ultraviolet light—the list goes on and on. Our human inability to detect these forces with our five senses does *not* mean these forces do not exist!

Discovering the forces that make our smart phones operate required human hypothesis, ingenuity, courage, and scientific breakthroughs. Remember that these forces are otherwise undetectable by our five senses. This process of discovery had to be repeated in order to harness their power and put them to work for us. All the while these breakthroughs and discoveries were being doubted and disparaged by the naysayers.

Countless, even infinite numbers of forces exist in our universe that are beyond detection by the five human senses. Remember, that does not mean they do not exist! We simply just haven't made the vast majority of these breakthrough discoveries yet.

Humanity is on the verge of a new era of discovery which will result in the greatest breakthroughs and discoveries in modern human history. New understandings of quantum physics and Einstein's theory of relativity point to it.

Watch closely for the results of scientific studies attempting to identify and define relationships between the forces of wave energies, electromagnetic forces, elemental magnetic forces, gravity, and the bonding energy forces within the structure of the atom itself.

A deeper understanding of the relationships between these forces will lead us to an age of science and discovery that will literally open the doors for mankind into the nature of time, space, and other dimensions.

When we step through those doors the relationship between astrophysics and the metaphysical will become clear. Hold on to your seats!

To that end, I will share with you some music and poetry from my youth that calls to mind who it is that I truly am, and how I came to be here in the first place.

In The Beginning

The First Man:

I think, I think I am, therefore I am, I think . . .

Big Technology:

Of course you are my bright little star,
I've miles and miles of files...
Pretty files of your forefather's fruit.
And now to suit,
Our Great Computer...
You're magnetic ink!

The First Man:

I'm more than that, I know I am, at least, I think I must be . . .

The Inner Man:

There you go man, keep as cool as you can.
Face piles of trials with smiles.
It riles them to believe that you perceive the web they weave.
And keep on thinking free . . .

Graeme Edge, The Moody Blues

Higher And Higher

Blasting, billowing, bursting forth
With the power of ten billion butterfly sneezes
Man with his flaming pyre
Has conquered the wayward breezes
Climbing to tranquility
Far above the cloud
Conceiving the heavens
Clear of misty shroud

Higher and higher
Now we've learned to play with fire
Go higher and higher and higher
Vast vision must improve our sight
Perhaps at last we'll see an end
To our own endless blight
And the beginning of the free
Climb to tranquility
Finding its real worth
Conceiving the heavens
Flourishing on earth

Higher and higher
Now we've learned to play with fire
Go higher and higher and higher

Graeme Edge, The Moody Blues

Chapter 4

Living Within the Community

Part 1
On Role Models

As a young adult I found myself in a rural community raising two children, my son Stephen and my daughter Sylvia.

We lived about ten miles down country roads from the village of Hammondsport, where the school and the extracurricular activities that my children wanted to participate in were located.

I ended up as a role model as a consequence of not seeing any sense in driving ten miles to drop my children off for their activities, then driving ten miles home alone, and then driving the ten miles back, alone, to pick them up, and then another ten miles home.

Spending as much time as possible with my family, not alone, had always been my main goal when I became their primary caregiver.

So I decided to stay for their activities, and eventually I accepted nominations to become part of the leadership corps, as a scoutmaster, assistant Girl Scout leader, 4H leader, baseball coach, etc.

Which is how, by spending more time with my children, I learned what it means to be a role model.

Role Models

- We become almost a surrogate parent to each participant in the group.
- We learn about the individual behavior patterns of each participant.
- We learn about the behavior patterns of the parents of the participants.
- We learn that every interaction with the group is being carefully monitored by the parents of the participants.
- Through this entire process we learn to communicate instructions in a variety of ways to reach each participant.
- This process teaches us to adjust our reactions for each participant interaction.
- By doing the above we can gain the cooperation of the participants, and the group will achieve its goals.
- We eventually will receive compliments and recognition on the achievements of the group and the participants.
- The group participants will begin to look up to us. Their parents also notice.
- We then are looked upon as role models.

Rudimentary? Yes. Just the tip of the iceberg? Definitely.

Being a role model is one of those things that's definitely best appreciated in the eyes of the beholder anyway. We never notice it ourselves. We don't stand out in our own minds! But a role model's service in the community is immeasurable.

Living vicariously through the experiences of each group participant, and sometimes even their parents, is rewarding.

Living vicariously through our own children's experiences is priceless!

On Leadership

I'll open this subject with excerpts from one of my favorite commencement addresses that I heard several years ago. It was given by Major General Martin Dempsey, a former Chairman of the Joint Chiefs of Staff in the White House, addressing graduates of the master's degree program at Duke University in May of 2014.

Major General Martin Dempsey on Leadership

> "I hope you understand and believe in action over admiration. We need leaders of consequence, no mediocrity, no bystanders, no ambivalence. Make it matter."

> "After four years of hard work, you young men and women on the field have crossed your academic goal line. But what's in your heart? You're all going to lead something. I know your resume, but what's in your heart?"

> "My real worry is that you won't confront that question. You'll quickly become too busy to give each moment the value it deserves, too driven to lead personally, too confident to be inquisitive, too certain to be approachable."

> "I had a mentor suggest to me once that from time to time I ought to ask myself a very simple question: When is the last time I allowed someone to change my mind about something? The more responsibility you get, the more important that question becomes."

So, what's Mike Sable got to add to the Major General's words of wisdom?

Within the context of leadership, to answer his question "What's in your heart?" you need to ask yourself about more than just what's inside your own heart. To lead, you need to ask the people you lead questions, and listen to their answers. Ask your subordinates for their thoughts, their views, their opinions, and their ideas. Ask what they would do in a given situation.

Responses to these questions will serve to:

- Maintain your own personal involvement with the decision being made.
- Maintain your own personal involvement with the people you lead and who hold you as a member of that group.

- Bring new ideas and new participants into the discussion-making process. (It's best to have several options to choose from when leading the way forward.)
- Allow more time for thoughtful discussion on the decision to be made, assuring all possible outcomes and consequences are considered before arriving at a final decision.
- Promote "buy in" among those subordinates who will be instrumental in the success or failure of the measures taken by leadership. When people feel included in the decision-making process, they are more likely to promote the success of that decision. Buying in often means doubling down.

Leadership and Safety

Sometimes, being a leader requires diffusing conflict first, in order to unite a group before leading the way forward.

Bringing the topic of safety into the discussion will usually help dissipate the conflict, since everyone is concerned with at least their own safety.

Discussing safety also provides a useful and important tool in finding common ground. Safety is critical if the group is to accomplish its goals. And spending time on discussing a unified safety plan redirects the group's focus away from the conflict.

Of course there are so many famous sayings on leadership. I reflect upon these often. Sometimes I find them useful in reminding myself of how simple it can be to offer people help.

Leadership is about more than leading nations, armies, corporations, teams, and other groups. It can and should be about sharing what we have learned with those around us. With that in mind I'd like to close with four of my favorites, which have served me well over the years:

- "Never ask someone to do something that you would not be willing to do yourself."
- "Point the direction forward but let others find their own ways to get there." (My own!)
- "Give a man a fish and he will eat well tonight. Teach a man to fish and he will never go hungry."
- "The efforts of the farmer that feed his own family feed the families that surround his farm as well."

Conclusion

As role models and leaders we have a bird's eye view of the magic unfolding as the behavior we model spreads out into the community around us.

The glimpses that we have of that magic in action is the fuel that powers our souls. It really is a two-way street after all.

A perfect example can be found in The Scout Oath, as we recited each week at our regular meeting of Troop 18, Boy Scouts of America, Hammondsport, New York:

"On my honor I will do my best, to do my duty to God and my country and to obey the Scout Law; to help other people at all times; To keep myself physically strong, mentally awake, and morally straight."

By serving other people as stated in the Scout Oath, I also serve to better myself. It really is a two-way street.

I hope and pray that my interactions with others have left each of them with a mark. A mark which serves to help them bring out the best in themselves, and the best in those they interact with.

In the end, I'd like to feel that I've touched the lives of others in ways that leave the world a better place.

Part 2
Giving Back to the Community

Shortly after I was diagnosed with ALS in late October 2018, I began to think about writing my book, *Legacy*. Let's share an excerpt from the last couple of paragraphs from this book's Introduction to understand why:

> *Another blessing I've been granted is time to reflect upon my life. Time to truly appreciate the people around me and revisit the wonderful places I've been to. Time to relive the many experiences I've enjoyed over the past sixty-plus years.*
>
> *I've lived a long and storied life!*
>
> *I've learned to count my blessings, and to encourage others to count theirs as well.*
>
> *I want to offer you all these memories and reflections in this book, Legacy. The time that I've spent working on this has brought back many great memories that I now get to enjoy again and share with all of you. What a wonderful gift has been bestowed upon me!*

At the time I knew which subjects I wanted to discuss in this book, and the things I've learned that I wanted to pass along to others. My daughter Sylvia knew how much scouting has meant to me, and suggested that I share some of my thoughts and passions about it.

My father, who was the treasurer of my own Boy Scout Troop 24 in Edison, New Jersey, also understood just how big a part scouting and serving as the Scoutmaster of Troop 18 has played in my life. So my Dad saw to it that my old group from Troop 18 was informed of my ALS diagnosis and my impending demise.

The Surprise Visit

Scoutmaster Mike, Morning of August 18, 2004, after the thunderstorms of night three,
Woodland Caribou Expedition, Northwest Ontario, Canada 2004.

Maria and I had just greeted my daughter Sylvia and her partner Eric who were joining us for dinner with my mom and dad. My sister Julie and brother-in-law Ray were also expected to join us. Or so I was told.

I didn't really notice all the activity underway next door at my sister Be's house. I did see both Eric and Sylvia go in and out of our house several times, but otherwise nothing out of the ordinary.

Then my sister Be came in and told me there were some people outside who wanted to see me. People, usually family, sometimes stopped by unannounced to visit since I've been housebound with ALS so this did not strike me as anything out of the ordinary. Be told me they all had masks, which would be expected due to the Covid virus and the condition of my lungs. I told Be to show them in.

A couple of figures appeared in the shadows of the dining room, the lights were off so it was dark in there. I recognized a couple of them as Ray's sons, my nephews, and a gentleman I did not know. He was carrying what looked like a framed picture or a plaque of some sort.

The gentleman stepped forward into the light, and then a lot of people were talking at once. I think they were asking me if I knew what was happening and telling me what was going on at the same time! The gentleman was introduced to me as the current Scoutmaster of Boy Scout Troop 18 in Hammondsport, Mr. Ian Walruth.

Troop 18 is the troop that I served as Scoutmaster for from 1998 until 2007, the years my son Stephen was in Boy Scouts, and also for a few years after Stephen had graduated from the Scout ranks as an Eagle Scout.

The Background and Traditions of Hammondsport's Troop 18

Troop 18 possesses a financial asset that is not commonly seen in other scouting organizations. In the late 1940s the family of Reginald Wood, a Hammondsport Eagle Scout who went on to serve his country in World War II and died in battle in 1945, created an endowment, The Reginald Wood Memorial to Scouting. In addition to building a Scout House for a place to meet, hold events, and store equipment, the endowment includes a parcel of land down in the village of Hammondsport which extends into adjacent wooded property and near the Finger Lakes Trail where there is now a new campsite. I'll tell you a little more about that campsite later.

The endowment makes funds available first to offset the costs of the property ownership and the maintenance and insurance of the Scout House. If additional funds remain then applications to offset the costs of the scouting programs and summer camp are considered for funding on an annual basis as well. Talk about giving back to the community!

Carrying On the Tradition

I stepped into quite a heritage of scouting program excellence when departing Scoutmaster Dave Drum handed the reins of Troop 18 over to LaRue McAfee and myself in early May of 1998. Over a long and storied history Troop 18 has distinguished itself as a leader (and a maverick of sorts) amongst the troops of the Thunderbird District, Five Rivers Council, Boy Scouts of America, which currently includes 139 units.

Under our leadership, Troop 18 continued a longstanding tradition for sending above average numbers of outstanding candidates to Five Rivers Council each year for consideration for the award of Eagle Scout. This is because Troop 18 has always been committed to offering an outstanding high-quality program for our scouts, adult leaders, and scouting parents.

Under my direction we made it a policy to offer at least one outdoor overnight camping adventure, rain, snow, or shine, every single month of the year! This was in addition to all the activities, both indoor and outdoor, that were happening at our weekly meetings.

None of the events we offered were ever considered mandatory. Some boys were not into winter camping, for example. So we also made it a policy to offer one indoor activity option every month of the year, such as visiting museums, or attending concerts, memorial services, state congressional sessions etc.

It has always been my belief that the ages of twelve to seventeen is the time to open doors for our children, not to close them. There were no mandatory requirements for event participation, or any participation requirement at all. We were careful to listen to the interests of the Scouts and always tried to balance our activity list based upon that. We also continued our weekly meetings throughout the summer, and whenever school was in recess. After all, the summer season is perfect for enjoying the great outdoors!

Additionally, Troop 18 was a dependable participant at *all* Council sponsored events like the Jamborees, the Spring and Fall Camporees, Raft Regattas, Summer Camp, Polar Bear Weekend, the Klondike Derby, The Mall Overnight Scout Promo, and more.

As if this weren't enough, to round out the experience, and with plenty of input from the scouts, we usually scheduled:

- A Saturday ski and snowboard trip at Swain in February.
- A night backpacking adventure with two nights of camping In July on the Finger Lakes Trail.
- Twice annual six-hour hikes performing trail maintenance for our sponsorship of the five-mile section of the Finger Lakes Trail where it passes by Hammondsport on the top of the mountain.
- A mountain biking two-night camping adventure each September on Bluff Point, from Keuka Lake State Park to the Garrett Chapel and back.
- An overnight three-story indoor rock wall climbing adventure every January in Rochester.
- Whitewater rafting each year in late April or early May, when the water in the Lehigh River was at its highest!
- Whitewater canoeing in early to mid-May—a three-day, two-night canoe and camping trip down the Delaware River from Callicoon, New York to Matamoras, Pennsylvania.
- We even went deep sea fishing in the Atlantic Ocean on a 95' charter boat out of Point Pleasant, New Jersey! Always looking to widen the experience.
- There's more, but we'll discuss the multiple-week annual "High Adventure" trips a little later in the book!

You might be wondering how all of this could be possible? Well, we had a schedule of activities we had developed and refined over a few years. It was tried and true. We knew what worked and what didn't. And we had established contacts at the other end who were familiar with who we were and what we needed. So setting up the trips was really a breeze.

But what was most important, enabling us to maintain such a busy schedule and such an expansive program? We had a lot of help from a crew of really great parents and assistant leaders who were hooked on going along with their scouts on these wonderful adventures. A great adventure is a great adventure, no matter how old you are!

Now, you may be wondering, how do you get parents to participate in scouting, eager to go along on the adventures together with the scouts? How does that come about? Well it doesn't just happen on its own!

When the boys would cross over from Cub Scouts to Boy Scouts at the annual Blue and Gold Dinner every February, as Scoutmaster I acted as the ceremony's host. While offering the new Boy Scouts my congratulations at the end of the evening, I always made it a point to mention that the first outing they'd be eligible to attend be our annual two-night camping trip, including a whitewater rafting adventure! I explained it would be "in the Lehigh River, this April, when the water is at its highest and the ride is the most exciting! And oh, yes, it's about a four-and-a-half-hour drive away." I told them we had photos from previous years' trips on display at the awards table, and they should be sure to check them out. The boys would immediately crowd around the display, with their parents close behind. Not only were the boys completely psyched about what they saw, their parents were, let us say, freaking out!

So I also made a point of telling those parents it was perfectly normal for a parent to want to accompany their son on his first bigger adventure with the Boy Scouts. And of course they were welcome to go along with him to assure his comfort!

Once a parent went on a trip like that, they soon realized how much fun *they* were having, and they were hooked. I must have recruited 75% of my adult assistants this way and I never lacked for adult participation. A great adventure is a great adventure, no matter how old you are!

A Few Things I Learned From My Years as a Scoutmaster

- Never forget the number one rule for leading group activities: Detailed and ongoing communication with the entire group is absolutely essential!
- At any of our weekly meetings there would typically be at least three or four sign-up sheets at our sign-up table, right up front, to let all of the boys and their parents know the status of the upcoming events. The sheets included the dates, times, costs, details, and the deadlines for the upcoming events.

- There was always an adult participant sign-up sheet for each event too, so we could recruit drivers and additional supervision.
- There were always take-home information sheets at the table for the scouts to give to their parents. We kept a small stack with each of the sign-up sheets, with a separate information sheet for each event, to keep any parents who were not at the meeting informed of the details of the activities that their scout was interested in. (Parents were always encouraged to attend our weekly meetings, not necessarily to be part of the scouts' meeting, but also to be included in the planning process. Another opportunity to recruit adult participation.)
- The take-home information sheet for each event included a list of Rank Advancement Opportunities that were appropriate for that particular activity. This gave the parents the chance to work with their scout, planning a route for completing the requirements for their next rank advancement. This was a great opportunity for parents to teach their Scout how to be a self-starter in life.
- After the opening of each weekly meeting, before turning it over to the scouts to run, I would spend a few minutes reviewing the status of the events on the table—that is, the sign-up sheets. Did we have enough participation? Did we have the required number of adults? Did we have the necessary qualified individuals to meet the requirements for a tour permit and had the permit been accepted? There were always deadlines set for making the final decision to either go or to cancel, if necessary.

So this is how Troop 18 has maintained its status as a leader in the Five Rivers Council—by continually offering scouting families the excellence and adventure of an outstanding scouting program!

Now, back to my introduction to Mr. Ian Walruth, the current Troop 18 Scoutmaster.

You remember Mr. Walruth, who I wrote about earlier? He had come to my home in Pulteney to present me with a wonderful honor! First he gave me a plaque thanking me for my service to scouting in Hammondsport that will hang on the wall of the Scout House as well!

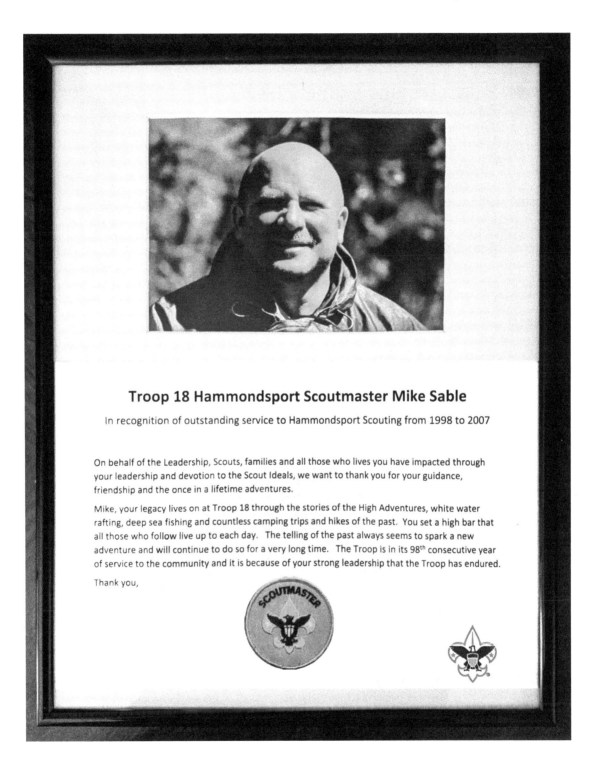

Troop 18 Hammondsport Scoutmaster Mike Sable

In recognition of outstanding service to Hammondsport Scouting from 1998 to 2007

On behalf of the Leadership, Scouts, families and all those who lives you have impacted through your leadership and devotion to the Scout Ideals, we want to thank you for your guidance, friendship and the once in a lifetime adventures.

Mike, your legacy lives on at Troop 18 through the stories of the High Adventures, white water rafting, deep sea fishing and countless camping trips and hikes of the past. You set a high bar that all those who follow live up to each day. The telling of the past always seems to spark a new adventure and will continue to do so for a very long time. The Troop is in its 98th consecutive year of service to the community and it is because of your strong leadership that the Troop has endured.

Thank you,

He also showed me a bronze memorial block, engraved with the words "The Mike Sable Memorial Campsite." This will be placed at the new campsite that was just created near the Finger Lakes Trail, on the Reginald Wood property that I mentioned earlier.

Apparently, I left a positive impression on Scouting in Hammondsport that has carried on to this day.

My father, Art Sable Senior, had let the Scouts in Hammondsport know about my battle with ALS, a terminal condition. The Scouts contacted my old Scouting troop and between my family, my old troop, and the Scouts, they decided to honor my service this way, and to visit me at home. They even brought along two Dutch ovens and baked cobblers just as we used to do on many of our outings!

The surprise "Scouts Visit Mike at Home" presentation of the "Awards of Appreciation"
November 13, 2020, Pulteney

L-R: Tim Ullrich, Evan McAfee, Jason Arnold, Kane McAfee, Ray Ullrich, Assistant Scoutmaster LaRue McAfee, Stephen Sable, Junior Walruth, Secretary Tony Smolos, David Ridge, Committee Chairman John Ridge, Scoutmaster Ian Walruth.

After the surprise visit, and the honors bestowed upon me that Friday night at my home, I'm guessing Troop 18 will keep sharing stories about our group and our adventures for many years to come.

High Adventure

Mr. Walruth went on to explain that even now, whenever new scouts join the troop, the conversation always seems to work its way around to a large easel-mounted map on display in the meeting room of the scout house. It's a detailed topographic map of The Allagash Wilderness Waterway. Assembled from several full size US Geological Survey (USGS) topographic maps by the Scouts themselves, it is marked up describing our route through the wilderness and our adventures along the way.

To read a bit more about Troop 18's two Allagash High Adventure experiences, and why they have marked us as "Mavericks" in Scouting, read my book *Troop 18: A Profile of Excellence in Scouting.*

Chapter 5

My Beloved Family

Mike and Maria's wedding day, December 27, 2015
Standing: Brothers Art and Andy, Mike and Maria, Sisters Lisa, Be, and Julie.
Seated: Mother Julia (MJ), Father Arthur (Big Art).

This chapter has three parts, each with several stories about events involving my family members and friends. Personalities shine through, and these recollections will bring those times to life again for everyone to relive.

Part 1
How Special is That?

My life has taken me on quite a journey—I've come full circle, as they say. And I'm thankful to have arrived back home. My home. This home where I've come to realize just how blessed I am. Blessed to have been born into the beloved family that surrounds me today. The family that has always been here for me, through all the good times and all the hard times.

The Family of Arthur and Julia Sable

While searching for the right way to begin this very special chapter, I thought about just how incredibly well this family treats all of its members. Especially the special way they have rallied around me while I'm fighting the battle of my life with ALS.

The very toughness of the battle I'm fighting with ALS contrasts sharply with the kindness and sensitivity that my family has treated me with. Let's talk about that word, "special," for a bit.

How special was it, in late February 2019, when we had all just decided to share the goal of seeing the asparagus come back up in the garden in May together? Not only had I beaten the odds of making it through the holidays, I'd even made it to my 60th birthday on February 24th!

My Uncle Matt SanAngelo (also written Santangelo) had recently passed away in the late summer of 2018. About fourteen years older than me, he was my mom's (Julia's) youngest brother. I was close to him, acting like his little tag along buddy when he was in his teens.

Instead of a traditional funeral we held a party to celebrate his life, just as he had requested before he passed away. That celebration made a very strong impression on me. It was truly a party to celebrate him and the life he had lived. Crazy Uncle Matt, as we used to call him, would have loved that party—such a wonderful gathering of family and friends. And the food! Yes, Uncle Matt would have loved that party!

HOW SPECIAL IS THAT?

So in February 2019, after my 60th birthday, I got to thinking. It looked like with any luck I would make it to May, anyway. The weather would have turned for the better by then. And Mom's restaurant on the west side of Keuka would be open in April, sometime around Easter, just like every year.

If I wanted to have a celebration of life something like Uncle Matt's at Mom's Waterfront Restaurant, wouldn't I want to be there in person and enjoy all of those great people and memories, and the food? Oh that food!

And so it was. All I had to do was say, "Wouldn't it be cool to have a celebration and be there to enjoy it too?" My sisters, brothers, Mom, Dad, and my children Stephen and Sylvia heard that, and took it from there.

The invitation:

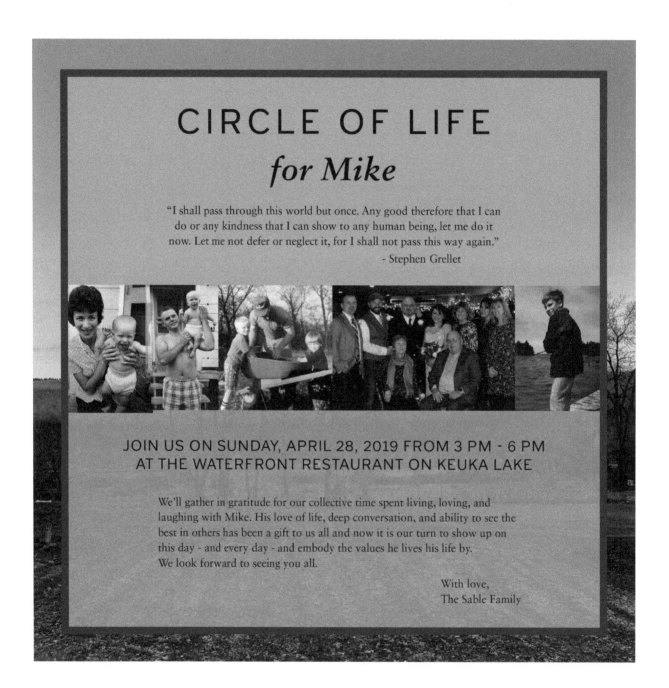

CIRCLE OF LIFE
for Mike

"I shall pass through this world but once. Any good therefore that I can do or any kindness that I can show to any human being, let me do it now. Let me not defer or neglect it, for I shall not pass this way again."
- Stephen Grellet

JOIN US ON SUNDAY, APRIL 28, 2019 FROM 3 PM - 6 PM
AT THE WATERFRONT RESTAURANT ON KEUKA LAKE

We'll gather in gratitude for our collective time spent living, loving, and laughing with Mike. His love of life, deep conversation, and ability to see the best in others has been a gift to us all and now it is our turn to show up on this day - and every day - and embody the values he lives his life by. We look forward to seeing you all.

With love,
The Sable Family

HOW SPECIAL IS THAT?

My sister Lisa knew I had played the guitar for over fifty years and that music was one of the loves of my life. She went ahead and contacted Athens Creek, one of my favorite bands and recording artists, based in Detroit. She told them about our family, me and my battle with ALS. She even offered to let them stay overnight at her home for lodging. They decided to play our party, at no charge!

HOW SPECIAL IS THAT?

Later that summer in August another of my favorite bands, America, was set to play a concert on the west side hill overlooking Keuka Lake. They have released dozens of outstanding albums going all the way back to the 1970s.

Tickets weren't cheap, but how often do you get the chance to see a band like that in concert, literally in your own backyard? My daughter Sylvia, her companion Eric, Maria and myself opted for the best, most expensive seats available, offered on a first come basis when you arrived.

On the day of the show we packed me up with my walking chair and ventilator and made the trip to the concert venue only a mile from our home. We arrived early, but still the line stretched back several hundred yards from the gates which were not yet open. People waiting in line noticed my chair and my disability right away. Sylvia picked up on that immediately, and she talked our way right up to the gates at the front of the line. With a few more words she had us passing through those gates that were then closed behind us.

HOW SPECIAL IS THAT?

Once inside, a gentleman named John Rodenhouse, the owner of the venue and promoter of the concert, introduced himself. He already knew my name, I assumed because he knew Andy and Artie, my brothers. He directed us to the front row at the foot of the stage and instructed us to "take whatever seats you like." No one else was seated yet.

HOW SPECIAL IS THAT?

During the opening act, I felt a tap on my shoulder. I turned around to find Mr. Rodenhouse. He told us that a couple of people were out back and were waiting to see me. Maria and I followed him back to the concession area.

But he kept going, past some trailers to a tent near the stage. I honestly didn't realize what was happening until I was right there with the band as they were sipping iced tea. Andy and Artie had set me up!

HOW SPECIAL IS THAT?

We talked about bands, music, Ovation guitars, life, and how beautiful the Finger Lakes are for quite a while. Then Dewey Bunnell, America's lead singer and guitarist who wrote the hit song "A Horse with No Name," looked over at my walking chair and said he was sorry to learn about my ALS. "Dewey, you shouldn't feel sorry at all," I replied. "I'm okay with being the local poster person to illustrate the plight of ALS. In fact they couldn't have picked a better guy for the job." He looked up at me and just smiled.

The band all commented about how cool it really was to just get to talk with us about the area and the people who lived here, instead of standing there and "just signing autographs."

And that was that. We all shook hands, and the band prepared to take the stage. Mr. Rodenhouse showed up in a golf cart and drove us around the crowd and back down right to our seats at the foot of the stage.

HOW SPECIAL IS THAT?

Part 2
The Invitation

Christmas Eve with Mike at Sister Be's Garage

Thursday, December 24, 2020, 5pm
9207 Main Street, Pulteney

"Maybe Christmas doesn't come from a store.
Maybe Christmas, perhaps, means a little bit more."

If Mike can't come to Christmas, Christmas will come to Mike!

No one fights alone and no one goes it alone in this family. So, we will brave the weather, stand together and give this incredible, funny, great spirited guy a Christmas to remember!

We have always done Christmas big. Huge, actually, and this year would be no exception. We are planning a SURPRISE "flash mob style" Christmas carol visit to Mike at his home.

We will gather at Be's next door and show our faces in small groups one by one as we come out of the dark yard until, by the end of the first song, we are all together under the lights for him to see, just like in the attached video! Well, maybe not so perfect but as best as we can! (We all know our family wasn't blessed with the gift of song!)

Yes, my family, obviously aware of my paralysis and knowing I could not attend any of our holiday activities, had followed my sister Be's lead and planned another incredible surprise to keep my spirits high during the 2020 Christmas season. Christmas caroling at Be's garage, the whole family there live, presented on video and projected on my 65" TV with the Bose sound system. The whole crew enjoyed dinner at my home, and we all spent Christmas Eve with one another as we always had.

Eric and Ray, The Masked Duo! Performing at Be's garage with all of the siblings, nieces, and nephews.

Thank you Sister Be for dreaming this night up and putting in the effort to make it a reality. And thank you to all of the carolers, I could not have asked for more. And you truly caught me by surprise! This family never lets down one of their own.

Part 3
Martin Sexton: Singer, Song Writer, Folk Artist

Video visiting with our friend, performing artist Martin Sexton, December 24th and December 27th, 2020 — a gift from my younger brother Art, sixteen years my junior.

Knowing I was a big fan of the local folk singer, songwriter, and recording artist Martin Sexton, Art arranged for us to meet once again. Ever since 2015 when Martin played a show for us at my mom's place, the Waterfront Restaurant, I had been catching up with his earlier recordings, following his career and his new work. Martin's guitar picking style is a lot like my own. His vocals and the stories in the lyrics of his songs have a timeless quality and are particularly relevant to our beloved Finger Lakes Region.

So for a special Christmas treat my brother Art contacted Martin and arranged for two dates for us to video chat with him, to talk and hear him play.

On Christmas Eve, Martin gave us our own personal video concert, performing a number of his tunes as a special treat! Then a few days later he joined us live again with more songs and conversation using the two-way video feature on our television with the Bose sound system. This evolved into a wonderful discussion on philosophy for the both of us. We talked about our guitars, the Finger Lakes, our lives, and shared our philosophies of life and how we were living them. How we got on the subject of philosophy is an interesting story of its own.

After greeting one another, Martin started talking in a sort of conciliatory, somber tone about my ALS and my overall physical condition. I was able to get him on the right track pretty quickly though, which I think initially caught my brother Art a little off guard. We laughed about it later, but for a minute I unintentionally had my brother worried I was starting an argument with Martin, which was the furthest thing from my mind.

I can understand why Art was worried when I consider the way it might have sounded to him. But being a musician myself I have a kindred faith in the spirit of an artist who expresses what Martin does through his songs. We talked a lot about his music. Our philosophies of life were similar, and we had taken similar paths to arrive at them. And we handled our guitars the same way too. I knew he would understand where I was coming from.

"Hold on there with feeling badly for me Martin! This really isn't a tough time I'm going through. Not at all. In fact I'd have to say I'm living through one of the finest moments of my life right now." After a pause, and a puzzled look from Martin I continued, "I'm doing things, seeing things, having conversations with people—like yourself, for example. During the holidays no less! Basically I'm living in a way I never would have thought I'd be living before I became ill. For anything precious that I may have lost because of ALS, I've been blessed with something taking its place that I never could have dreamed of. My situation has made me slow down and become aware of what I otherwise might have missed. Some of that turns out to be vividly clear, and what I find very close to my heart now that I can take the time to see it."

If you've ever listened to Martin's songs then you know what I said hit home with him. He truly appreciated that I was able to touch him that way. Who knows, we might hear some of those thoughts and emotions in a new song from him soon. As for me, I truly appreciated hearing how Martin has adopted a philosophy similar to my own. He's endured some of the same hardships and life lessons that I have lived through, and even some that he might still be living through. I will continue to have faith that I can truly read the heart of a kindred spirit through the music he plays for us. Thank you Brother Martin. And thank *you* Brother Art!

Chapter 6

Parents and Parenting

Part 1
Parents

Arthur A. Sable and Julia M. (Santangelo) Sable
August 31, 1956

Arthur and Julia's Family Photos

Art and Julie in high school

And after 60+ years, Art and Julie these days

Meet Art and Julie Sable's six children

Michael Andrew Sable
Born 1959

Julie Marie (Sable) Ullrich
Born 1960

Elizabeth (Be) Jeanne Sable
Born 1962

Lisa Ann (Sable) Cole
Born 1963

Andrew Arthur Sable
Born 1975

Arthur Joseph Sable
Born 1977

The Family, A.D. (After Diagnosis)
Dad, Lisa, Mike, Be, Andy, Julie, Mom, Art Jr.

1966. Time for the famous Robert Hall jingle,
"When the prices go up, up, up, and the values go down, down, down,
Robert Hall will show you, the reason they give you, High Qual - ity, Econ - omy!"

Always dressed up for the holidays!
Dad Art, Mom Julia, Mike, Lisa, Be, Julie.

Mom's Gals
Tiffany (Andy), Maria (Mike), Lisa, Mom, Missy (Art), Julie, and Be.

The Vacation Series

Six Family Vacations
1967–1972

Mom and Dad tried hard to ensure our family would enjoy unique vacation adventures together every summer while school was in recess. The themes and the venues chosen for these family vacations always included a bit of historical significance that we could enjoy, along with outdoor activities in rural settings. And so it was to be as we embarked on our adventures from our home base in the suburbs of New Jersey.

- 1967 Cape Hatteras
- 1968 Thousand Islands
- 1969 Chincoteague Island
- 1970 Lake Champlain
- 1971 Cape Cod
- 1972 Keuka Lake

1967 Cape Hatteras

Mom and Dad were close with our Aunt Lucy and Uncle Joe Farris. Lucy was Mom's younger sister, and Dad and Joe shared a love for fishing and boating. So the young parents decided to bring both families together to enjoy their first summer family adventure.

When the four Sable and three Farris children were old enough for a week-long family vacation, Cape Hatteras North Carolina was the choice. Located on the beach with a cool lighthouse, historic Kitty Hawk just a short drive away, with fishing for the dads, sand for the kids to play in, and picnic style cooking outdoors, we had all of the fun activities we could have wanted in easy reach. Joe and Lucy owned a Volkswagen camper, and my mom and dad rented a pop-up camper. The families rented campsites on the seashore of the Cape, and camping we would go!

I went over the dunes to the ocean with my dad and Uncle Joe early the first morning. They were fishing right in the surf just beyond the breaking waves. They were able to cast their lines out that far thanks to the super long, specialized surf casting rods they were using. I wasn't able to fish with them because I was just too little to cast those long rods. But I did catch dozens of fiddler crabs that morning digging in the sand with my sister Julie, and we had a great time anyway!

When we went back to the campsite for lunch my mom and Aunt Lucy grilled up burgers and hot dogs. The seagulls were going crazy trying to get the food and they did manage to steal a few hotdogs right out of the little kids' hands, all the while squawking and pecking at each other! What a scene that was—the little ones crying, the birds fighting and flapping their wings, and the adults trying to shoo the birds away!

The youngest children finally went down for a nap and Dad and Uncle Joe settled down to mess with the fishing gear for a "night fishing adventure" planned for that evening. They took me with them when they left camp to get some special bait. I'll never forget what happened when we returned to camp and checked the bait.

Apparently, ever since lunch the camp picnic tables had been under a continuous assault by the seagulls who had picked bits of food out of the garbage and then proceeded to attack any food related items not secured in the campers or locked up in the coolers. What a mess they had made!

Uncle Joe got the idea that these birds were so reckless he and my Dad were going to have to "teach those gulls a lesson." Dad and Uncle Joe baited up their hooks, and with those long rods Joe and Dad casted up into the air—they actually hooked and pulled a few of the frenzied gulls right out of the sky! After watching a couple of gulls losing the battles the flock scattered and didn't bother us again.

The historical significance of the Lighthouse and the Kitty Hawk visits were somewhat lost on the little kids, but I remember how impressed we older children and the adults were. The fishing had been mildly successful, so Dad and Uncle Joe were satisfied. I think the sand and the beach and collecting seashells were enjoyable for all of the children. And the activities included a first for me—sack races and three-legged races!

All in all it was one great big bonding experience for our two families. The Sables added three sisters and the Farris girls got a brother!

1968 Thousand Islands

The Sable Family once again rented a pop-up camper, this time heading north to Cape Vincent in the Thousand Islands of the Saint Lawrence River, in Ontario, Canada.

Highlights of that vacation included a day trip to an amusement park located near the Thousand Islands Bridge on an island in the river. We kids had our first experience with a zip line at that park, and Julie and I were only eight and nine years old then.

We went through Customs while in the car. None of us children had ever been out of our country before—prior to that trip it had been a big deal for Julie and me just to count up the states we'd been to! We ventured into the town of Gananoque and saw the huge Northern Pike and Muskelunge mounted on the walls of the sporting goods store. Gananoque was a quaint little town, like one you'd see in a story book. Mom enjoyed the gift shops the best. We ate lunch in the local sandwich and coffee shop.

I was fascinated with the boats docked at the camp. Before that trip the largest outboard motor I'd ever seen or operated was six horsepower. But these outboard motors were fifty, seventy-five, and even ninety horsepower! That kindled an interest in me. Later on in my teen years, I became a factory-certified mechanic for three famous brands of outboard motors, before I had even graduated high school!

Back at the camp the swim area had the clearest water we'd ever seen. It was also the coldest water we'd ever swam in. And the fishing was unbelievable!

The local kids fished right off the docks at the camp for yellow perch. Julie and I watched what they were doing and when the schools of perch came through it was nonstop—drop in the line and pull out a fish—as fast as we could go!

We were used to releasing the fish we caught. The local children looked at us a little bit oddly when they saw us do that. They explained they were fishing because that was how they provided dinner for their families. The parents had the children provide the dinner for their families! They had a big wooden table on the beach where they cleaned and filleted the perch, and boy could those kids crank out perfect fillets, in less than a minute per fish. (They had been given a quota to fill and a time limit to return home.)

We quickly became their friends when we handed everything we caught over to them. That meant they'd meet their quota for the day early and have time to swim with us. They told us they usually didn't have much time to play.

I learned a valuable lesson that has stayed with me all these years, about how different life can be in other places, even for people our age. And we weren't even all that far from home.

1969 Chincoteague Island

Virginia, at the Atlantic coast again. This time we would get to see the famous herd of wild ponies that Chincoteague Island is known for. And we had the Farris family along to enjoy a shared vacation with us once again! Always memorable when this group of cousins gets together.

I bet you didn't know there are wild ponies on an island in Virginia. Very cool. When Dad came home from work one day that spring to announce we were going on vacation to a place with wild ponies we were psyched!

Turns out small ponies with long manes lived wild on about half the island. The ponies and the people were kept on separate parts of the island divided by a fence so everyone stayed safe. We were able to go to a parking area next to the area where the ponies usually were and got to see them up close in their own home in the wild. You could tell these animals were not pets!

Once again, my parents had rented a pop-up camper, and we really had the routine down by this point. We knew the steps to convert the camper interior from living-in, to dining-in, to sleeping-in; we were all old enough to help that year and those daily chores went off without a hitch!

Highlights of the trip included fishing as always. But Uncle Joe and Dad did their fishing without me, and this time I went on my own.

The first day I was so eager to go fishing, but Dad and Uncle Joe were still busy setting up the campsite, shifting the two camper spots so they would face each other like Mom and Aunt Lucy wanted. I suppose it was nicer that way, plus they could keep track of the kids coming and going more easily. The kids, mind you, not the young man in the group!

So back to me, down by the waterfront fishing by myself. Well not really—by myself, that is. Seems that a nice Southern family was also on vacation that week and had their campsite all set up right there by the water.

On my second or third cast out with the spinner bait, low and behold I had a hit!

Turns out her name was Anna Lee and that was her mom and dad's camper there so nice and close to the water. She was ten, the same age as me, pretty, and said she was single. That's all it took for us to strike up a conversation. We talked while I casted out the spinner again and then BAM! I had another fish on. A real fish this time!

Well Anna Lee went a runnin' right overtaher campa cross de street, all dah while a yellin', "Daddy loook Daddy loook, Miiichael cawt a fiiissh!" (Oh that Southern accent of hers made my heart skip a beat! She was soweet!)

Course her Paw had to check in regarding what my intentions were, and he came to understand they were honorable.

Meanwhile I guess my absence had been noticed by the girls who knew I'd gone fishing. Of course it had to be Denise and Pam that busted me with Anna Lee and turned me in to the authorities. I never did live down that I'd found a girlfriend that week. And a wonderful week it was!

Back to the vacation adventure. This time we also got some Maryland blue crabs and bought some clams. I ate my first raw clams on this vacation. Dad and Uncle Joe were downing the raw clams and steamed Maryland blue crabs as fast as they could, chasing them down with Schaefer beer. But after the night I spent clutching the toilet it was quite a few years before I tried them raw again. I found out I got sick because I didn't chase those clams down with beer. Today they are one of my favorite foods—with the beer of course!

One evening at about dark the entire campground assembled as a group outside the office building where they checked the guests in and out. There was a single television set up high on a board above the entrance so everyone could see. The date was July 20, 1969. And . . .

THE EAGLE HAS LANDED!

Yes, we watched from Chincoteague that night as Neil Armstrong took his first steps on the moon.

1970 Lake Champlain

Lake Champlain, which runs along a considerable length of the Northern border between Upstate New York and Vermont, was our family vacation destination for the summer of 1970! Instead of a camper, that year Dad had rented a cottage way up on the northwest side of the lake. This location held some tantalizing glimpses into what the future would hold for the entire Sable family.

To start with the rental was part of a group of cottages on Lake Champlain that went by the name of "IdleHurst, Quiet Hillside Housekeeping Cottages for Rent." Fast forward fifteen years to the west side of Keuka Lake in the picturesque Finger Lakes region of West New York. My father Art Sable formed a property owner's association that he called "IdleHurst Beach Club," envisioning one of the very first property developments of its type in the Keuka Lake area.

That business later expanded to include the construction of several custom built homes in the Finger Lakes region. I always admired my dad for his vision and his entrepreneurial approach to business.

Getting back to that Lake Champlain vacation in the summer of 1970—we had invited Nana and Pop Sable to join us that year. Of course fishing would be a highlight once again. This time the prize was Northern pike.

Our Northern Pike Recipe

Put my pop Andy Sable, my dad Art Sable and me in an open 14' aluminum boat. Add three fishing poles and a small outboard motor. Garnish with Williams Wobblers and Thomas Spoon fishing lures and add a single cheap cigar. What do you get? The incomparable sharing of a familiar and mutually enjoyed pastime spanning three generations! Hard to match *that* when it comes to having fun and making the kinds of memories that last a lifetime. The Northern pike and the smallmouth bass surely felt our presence while we were there. The *average* fish weighed in at four to five pounds apiece! And what about that single cheap cigar, anyway? That was Grandpa Andy's *secret weapon* whenever we went fishing. If the fish weren't biting he would threaten them, "Look, if one of you doesn't give in and start biting soon then I'm gonna have to light up the cigar . . . " Usually a warning was enough. But when it wasn't those fish really ended up paying the price when he lit that baby up.

For me, my growing fascination with boats turned yet another page on Lake Champlain, where I actually started a new chapter with my discovery of the marine industry. This body of water was vast enough to attract a number of large sailing yachts exploring the shorelines of the islands and coves. These larger cruising sailboats really caught my attention. My dad and my grandfather taught me a lot about them, like the differences between a sloop, a yawl, a ketch, and a schooner. I learned about the differences between fixed keels and centerboard boats. Years later my interest in sailing would even lead me away from our family boat business. As a young family man in Ithaca I worked as a sales manager for McPherson Sailing Products where I also served as racing crew aboard several sailing yachts. Renowned yacht racer and business owner Don McPherson and his wife Carol were instrumental in developing my sense of business savvy at McPherson's, which served me well in the multi-career life I still had ahead of me.

This year's vacation saw blossoming maturity and a close relationship developing amongst the Sable siblings. A lot less of the whining, "when are we gonna get there?" while a lot more intelligent questions were asked about the places we visited. We enjoyed the day trips away from the cottage and spending the day at the lake. We immersed ourselves in the history of Fort Ticonderoga for example, spending time there with real cannons still perched atop the walls and the like. And instead of just wolfing down the real Vermont maple candies being created before our eyes we asked questions and tried to understand the process we were witnessing.

(We did eat the candy as well!)

Yes, some of the childhood innocence and the simple raw excitement of new adventures that we had felt on previous vacations was gone for good. But I could sense that the common experience, the blessings of sharing these new adventures and making memories together, was strengthening the bonds between us. These vacation adventures formed some of the lasting bonds that keep our family so very close today, even after all of these years.

I remember we made a day trip up to the City of Montreal, Quebec Province, Canada. We went specifically to visit the site of Expo '67. The International and Universal Exposition or Expo '67, as it was commonly known, was the latest rendition of what we used to call the World's Fair. Expo '67 was originally held from April through October in 1967. At the time it was considered the most successful world's fair of the 20th century with sixty-two nations participating.

I recalled that the "old" World's Fair I had heard about as a young child had been held in New York City in 1964. I remembered that whenever my parents had driven us past the site in Flushing Meadows Park I was always so impressed by the iconic giant globe of the Earth sculpture, which was still was in place in 1970 (and for years after the fair was over).

So with those memories behind us, Mom and Dad were very interested in seeing what Expo '67 had been all about. And to top it off, unlike the site of the World's Fair in '64 in New York City, Expo '67 was still open and operating in the summer of 1970!

NYC Site of World's Fair, 1964

Montreal, still going well in 1970 when we visited!

One display that really stood out for all of us was the German Bavarian Pavilion. It was lunchtime and we were looking for a place to eat. There was a cool looking place in the Bavarian Pavilion serving lunch right on the water, so we decided to see what they had to offer.

We were greeted in German and seated in a festive atmosphere on the deck over-looking the edge of the waterfront boardwalk. The lively music was played by men dressed in white shirts with colorful suspenders, and plaid *skirts* with high colorful socks pulled up to their knees! I remember an accordion, an upright bass, a small kettle style drum, and a few wind instruments. Our waiters explained that the celebration being recreated that day was Oktoberfest.

While we waited for the staff to bring us a sampling of the dishes in keeping with the Oktoberfest theme, we had the chance to experience some of the local color working next to where we were seated but down on the water. The local Montreal children were hard at work, just as the children had been two years before in the Thousand Islands. Here they were using canned corn strung out on long hooks with weights at the ends of *hand lines* that they tossed out into the waterway. They were fishing for carp—big ones—*to feed their families at home.* This was not playtime for them. Once again, we witnessed firsthand just how different life could be for children our age in other cultures. And once again, we were really not that far from home. That had an impact on us.

Soon the waitstaff brought out the food and as part of the experience *stayed with us,* explaining what each dish was and how it was made as they served us whatever we wanted to try from the platters. It was all a wonderful experience combining food and entertainment. We savored several types of sausage and a great bratwurst, both grilled and boiled in beer. We enjoyed a nice, stiff crusted and airy bread for holding the various relishes and condiments. The staff even had us trying different types of mustard and horseradish root. And of course there was the best sauerkraut I ever had, with a snap and a crunch to it. It was that fresh! Expo was a noteworthy and formative culinary and cultural adventure for all of us, adults and children alike. I'll never forget it. That lunch was over fifty years ago! That day also foretold what the future would hold for this family that would one day own and operate a marina, two restaurants, and an entertainment venue on the water in upstate West New York.

Our Family Vacation Adventure to the IdleHurst Housekeeping Cottages on Lake Champlain was a maturing experience for the Sable siblings, individually and as a unit. And I learned even more about the marine industry on that trip. Not so apparent at the time was how closely these vacation experiences would foreshadow the critical roles that boats, restaurants, and waterfront properties would later play in all of our futures, together and in our own personal lives.

1971 Cape Cod

With our family vacation to Cape Cod, Massachusetts in the summer of 1971, the Sable family broke new ground in a few ways.

For one, we were headed to a more populated area than we had visited before. And a place with deep colonial history.

As a part of this vacation Mom and Dad planned to take our family out to dinner at a more upscale restaurant than we were accustomed to with the children so young, aged seven to twelve.

We planned two all-day adventures that required traveling some distance away from our home base vacation rental.

Our rental was not located directly on a body of water. This vacation house was more substantial than the modest cottage we had rented at Lake Champlain, and certainly not camping by any stretch of the imagination. That was okay.

One of the two day trips would expose us to a part of American culture that we young Sables had not experienced before. (I'm not sure that was part of the plan though.)

We had rented a house on a lake located just where Massachusetts begins to narrow down into the peninsula, before crossing the bridge onto Cape Cod. The house wasn't exactly on the lake, but it was right across the street. It was a nice lake, albeit in a more residential neighborhood, with family summer homes and not many vacation rental properties. That didn't affect our enjoyment of the lake, it was just a bit different than what we had anticipated. (The property we stayed in was a lake house in an area very similar to where we would call home just two years later, on the West Side of our own beloved Keuka Lake!)

We arrived after noon, settled in and enjoyed a late lunch leftover from the drive while Mom and Dad looked through the local summer vacation guide publications we found waiting for us. And as for the four of us kids? We quickly changed into our swimsuits, grabbed towels and fishing poles, strolled across the street and went down some stairs to the section of lake frontage designated for our use.

The lake was large enough to accommodate powerboats pulling water skiers, something I'd never seen before. I watched, fascinated, as the neighbors pulled their children up out of the water on skis. My sisters and I talked about what it would be like to live in a house on a lake with a boat right out in the front yard. And after watching the action next door to us, I wanted to learn how to waterski! And so a new chapter opened in my learning experiences on recreational boating—a recurring theme for me on our summer vacations. Once again, our Sable family vacation offered a glimpse into what the future held for us.

Julie and I immediately checked out the fishing. A few casts from the little dock on the beach with a Mepps Spinner bait confirmed a healthy population of yellow perch, so the fishing would at least be active and enjoyable. Besides my dad, my sister Julie had become my closest vacation fishing buddy over the years, and was right by my side. We spied a small aluminum rowboat with a couple of oars aboard and later that afternoon got permission to take it out on the lake to fish, just the two of us! How cool is that?

We were only eleven and twelve years old. We stayed, just as we were told, within sight of Mom and Dad who were on the beach with Betty Jeanne (Be) and Lisa. I suggested using a red and white Daredevle Spoon Lure to Julie. I attached a short leader to the swivel just as I had learned from fishing with Dad and Grandpa, and showed her how to cast and retrieve at the proper speed. Once, twice, then BAM, fish on! The rod bent down over with the tip in the water.

They could hear our excitement and hollering from shore. The rod and reel were light and the line was only eight pound test, which meant we had a light drag setting to allow the fish to run and tire out without breaking the light line. Julie got the fish near enough several times for us to catch a glimpse of what we were dealing with. It was either a very large pickerel or a Northern pike, maybe a seven- to ten-pounder—a really nice sized fish! Anyway the rod stayed doubled over. I never saw Julie so excited while fishing before. The fish was so big it was actually moving the boat around! The fish would make a run and she'd work him back in—two, three, four times.

Finally Julie got the fish close enough to the boat for me to try to net it. As a twelve-year-old trying to handle the net while leaning over the side of the boat, it was a little too much for me to stay calm. Plus I was quite excited myself, I had never netted a fish this big before! But I had already learned from watching Dad and Grandpa. I knew you never grab at the line and try to lead the fish into the net. I knew I could do this.

Here's poem of sorts. Read the next paragraph with a rhythm:

This fish was so big! Both of our hearts beating so fast, we didn't want to lose him! I tried from behind, I tried from the front, his eye looks at me, he puts his head up. His mouth opens wide, the lure down inside, he looks at me. . . Again. Net under his tail, Julie raised the rod high, I grabbed at the line . . . I GRABBED AT THE LINE? The fish closed his mouth, he looked away. He shook his head once, then he swam away! We still remember that day my sister and I—You NEVER grab the line.

For a day trip away from home base, Mom and Dad always liked to mix it up. Usually they were met with a lot of whining, "Doo wee haave too . . . Why can't wee juust staay heere?" The young ones would usually still be recovering from the initial drive to our destination, and they'd want to stay put and enjoy the lake or the beach right where we were. That's easier, right? But Mom and Dad usually had other plans and the kids sometimes just couldn't understand why.

This year would be a little different for a few reasons. First, the drive from our home in Edison to the rental in Massachusetts had only taken a little over four hours. Second, our group was noticeably maturing. Julie and I were likely to be at least curious about what Mom and Dad had planned, and Betty Jeanne and Lisa really couldn't argue against the four of us effectively. Third, this day trip sounded really cool.

We headed out onto the Cape to the ocean port city of Hyannis Port. Along the way Mom and Dad filled us in about the history of the Kennedy family who were based there, including John F. Kennedy, brothers Bobby and Ted, their wives and children, and of course the patriarch, Joseph. The history of the family, their triumphs and their tragedies, PT 109, and their bootlegging during Prohibition all proved fascinating and a lively question and answer session ensued as we approached our first destination at the port.

The plan was for us to board a passenger ferry for the ninety-minute ride out to Nantucket Island! Again for me this included a study—a quick study this time —of the various types of vessels found in this more commercial marine environment. And on our way out of the harbor the ferry was overtaken by a rather luxurious classic style mahogany yacht. Over the loudspeaker came the announcement that it was the Kennedy family aboard that yacht and we all waved at them while they waved back!

But we all were more focused on what we would find out on the island itself with its rich history in seafaring and the whaling industry. The lifestyle on the island was like nothing we had experienced before. No automobile traffic, for starters.

The shops that we first thought were modern recreations of life on the island long ago —the boat builders and the sail lofts, the cordage shop, the fishnet and lobster trap makers, the bicycle shops and the small forging shops producing boat hardware—all of this was real life hundreds of years ago, and in many cases those lifestyles and trade occupations continued virtually unchanged to this day.

So many parts of our country's history and the multitude of roles filled by this small but ideally located island and its port are truly astonishing.

We had lunch on a brick covered plaza between buildings that dated back more than 300 years.

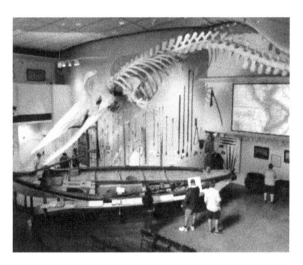

The whaling museum was *so very cool!* Try to imagine the scale of the battle between Man and Whale. Think about mounting an assault on that animal with a harpoon such as those on the wall, whilst rowing and handling the craft pictured, in the middle of an angry ocean. This gives us insight into the dangers and difficulties inherent in 19th century whaling.

Nantucket Island certainly ranks among the top three of the most interesting and important historical places that our family visited over our six years of Summer Vacation Adventures.

And how about dinner out, with proper table manners! Mom and Dad decided the time had come to introduce us to having dinner out together in a restaurant. That is, not at a truck stop, burger joint, pizza shop, or diner. Something a bit more upscale in atmosphere, menu selection, and service. The type of restaurant where we children were expected to address the waitstaff with "yes, sir" and "no ma'am." Where Dad might have a cocktail before dinner. Where there was an aquarium in the dining area with live lobsters!

The children weren't issued placemats for coloring and a box of crayons here. And we were expected to behave with each other too. Not that such an experience was supposed to be fun for the youngest of us. But with Mom and Dad directing Julie and I, the thought was that Betty Jeanne and Lisa would fall in line with their older siblings. And we'd all be rewarded with the pride of acting like "young ladies and gentlemen." I can happily report that on our very first "dinner out" with Mom and Dad all went smoothly. Mission accomplished.

I ordered the swordfish steak for my first real dinner out. I'd heard about swordfish before, and knew what a swordfish looked like from the fishing shows I watched on TV. When Mom asked me if I knew what swordfish steak tasted like I had to say no. But Dad let me order it and taught me how to dip it in the tartar sauce. I enjoyed my meal. With some help from Mom and Dad with meal selection the experience was positive for the entire family, and it would be fine to have dinner out again soon! Mom and Dad told us so. That was our reward. And that was more than enough.

Now this may seem insignificant to those of you who grew up eating in our family owned restaurants, ordering chicken cordon bleu as an eight-year-old. But back in the days before we owned The Lakeside and The Waterfront Restaurants that's how it was. We had no experience having dinner out! We ate dinner at home every night, and it was pretty basic fare. Corn fritters and Shake 'n Bake pork chops. So for Mom and Dad to feel comfortable taking four children ages seven to twelve out was a big step forward for our family in social settings. After the Cape Cod vacation Pop Santangelo would sometimes take us out to dinner at his country club, and he knew from then on he never had to worry about our manners!

For our next day trip we planned to drive way out on the Cape, with a stop at Cape Cod National Seashore for a swim in the ocean. We would continue on to Provincetown at the very tip of Cape Cod.

Mom and Dad knew Provincetown was known as an artist community and figured there would be lots of shops with artists busy painting on street corners. Reflecting the times, we also expected a very festive atmosphere. It was every bit of that, with revelers packed shoulder-to-shoulder in the streets so cars could not even pass through!

Little did we know we were about to have our first introduction to the liberal way of life and free loving atmosphere prevalent in Provincetown.

That surprise went very well for all of us. Julie and I were cognizant of the atmosphere around us, but for Betty Jeanne and Lisa? It all went right over their heads, while we talked with the artists and all enjoyed a very good lunch from a steam cart on a street corner.

Provincetown was a classic seaside town with cottage style houses and narrow cobblestone streets in the old parts of town. Mom didn't find any works of art that caught her eye that day, though she did enjoy just looking around and visiting with the shop owners. As for me? I found out the ocean was way too cold for swimming way out on Cape Cod!

A few days later on the drive home to Edison we planned our departure so we'd be able to stop and spend part of the day at Mystic Seaport in Mystic, Connecticut, where we visited the famous Maritime Museum and Seafaring village.

The site is an actual operational 19th century seaport and a historically accurate seafaring village. A fantastic collection of restored and recreated boats and sailing ships from the period were waiting for inspection docked at the piers, including the oldest remaining wooden commercial sailing ship, the Charles W. Morgan. Some of the craft were undergoing refurbishment and restoration work in the shops, on the boardwalk, and at the shipyard.

The accompanying seafaring village was recreated from more than sixty rare commercial historic buildings that had been meticulously restored and then carefully moved to the site.

This operating 19th century village was staffed with true craftsmen practicing their trades to show what life was like in the period. We visited a wide variety of shops including the print shop, the tack shop, the hardware store, a candlemaker, a glass shop, a fabric weaver, the general store, the saloon, and the village bakery, where they were baking bread, pressing cider, and making apple butter that day. Most of the craftsmen were explaining the details of their trade, and samples of the goods they produced were available for purchase. We got some apple butter. Yummm!

The visit to Mystic Seaport may sound similar to Nantucket Island, but the differences between the two lifestyles really stood out to us, especially after visiting both locations only days apart.

The lifestyle of the islanders on Nantucket revolved entirely around the sea, its rhythm of life controlled by the arrivals and departures of the tides and the whaling ships. The traffic of goods to and from the mainland was based solely on the exports and the needs of the island's occupants, which revolved exclusively around the whaling industry.

In Mystic the lifestyle was much more diverse. The shipping was based much more on the export of goods from the interior of the mainland. And the craftsmen in the shops provided goods and services for the much wider diversity of lifestyles found on the mainland. And the merchant ships and their crews had somewhat different needs from the whaling ships and their crews.

Just to be able to make these comments and comparisons between the lifestyles of people, whether they were from 1971 Provincetown, or Nantucket Island and Mystic Connecticut in the 19th Century says an awful lot about our Summer Family Vacation Adventure to Cape Cod, Massachusetts in 1971. It reflects that we children were growing up, and that Mom and Dad were doing a great job guiding us along the way. And lest we forget, dinner out was fair game from now on!

1972 Keuka Lake

Keuka Lake followed Cape Cod as our vacation destination in 1972. The Farris family joined us once again and we headed to the middle of the Finger Lakes region of West New York.

At Cape Cod in 1971 it became apparent that the Sable children were starting to grow up. For example, we'd learned to go out for dinner with Mom and Dad and could be trusted to behave. But the growing up went deeper than that. What we'd find entertaining and enjoyable within a vacation setting was beginning to shift as well.

We started to notice the other families around us. Not so much the other families that were also on vacation, but the families that actually *lived* where we were vacationing, year-round.

Remember the families at the lake we stayed at on Cape Cod? The children there could walk into their front yard and instead of finding a lawn to mow there was a *lake!* A lake where they could swim, or fish, or even go waterskiing behind the boat parked at their own dock! What would it be like to live in a place like that? (And just how does this relate to our vacation locale for 1972?)

In the last six years or so, at least as far back as our first family vacation with the Farris family at Cape Hatteras in 1967, it seemed as though whenever the two families got together, whether for a holiday or even just a short weekend get together, the adult conversation always seemed to drift to the subject of a small business that the two families could own and operate together.

So what does that have to do with the children growing up? And what does it have to do with Keuka Lake where we joined the Farris family for our 1972 summer vacation?

Dad and Uncle Joe had taken a short vacation of their own in the spring of 1972. Just the two of them. They were off on a trip shopping for a business to buy and operate as partners. They felt like they needed to strike out on their own, make their own way in the world, and make their own decisions. To take a risk. To take control over their lives once again. To decide for themselves just how the children would be brought up. Ultimately, they hoped to enjoy their own lives more, while also setting the best example for their children.

So on that trip they'd made a swing through the Finger Lakes and visited Keuka Lake. They returned home with some ideas to discuss with Mom and Aunt Lucy.

As I said earlier, we children were growing up a bit. Those kinds of conversations—about buying a business, quitting jobs, picking up their families and moving us to a new home in a new state—they did *not* go unnoticed!

And our parents really weren't being secretive about it or trying to hide anything from us at all. And that's where this story starts to come together. The plan was to take both the Sable and the Farris Families on a summer vacation together based out of Keuka Lake, so we would all get to take a firsthand look at what Dad and Uncle Joe had been considering for a family business.

The vacation part of the plan was simple. We'd stay on Keuka Lake, a gem of a lake located smack in the middle of the magnificent Finger Lakes region. It was about a five-hour drive from our home in Edison, New Jersey and four hours from the Farris family home in Albany, New York.

As was true with any lakefront vacation we'd taken before, there'd be fishing, swimming, playing on the beach for the younger ones, dinner out, and taking a look around at the lifestyle in the area where Dad and Uncle Joe had apparently seen a few businesses on the market that had caught their attention. We kids were curious, excited, and a little bit nervous too, all at the same time. In July of 1972 we set out for the Viking Resort on the east side of Keuka Lake.

I'm sure we had heard on the national news back home in Edison about Hurricane Agnes, a slow moving hurricane from the that had crept up into the Ohio Valley from the Gulf of Mexico. It had basically stalled there causing a week straight of heavy rains and horrendous flooding that had inflicted millions of dollars in damage on the region.

What we did not know at the time was the geographical relationship between the Ohio River Valley and the Finger Lakes region. And that a great deal of that week's heavy rain had fallen onto the watersheds of the rivers and streams crisscrossing the Finger Lakes! The rain that fell flowed into and through the lakes until the areas downstream began to flood.

The Corps of Engineers, the authorities in charge, had given the orders to start to retain the water in the lakes. Once issued, those orders apparently weren't to be rescinded until the flooding downstream had begun to recede. All the while it kept raining for another week.

The water had nowhere else to go, so the Finger Lakes also flooded. Seriously. Enough that the authorities closed the lakes to boating activity—for the entire summer. The lake frontage properties were destroyed. Our hopes for a lakeside vacation were literally washed away with the lakefront real estate!

I distinctly remember the moment when the devastating impact of Hurricane Agnes became apparent to us for the very first time as we were driving to Keuka Lake from Edison. Along the way Dad was explaining to us all about the Finger Lakes, the wineries, the grape vineyards, Corning Glass, all of the Finger Lakes region highlights in general. Our anticipation grew as we continued up Route 81 from Scranton towards Binghamton.

Looking out the windows, the mood in the car abruptly changed when we first noticed the extent of the destruction that the flooding from Hurricane Agnes had caused. Way off in the Ohio Valley? No. Right where we were headed!

The bridges on Route 81, and then Route 17, had whole fallen trees lodged in the bridge structures and the guardrails. The flood waters had receded some but were still flowing at what were well above record elevations. This was three weeks after the peak of the flooding. The water at its peak elevation had reached twenty-five feet above the roads near Corning, New York, submerging the second floors of the homes under several feet of water! Just trying to imagine the scene of these homes as water rose past the second-floor windows was more than I could fathom. I thought about our home back in Edison. What would it be like to return home to the complete destruction that the families who lived in these houses had faced?

We greeted the Farris cousins upon our arrival at the Viking Resort with an air of heaviness and disappointment hanging over us.

Upon checking in, the owner of the Viking Resort, Ken Christiansen, made it clear that all plans for activities involving the lake were canceled. Aside from the swimming pool at the motel portion of the resort, this vacation wasn't going to be much fun for the youngest children.

Speaking for myself, the eldest of the seven cousins at thirteen years old, I was very much looking forward to learning more about the businesses that Dad and Uncle Joe planned to take us to visit.

The adults had already honed in on two Keuka area businesses: a marina at the north end of the east branch of the lake, Hopkins Marine Service, and a diversified metal fabricating firm in Hammondsport known as Clark Specialty Company.

So there was quite a bit for the adults to discuss after dinner that first night of our vacation. I remember they talked about Stan Clark and Clark Specialty first. Among the variety of existing contracts the firm had for fabrication of sheet metal products, in the past the company had produced a small line of riveted aluminum rowboats ranging from ten to sixteen feet called Keuka Kraft.

Stan Clark, the owner and president of the company also owned and operated a marina business at the south end of the lake in Hammondsport. That business and property were more interesting to Art and Joe, but Mr. Clark was mainly interested in selling the metal fabricating business and had only offered the marina as a part of the deal if it was to be sold along with the specialty company. Combined, the financing required to buy the two businesses together was beyond what Art and Joe could secure through the local banks.

The next morning the two families loaded into our cars and made the trip to Hammondsport. We pulled into the parking area for Clark Specialty Company just to get a look at the scale of the operation. It wasn't a huge facility, but judging from the number of employee vehicles parked there—maybe around forty—I certainly wouldn't consider it a "Mom and Pop" operation. The overall appearance of the buildings and the parking lot was not what I expected. Let's just say the entire operation was a bit worn and rough around the edges.

The adults had decided the night before to continue the tour up the west side of the lake, and then around the bluff, the peninsula that divided the east branch from the west branch of Keuka Lake. That would bring us to Penn Yan where we'd stop by the Hopkins Marina operation to look it over before continuing on back to the Viking Resort. At that point we'd have completed the trip around Keuka Lake, about sixty-seven miles.

Less than a half mile up the West Lake Road from Hammondsport we pulled off to the right and went down a steep driveway to Clark's Boat Livery. Art and Joe had described a long narrow lakefront yard area with a steep bank back up to the Lake Road to the left (west). A long sea wall to the right, running north and south, had been holding the driveway and a cramped parking area in place. The sea wall had also been creating the deep water for a marina with about seventy-five boat parking spaces, or slips.

About half of the slips were exposed, the others were covered under a series of roofs built right above of the docks on sets of maybe six or eight boat slips each, like boat garages over the water. The entire flat and useable property was only maybe one hundred feet wide by maybe six hundred feet long, north to south.

There had been a bait shop, a small office with a ship's store, a gas dock, a boat launch area, and a boatyard where boats had been cradled for storage and repair. Key words in the above descriptions of the property from the night before: "had been."

What remained of the operation was a far cry from what Art and Joe had seen the last time they visited. The flood waters were still above the sea wall and over the tops of the gas dock and the boat slips, and the waves from the light breeze that day were licking the edge of the driveway.

There was a silence as we all stepped out of the cars. Mom and Aunt Lucy held the little children close to the driveway as Uncle Joe, Dad and I walked ahead to survey more of the damage. Boats that had broken loose from the docks were laying haphazardly around the yard, which basically was impassable from where we had stopped at the base of the driveway. Some boats were sunk in place at their slips, while others were up on top of the docks. The roofs of several of the covered boat slips had collapsed onto the boats and were rocking back and forth, squeaking as they shifted against the remaining sections of the sea wall which had all but washed away. The gas dock and the launch area were buried under debris from neighboring properties and even whole trees, roots and all, were tangled in a big floating mass of debris pinned against the shoreline.

The entire marina operation had not only been destroyed, erosion from the waves and flooding continued to cause more damage. It was hard to imagine getting this marina back into operation. It was even harder still to imagine starting a new business at a location that had sustained such damage. Much of the property had literally washed away and into the lake! A sense of disappointment emanated from Art and Joe, and I was feeling a bit of the same, even though I hadn't seen the property before. As for my mom and Aunt Lucy? With Art and Joe feeling so down about the whole situation, I guess there was no way for them to get Mom and Lucy fired up about the idea now.

And my dad and Uncle Joe had been so excited about it just the night before. They couldn't wait to show us this marina. I'll admit I had already gotten excited about a marina becoming our family business. And I could tell Art and Joe had been hoping they could talk Mr. Clark into selling them just the marina without the Specialty Company. But what we had seen that day had dashed all hopes of ever getting Mom and Aunt Lucy on board.

We continued on up the West Lake Road, past a few smaller businesses—a bait shop (Jake's), a bar (The Wheel Inn), a hot dog joint (Dottie's Dog House) and a small yacht club (KYC). We finally stopped at a place called Bud's. Marina, that is. Fiberglass Boats. And Chrysler Outboards!

The place was just the right size. Yes, it too was a mess from the flood. (And probably some from before that!) Bud said the place was not for sale. But Bud's wife Ruth kept sticking her head out the windows of the apartment overhead and yelling down at us, YES! Yes! We'll sell the Marina! Bud! BUUDDD! YES! WE'LL SELL THEM THE MARINA!

We continued on up the road, past the Knotty Pine Inn, past Kelly's Marina (not for sale), out onto The Bluff and to Johnson's Marine Service (not for sale), and finally to Hopkin's Marine Service. Penn Yan, on the original list. Last stop of the day.

I got to hang out with my dad and Uncle Joe while they talked with Dave Hopkins. Nice place, and not a whole lot of damage from the flood. Dave wasn't under any real pressure to sell the place. He had listed it "just to check out the market." He'd consider selling it. But for a price that turned out, in Art's and Joe's minds, to be too high to make ends meet.

And, as they say, the rest is history! Yes. That was the last of the family vacations for the Farris and the Sable families.

See chapter 8, Family Stories, for the rest of the story.

Principles, Life Lessons, and Parenting

Throughout their lives, my mom and dad have learned many principles and life lessons that they wanted to pass along to their children. They also inspired us to develop our own to pass along to our children one day.

In this part of Chapter 6 we all share family memories. I'm sure we will all enjoy the memories this section will bring back to life for us. Additionally our own families will gain insight into our generation of the Sable family and how we were raised. No doubt Mom and Dad will enjoy reading this too!

From Mike

I learned a great deal about parenting at home from the example they set in how they decided to raise us.

The First Swimming Pool

Even back at the Avenel home, our first home, we always had water to play with, in addition to the classic sandbox with the little buckets and shovels. I remember starting out with the lawn sprinkler when we were very young on hot summer days.

The Avenel Home
324 Woodruff Avenue
Avenel, New Jersey

We also had one of those single-piece hard plastic kiddie pools. Mom always rubbed us down with suntan oil—there wasn't any sunscreen back in the day. Remember how cold the water was right after Dad filled the pool with the hose? Of course the sandbox buckets always migrated over to the pool at some point, which meant a water change almost every day!

When we moved to the Edison house our family was always strapped for extra money with four small kids. Yet our parents always made it possible for us to have good clean fun right in our own backyard! They set up a three-foot-deep frame pool with a liner and a filter, assembled over a raked sand ground cover. I'm sure it cost an awful lot of money for a tight budget, but the kids had a pool right in the backyard!

The Edison Home
30 Stephenville Parkway
Edison, New Jersey

The Ice Skating Rink

We inherited a brick patio laid in sand that covered a quarter of the area of our backyard in Edison. It was irregular in shape, conforming around the landscaping and a good sized maple tree. Not an easy thing to do, but Dad was able to frame out a form of 2 x 4 lumber that covered the patio, and then he lined it with heavy-duty plastic. When the weather was cold enough, he flooded the area with the garden hose. A couple of weeks later it was Christmas and Santa brought all four of us our own pair of figure skates! We all enjoyed learning to skate and building the ice rink became an annual tradition.

The Monkey Bars

Again working with a tight budget, Mom and Dad saw to it that their children had a swing set with a slide, and a set of monkey bars for climbing, right in the backyard. I recall bringing a scrap piece of plywood to the top of the set with a couple of folding lawn chairs. Sitting up there in the mid to late 1960s I saw the fires burning from the Esso/Humble Oil refineries in Carteret for several days after the accidental explosion. (Yes, back then explosions like that were accidental!) On a more historical note, from the same perch I watched, over two summers, as the Twin Towers of the World Trade Center made their way up to the height of the Chrysler Building, then the Empire State Building, and finally beyond and alone into the sky to stand as the tallest buildings in the world.

The Fire Pit

This was Dad's vision. Our first fire pit, built of brick and sunken right into the backyard brick patio. With logs for bench seats. Kids love campfires! What a great place for weekend parties, roasting marshmallows, and hosting barbecues with family and friends. Another reason for the children to have fun right in our own backyard!

The Inground Pool and Deck

When our three-foot-deep pool was not enough to contain and entertain the children any longer—here comes another budget conscious brainstorm from our father! Dad had a local contractor named Sal Cursi come over with his backhoe and dig out an area for a sunken inground pool just beyond the backyard brick patio! More about that budget conscious inground pool brainstorm in a moment.

The Family Room Addition

Sal Cursi had built Pop Santangelo's home next door, and he also dug out the foundation for, and framed in, our large family room addition, extending from the back of the house and next to the fire pit, the brick patio/ice rink, and later the new pool. After Sal gave him the start, our father finished this family room addition. HIMSELF. One step at a time. Paycheck to paycheck.

That Inground Pool

Now Dad had found a way to fit something more into this small backyard—a sunken pool! With a wooden boardwalk style sun deck to boot. (And don't forget about that swing set and the monkey bars.) How could Mom and Dad have envisioned all of this in such a small place, with little money, and four children who were growing up quickly? We would now have every reason to keep ourselves entertained at home when we were not in school.

So Dad actually built in this pool himself. He found a used 5' deep by 20' diameter above ground pool and assembled it over sand in the area that Sal had dug for it. Dad removed the earth by hand from about a third of the side of the pool hole facing the house and filled in behind the pool, creating a ground level base for the wooden sun deck he constructed on the far side. Being a creative guy Dad got a load of grey boulders to landscape and camouflage the exposed part of the pool, which became the pool filter and service area.

This was a huge project for one man to take on by himself, but he had his wife to support his efforts and see to his children's needs daily. I am sure that I have not, to this day, seen such a couple so devoted to their four children, and working as such a team, to give us all a home that we had no reason to leave. Everything we wanted and needed was right there for us in our own backyard with Mom and Dad.

I could go on and on about countless other things that Mom and Dad provided for us while on the tightest of budgets and schedules, but I just really want to say: Thank you for all that you did for us, Mom and Dad!

From Julie

Mom and Dad taught me that the world is bigger than our backyard, yet small enough to not be afraid to get out and see it. I wanted to return that gift to my children. We have sent many of them to places we have never been to ourselves. Some of them have been all over Europe and even to Australia. This idea that the world goes beyond our backyard also inspired our family trip to Peru. Talk about mountains! We wanted our children to know the world was within their reach. And all of this started with a school trip to France and Switzerland! Thank you Mom and Dad.

From Dad to his daughters: Go to college so you never have to depend on anyone to take care of you.

From Mom: Always put family first.

Another Dad lesson: Work hard and play hard, but work hard first.

From Be

First let me say that *the best gift Mom and Dad ever gave us was each other*! We are each other's best friends and there's no one in the world I'd rather hang out with than my family! I think we all feel this way because of the way Mom and Dad brought us up—always close, doing things together, family vacations every year growing up, sharing, learning, finding adventures in our own backyard, and later in life, making sure our holidays were spent together, family dinners and happy hours at Mom and Dad's on a regular basis, and family work parties to help each of us out when we needed it most—basically, anything that would bring us all together!

The importance of a strong work ethic was instilled in us at an early age. Work hard and play hard and make sure no one can ever call you a slacker. We were taught to have respect for our elders, always say please and thank you, look someone in the eye and give them your full attention when being spoken to, be courteous and kind and if you say you're going to do something, you better well do it! Be proud but also be humble. Take time to smell the roses and enjoy the little things in life. Mom always taught us to never go to someone's house for a meal empty handed and that when returning a plate, make sure you return it with some deliciousness on it!

These life lessons may sound small but, added up, they create the kind of character that we all should strive for, and if I may say so, all my siblings already possess. And we learned it all from Mom and Dad! Two amazing human beings who took the time to teach us right from wrong, good from evil and how to love! Brothers and Sisters, thank you for being my best friends and for always sharing your children with me—it means more than you'll ever know! Mom and Dad, I love you and am forever thankful.

From Lisa

Everything of value that I know today, I can relate to Mom and Dad somehow. It's like the book *All I Really Need to Know I Learned in Kindergarten.* I could change that to *All I Really Need to Know I Learned from Mom and Dad.* Let me relate several points from that book to my upbringing:

Share everything – Mom and Dad don't have a lot today, mainly because they gave it all to us. They never hoarded their money or their "stuff." What was theirs, was ours. If we were in need, they provided. They shared their wealth, their love, and their time, and taught us to be the same way. We are a giving, generous family because of them.

Put things back where you found them – hmmm . . . not all of us kept this value. I still can't find anything!

Clean up your own mess – We had to always do our chores, one of which was to clear your plate from the table when done. I think I may even remember Mom throwing things of mine away if I left them laying around.

Say you're sorry when you hurt someone – physically or emotionally. We had to look each other in the eye and apologize. I use that same strategy to this day in my classroom. It's so important!

Warm cookies and cold milk are good for you – we were sent next door to Nana Rose and Papa Mike's for this!

Live a balanced life. Learn some and think some and draw and paint and sing and dance and play and work every day – Mom and Dad both taught us to be hard workers, yet still play. Go outside until dinnertime. Play in the creek. Collect bugs. They were perfect role models for what a worker should be. To this day, they are still working, physically and mentally on their businesses they created for all of us to enjoy.

Hold hands and stick together – Well, we as a family may not hold hands, but we sure do stick together. If anyone hurts one of us or our kids, you can bet your bottom that the whole family will be on their case! If we disagree with one another, we agree to disagree and move on. Mom has taught us that God and family are what is important in life.

The Golden Rule – we were *always* taught this, over and over and over. I think we knew this before we knew how to walk.

Here are a few additional things I am grateful I learned from Mom and Dad:

- Always keep your car's gas above half full in case of an emergency - from Dad
- Cook chicken long enough so you don't end up with MJs half baked chicken. (Maybe that's why I burn everything I try to cook.)
- Be careful riding an escalator. If you step on a crack, you probably will fall and kill yourself. Hold on tight, hold your breath, and be scared to death every time you get on one.
- Look people in the eye.
- When you meet somebody and want to remember their name, use the Dale Carnegie strategies and repeat the name several times while making some type of association in your head. I'm still horrible at this!
- Good work ethics, honesty, loyalty.
- And last, but never least—the importance of FAMILY

F - faith, forever, fun, food
A - affectionate, active, awesomeness
M - making memories
I - Italian feasts, important
L - love, laughter
Y - Young at heart

From Andy

My story starts as a young boy growing up with a younger brother/best friend. I feel extremely fortunate that Mom and Dad made the move from New Jersey to Keuka Lake and gifted us with this unusual (I guess by today's standards) freedom of being able to run free in the woods right outside our home as kids.

From the start, I loved the outdoors and really disliked anything city. As if it couldn't get any better, Art and I came home from school one day and there was a large enclosed truck in our driveway in Lakeside. Dad was there with the driver and yelled "Come over here boys!" They were just about to wheel out two brand new Yamaha 80cc motorcycles! Art and I couldn't believe it, we were thrilled! I can't remember when Dad talked to us about the repayment schedule, but he made it clear to us we were responsible for paying him back for them (they were around $900 each I believe).

This was my first introduction to being held responsible for a debt, and it taught us each a solid work ethic and financial responsibility from a very early age (I think this happened when I was around eight or ten years old). I remember hiding every dollar I would make in my sock/underwear drawer, thrilled that I was that much closer to paying Dad back! My memory is terrible, but I believe we both paid him back within two years. And you know what he did with the money? He put it right back into a bank account for each of us. This again caught us completely by surprise and yet taught us another valuable lesson—selflessness.

We were definitely spoiled as kids, but had a mother that balanced this perfectly. I remember Mom saying many times that you don't do anything to someone that you wouldn't want done to yourself. Yes, we were spoiled little brats, but I feel like Mom truly gave us the ability to be "good human beings" and treat others with respect. No matter how much trouble we got into during the day—and with the new motorcycles, it was a lot—she would always be there to tuck us in at night and say I love you. She would usually come straight from the restaurant next door, no matter how busy they were, and I always remember she had that "restaurant smell" in her clothes that you could smell the second she walked into the room. MJ taught us love, family, respect, and responsibility. For this, I'm forever grateful.

From Art

I've been contemplating many different topics for this section of the book for weeks. But I keep coming back to one thing. FAMILY. We all have thrived in our own ways because we always have that support to fall back on—a safety net to let us spread our wings. There is no other family with such unconditional love and support. No matter what happens to me, my wife or my children, I *know* my family would drop everything to help.

I have seen the happiness, confidence, safety and security grow in my children over the years. Thank you, Mom and Dad, for providing me with the tools to pass on to our beloved boys.

Others come and go, but our family is always here to stay with unconditional support and no judgment. It's something I think about often and never take for granted.

Oh, and we're a damn riot together too!

The World Travel Series

Our mom and dad seemed to instinctively understand that a lot of what they wanted to teach us before releasing us into the world could be instilled by having us see what the rest of the world was like beyond our own backyard.

I think the experiences they both had overseas had an influence on their own lives, and they believed we would grow from our overseas travels as well.

Dad had actually lived in France as a teenager. Pop Sable had been a key member of the group that had pioneered the development of radar for use by the United States military prior to World War II. After the war the technology continued to advance, and with the Russian threat to our nation growing in the 1950s Pop was asked to continue his work in Europe. The United States planned to use radar as a defense, providing advance warning of Russian aggression.

Pop moved his whole family to Paris while he completed his service. Dad was a teenager at the time and he and his sisters attended the American School in Paris while they lived there.

Interesting side note: When Pop Sable returned to the United States with his family they crossed the Atlantic Ocean aboard a ship, the Andrea Doria. The very next time the Andrea Doria set out on the Atlantic Passage for America was the last time it was to sail. The Andrea Doria was shipwrecked, sinking off the coast of Connecticut.

Pop often spoke about the Andrea Doria and that tragedy at family gatherings when I was a child. His experiences aboard the ship, and the tragedy that befell it on its very next crossing to the United States, had a profound impact on our grandfather. I believe his experience at sea was behind the respect and love Pop had for the ocean for the rest of his life.

When we lived in Edison, New Jersey, Dad was the operations manager for SeaLand Shipping in Port Elizabeth. He and Mom traveled to San Juan, Puerto Rico, where SeaLand had established a major presence as the innovator of container shipping. Malcolm McClean, who headed up SeaLand, pioneered container shipping. The route between San Juan and Port Elizabeth had established company owned terminals at each location, bringing the concept of container shipping into its own as the predominant means of shipping worldwide today.

The next step for SeaLand was the European mainland and a connection in the Netherlands. Mom accompanied Dad there, enjoying her travels for the duration of his assignment coordinating the operations of the SeaLand terminal there.

As a sixteen-year-old sophomore in Hammondsport in 1975, I had my own opportunity to travel to Europe. Once I returned from France and Italy I told the family all about the trip and how it had affected me. After that, Mom and Dad decided such an experience would benefit all of us, and they made the commitment to send each of their children on a similar adventure of our own choosing, possibly at a slightly older age. And so it was! Enjoy our recollections of those adventures in The World Travel Series.

Mike in France and Italy

I came home from school one day in the winter of my sophomore year in high school and announced to my parents that I was planning on participating in a program entitled The American Institute for Foreign Studies—Springtime in Paris.

In French class that day, the opportunity was presented to us to travel abroad and experience the French language in its truest form. I also recognized immediately the opportunity to see what life was like in other parts of the world first-hand, and also the chance to follow in my dad's footsteps. He had lived in France as a teenager.

I was really looking forward to getting a fresh view of a much bigger world that I was sure was out there. I had actually enjoyed our move from New Jersey. Hammondsport, New York had offered me the opportunity to present myself as whoever I wanted to be. (*I had even made the cut to play for the varsity baseball team as a freshman!*) When I met the kids in Hammondsport, I was freed from the bonds of the New Jersey suburbs where the racial and social tensions of the last decade had continued to linger. The move to Hammondsport had freed me from the discrimination that had been imposed on me by the New Jersey school administration simply because I am white. This experience in France would once again offer me the chance to enjoy that feeling of leaving it all behind. I'd have the chance to see for myself how young people in France and Italy dealt with racism. Plus I would be the only student from my class in Hammondsport participating. I'd be truly seeing what other people in the world see without having a constant reminder of my life back home sitting there beside me.

My parents were easier to convince than I had expected. We decided to split the cost 50/50 and in April 1975 I found myself waiting impatiently at JFK Airport in New York City for the arrival of the Boeing 747 for my first airplane ride ever, and to Paris to boot!

(An interesting side note here is the reason I had to wait for this 747, which arrived nearly ten hours behind schedule. World Airways had loaned many of their 747s to the US government for the evacuation of Saigon—in April 1975 the US embassy in Saigon was under siege. Our military was scrambling to get the last of our troops, support personnel, and whatever South Vietnamese patriots we could rescue from the rooftops and out of the country as Saigon was being overrun by the Viet Cong.)

My first day in Paris we hit the ground running. Our bags were loaded from the 747 into the motor coach to begin touring the city! We spent three days and two nights exploring Paris, visiting all the standard historical and cultural attractions. Places like the Louvre where I saw the Mona Lisa with her mysterious grin, the Eiffel Tower with that extraordinary view of Paris, and L'arc de Triompe where I posed for a photo in the exact location my father had back in the 1950s. Years later my daughter Sylvia would have her photo taken at the same location!

Art Sable
1954

Mike Sable
1975

Sylvia Sable
2020

During our free time, adult supervision was liberal. With a few new friends I explored the culinary attractions of the city by day, enjoying my first experiences with French cuisine and fine wine at the sidewalk cafes. I was sixteen years old at the time, getting my first glimpse into what life might be like when I became an adult. I had something to shoot for if I played my cards right.

We visited the Sorbonne (the university) on the Left Bank of the Seine. The students were Communists and I saw up close how the United States is viewed in other parts of the world. I kept my mouth shut so as not to reveal my American accent while I watched them marching and cheering the defeat of the United States in Vietnam! Not what I had expected . . . It made me think first, slow down a bit, look around, and learn to put myself in the other guy's shoes before making assumptions or passing judgment.

By night we roamed through the entertainment districts. I remember a nightclub in a basement under a theater where disco was the rage. We danced and drank wine with the locals and learned that the rooms we were partying in had been part of a series of dungeons used for executions in the 14th and the 15th centuries.

The words scratched into the stone walls were the end-of-life accounts of the condemned. The prisoners who left these writings had been left to slowly drown, locked and chained in their cells as the spring season brought the rise of the River Seine and, over a period of days, flooded the dungeons.

We stayed out too late that night, not knowing the subways in Paris closed at midnight! After hiking across the city for most of the night we packed up, boarded the bus, and headed down through the French countryside from Paris to Nice on our way to the Mediterranean coast.

Along the way we visited several historic buildings and locations, cities both large and small including the Avignon, the Palace of the Popes, vineyards and wineries, cheese caves, dairy farms, and even a famous French perfume producer. I gazed out the coach window for hours at the rural French countryside, the farmers, the small towns, the vehicles on the highway and the people inside. It all looked so different from back at home, yet somehow with so much in common too.

After an overnight stay at an old stone French country inn—old style with shared toilets, bidets, and showers—we arrived at the French Riviera and the city of Nice, France. After enjoying the best seafood dinner I have ever eaten we spent the night in a fine resort hotel and headed for Italy the next morning.

On the way we stopped at Eze, a quaint little medieval village perched on a cliff overlooking the Mediterranean. But this little village was not built upon the cliff, it was literally carved out of the bedrock that formed the cliff jutting out over the sea! This was a village of craftsmen with their little shops built into the caves and their wares on display outside in the narrow, carved out alleyways. I bought a silk scarf and a pottery bowl that caught my eye to bring home for the family. I'll always remember the simple yet elegant way the people of Eze lived and the pride in their voices as they showed us how they made their products.

Our route to San Remo and the Italian Riviera took us through the principality of Monaco and the city of Monte Carlo. We spent our lunch hour there window shopping the exclusive shops that lined the streets of this beautiful city, not even asking the price of things. Very few items even had prices attached. The yachts at the marina were enormous! Most of the vehicles were chauffeur-driven, and except for the windshields all other glass was blacked out. Parts of the streets I walked down were part of the famous Monaco Gran Prix course which winds through the narrow streets of the city.

We spent the late afternoon and evening in San Remo, Italy and had another great meal. In general I found the atmosphere there much more relaxed and less intimidating than Monte Carlo.

Later that evening the bus brought us back to Nice where we boarded a night train for Paris. That was quite an experience with the sleeping cars equipped with bunks, blankets, and pillows! It was a bit noisy and too rough of a ride for me to get any real sleep, so I made my way to a coach car and enjoyed conversation with some of the French passengers. They were friendly and less presumptuous than the Parisians I had met. And they didn't even mention what was happening in Vietnam. When we arrived in Paris we had some time to wander around before departing for London and our flight home. Being near the airport it was a bit more of an industrial area and I really can't recall anything special there, although the food continued to be outstanding!

Overall my experiences overseas taught me a great lesson about putting our role as United States citizens into perspective as part of what is a *very* big world out there.

There are so many other ways of life beyond our borders that I never would have imagined. This has left an impression on me. I am now more convinced than ever that all people, from all walks of life, from all parts of the world and from all nations and ethnicities are part of one common humanity.

We all share responsibility for caring for one another as human beings. And we all share this same planet. We must all come together and realize that ultimately, to succeed as human beings in the Big Picture, we must embrace that diversity which exists amongst us. We must learn to use that diversity to identify and to fill all required roles to protect our species and our planet in order for any of us to survive the Big Picture. There are just so many big challenges to our survival that we have yet to discover out there.

Julie in Europe and the World

This is my favorite story to tell, as it is the beginning of the rest of my life. Mom and Dad sent me to France and Switzerland. France was lovely, lots of guys with purses and everyone speaking English! Beautiful cathedrals, wine, bread and cheese for every meal. Lovely. But this is not what has stuck with me all these years. Funny, since I can rarely remember most things. Anyway, one night we took the night train from France to Switzerland. We arrived at night in the dark, got our hotel rooms and went to sleep. The next morning I opened the curtains to the sliding glass door that led to the balcony. I remember as if it were yesterday—I fell backward on the bed and could barely catch my breath. The most majestic mountain towered over me, taking my breath away! My life changed from that day on. That educational trip, a gift from Mom and Dad, sparked a hunger inside that would shape the rest of my life. You see, from that moment on I could never stop looking for mountains. Always wanting to find higher ones and climb to the top. It drove me to part of every mountain range in the continental U.S. It took me to the top of the highest peak, Electric Peak, in Yellowstone. It took me to Mt. Rainier. As I flew in the airplane below the peak which reached above the clouds, I knew I had to climb as high as I could. And climb I did, where only mountain goats dared to join me. It took me to the Rockies, on a vision quest in the Sierra Nevadas, several trips to New Hampshire and countless other climbs. That first trip started a love for the mountains that I've been told I passed on to Andy and Artie when they were young. To this day, I look for mountains that compare to the Alps in Switzerland and I hope to return to them someday soon. That gift from Mom and Dad also taught me the world is bigger than our backyard, yet small enough to not be afraid to get out and see it. I wanted to give that gift to my children. We have sent many of them to places we have not yet been. Some of them have been all over Europe and even to Australia. This idea that the world goes beyond our backyard also inspired our family trip to Peru. Talk about mountains! We wanted our children to know the world was within their reach. And all of this started with a school trip to France and Switzerland! Thank you, Mom and Dad.

Be's Trip Overseas

When I was in my junior year in high school, Mom and Dad sent me to Europe on a school trip, just like my brother and sister before me. The year I went the itinerary was to France and Spain! I was so nervous because I didn't know anyone but quickly made friends. What a trip! France with all its beauty and history was amazing. I remember roaming all around Paris with its cobblestone streets, the cafes along the sidewalk for lunches of bread and cheese, the amazing Eiffel Tower and, of course, being a teenager, the freedom to go to nightclubs—even though we had to sneak out after lights out! I also remember how far ahead Paris was in terms of fashion. I took a picture of a girl wearing pink and purple together, in one outfit. It seemed weird and kind of ugly to me at the time as I had never seen that combo before back home. Fast forward a few years and you saw pink and purple all over NYC! After three years of language study in school, my French was OK by my junior year but it was so hard to understand anyone because they spoke so fast. I was able to pick up bits and pieces so I knew what they were talking about, but definitely was not able to hold conversation—ugh. Lesson learned, pay attention in class. I absolutely loved France and can't wait to go back now that I'm older and can appreciate it even more!

Soon we were off to Spain. Unfortunately I don't remember much about this beautiful country, except for the bullfights. Yes, they took us to a real, live bullfight! It was amazing. And scary. And wild. A stadium full of roaring fans and those bulls—wow! Just like you see on tv! Needless to say, my next trip overseas will definitely include Spain to make up for all I missed back in 1979. All in all, it was an absolutely incredible trip that instilled in me a love of travel. I have Mom and Dad to thank for my greatest passion!

Lisa's Trip Overseas

I went to France and Switzerland in eleventh grade. I was the only student from Hammondsport to go on a foreign language trip, so I joined a group from Horseheads, New York. Luckily, I made a friend right away and we stuck together the whole trip. We met some boys who were in the American school overseas and had a blast with them. We snuck out every night. We partied and learned how to have cocktails as teenagers. We saw their school, which I assume was the same one our father went to years before as a student when Nana and Papa Sable lived in France. I also remember being in some store in France, knocking over a shelf and merchandise went all over. I ran out of there with the store owner running after me, yelling something in French that I hadn't learned in class. I also learned the phrase *va te faire foutre* from those French boys. You can look up the horrible meaning of it. They thought it was funny to teach us and have us say it to passersby. The best part was sitting at the base of the Alps enjoying a bottle of wine and eating cheese. I felt so grown up! The majestic views in Switzerland made the trip well worth it. Although my memory is poor, that view, and that day, will live with me forever. I'd go back to Switzerland if given the chance, but I have no desire to go back to France. I thought it was dirty and the people were mean to Americans. Hopefully this has changed over the years. I am grateful to Mom and Dad for the opportunity to travel. I think if I could do that trip all over again, I would wait until I was a little older and could appreciate more than the social aspect of it all. Looking back, I am so happy I was able to experience other countries, because at this time in my life, I don't think I will ever head overseas again—although an African safari and a trip to the Egyptian pyramids is on my bucket list!

Andy in Florida

This story begins in my senior of high school and would shape the rest of my life. It emphasizes the love and support that was always, and still is, present from family. Being a member of the Sable family is truly sacred to me.

My love for the mountains was instilled early in me through camping trips with my sister Julie and later learning how to ski and snowboard in high school. Ski club was my absolute favorite part of high school and made me long for mountains even more. A big debt of gratitude here again to Mom and Dad as ski club wasn't cheap, and times were very hard as Dad struggled to keep the marina going.

As a senior in high school, I set my sights on forestry and was accepted into Paul Smith's College to become a forest ranger. In typical fashion, Mom and Dad offered complete support and even took me on a road trip up to Paul Smith's and Lake Placid that winter so we could check it out together.

Just a few months later, I would get the invite to work at Ron Scarpa's Watersports and pursue a possible career as a professional athlete. I was at a crossroads—college, or barefoot waterskiing? Sitting at the dinner table with Mom and Dad that night, we decided I would probably never get an opportunity like that again. They both looked at me and said, "You could always go to college if barefooting doesn't work out."

Needless to say, it worked out and allowed me to meet countless incredible people, travel to Europe and Scandinavia, and all over Canada and the US. The people I met and the places I traveled to provided a priceless education and experience that would not have been possible in college.

Art in Europe

My love of travel certainly originated from Mom and Dad's support for it. I've been overseas a few times now and even got engaged on the Island of Capri off of the Amalfi Coast in Italy—an amazing trip. Traveling internationally is certainly something we will do with our children soon.

My first trip was during my senior year of college, and Mom and Dad supported it and encouraged me to go. It was for school credit—Senior Symposium—and there were twenty-two of us (twelve of us were Sigma Chi fraternity brothers) venturing throughout Italy, France and Germany. Our chaperone was amazing. She made us get up early and had a set agenda to see all of the important historic sights. Then, most importantly, she gave us from 2:00 p.m. on every day to do as we wished. We met so many interesting people along the way who we would not have without our independence on the trip. There were even two guys who took a train with us to Amsterdam for the day! To highlight how lucky we were, we crossed paths with another Roanoke College group on the streets of Florence one day. They were pretty miserable—they had all day, every day fully scheduled and had minimal freedom. Their jaws dropped when we told them we had most days free to explore after we soaked in the important history of each area.

Another incredible thing our chaperone implemented was she made us keep a daily journal and even graded us on it. Below are some highlights from my journal.

May 5, 1998 - Rome, Italy

Buonanotte! My first day ever overseas . . . So far, I'm very impressed with the Italian people . . . upon our arrival, Harlow, Carter, and I were enjoying a few drinks at the smoke shop (vodka and orange Fanta) when, all of a sudden, a glass accidently spilled over. It had shattered all over the floor and I feared the owner's reaction. To my dismay, they were very understanding and allowed us to stay, cleaned up the mess and served us more.

May 7, 1998 - Rome, Italy

. . . It was off to the Vatican City! It's two days after the 1st murder ever in the Vatican and word is all over the US. When I talked to Mom on the phone, she informed me of this.

This has been the best day yet by far. The Sistine Chapel was astounding. I must have sprained my neck from looking up at 'The Last Judgement' for so long. The attention to detail Michaelangelo used was intense . . . The thing that made this day so great was touring St. Peter's Cathedral . . . the hike to the top of it was hell but well worth it. I was able to view the entire Vatican City, part of Rome, the Pope's house and the Sistine Chapel . . . goodbye Rome, hello Florence!

May 10, 1998 - Florence, Italy

It's the last full day in Florence . . . The most beautiful setting I've seen yet came tonight at dinner. Dr. Au picked an incredible place to view the sunset and grab a bite to eat . . . I could see the Duomo, The Arno River and the buildings and mountains that make up the city. The Arno curved into the dark red sunset with the bridges crossing over adding to the depth of the scene.

May 12, 1998 - Venice, Italy

. . . Later in the evening, we all decided to relax in peaceful St. Mark's Square . . . and I saw Nick Nolte! Poor guy had people all over, in Venice, Italy nevertheless, asking for a picture. I don't blame him for saying no, I wouldn't either.

My overall, general impression of Venice is that it's a mellow, peaceful city (and expensive) and appeared to be a popular place for honeymooners. I'll have to keep Venice in mind if I decide to get married someday. Whoa, that's scary! ☺

May 14, 1998 - Paris, France

. . . Wow! A word I'd use to sum up Versailles. How can one family gain so much money and power and leave the rest of the city in shambles and poverty . . . I thought about Louis 14th walking around his castle in his elaborate robe stumbling over the thought of 'which room do I want to see today?' He had so many different mistresses that he wouldn't let live in his house, including his wife.

. . . walking through the Hall of Mirrors, I imagined the gatherings they'd have with the abundance of food, nobles and elaborate clothing. All of this while they throw their breadcrumbs to the citizens.

May 18, 1998 - Munich, Germany

. . . somebody had a crazy idea to go straight to the Hofbrauhouse for drinks. So, sure enough, Alex, Carter, Harlow, Brian and I went. I was amazed at the differences in German and American cultures. It was 10:30 am and people were reading newspapers and drinking liters of beer . . . old and young . . . I couldn't get over it.

May 19, 1998 - Munich, Germany

The walking tour of Munich was very interesting. Seeing the buildings that Hitler worked in and the streets he walked was something . . . Dachau (concentration camp) was a very emotional experience . . . it's certainly not something you go back to see again . . . but everyone should see it once. Many of us left with a very ill feeling in our stomachs.

May 20, 1998 - Munich, Germany

Today I went out with my native friends of Munich. Anita picked me up and took me to her restaurant. There, she gave me a 4 course, delicious meal and many drinks . . . no charge. I guess we treated them well at my mom's restaurant years ago ☺ Later on, Christian and Renate met us there . . . I also got to see parts of Munich most tourists don't get to see! We went clubbing until 3am! . . . Christian drove me home in his new BMW!

May 22, 1998 - Munich, Germany

Mike's bike tours rocks! Especially with Haynes, one of the funniest guys I've ever met! . . . I learned that statues that have a horse with one leg up meant they were wounded in battle- 2 legs up they died in battle. Haynes told us that 4 legs up meant they were on drugs out of the hippy era and you can recognize them because they were tie-dyed.

I hope someday to purchase real estate in either Tuscany or the Amalfi Coast and spend a lot of time there each year with my family. Thank you, Mom and Dad!

Family Ties

Family. Tradition. Relationships. New experiences. Sharing memories of the times we've spent together.

All of these flow back and forth, like rivers forever crossing the generations. This is what forms us. And this is what ties us.

Yes, these times are part of what makes you and I who we are today, and foretells who we shall become tomorrow.

To close this chapter I'd like to share some lyrics from the Crosby, Stills, and Nash song "Teach Your Children:"

> You, who are on the road
> Must have a code that you can live by
> And so, become yourself
> Because the past is just a goodbye
>
> Teach your children well
> Your father's hell did slowly go by
> And feed them on your dreams
> The one they fix, the one you'll know by
>
> Don't you ever ask them, "Why?"
> If they told you, you would cry
> So just look at them and sigh
> And know they love you
>
> And you, of tender years
> Can't know the fears
> That your elders grew by
> And so please help
> Them with your youth
> They seek the truth
> Before they can die
>
> Teach your parents well
> Their children's hell will slowly go by
> And feed them on your dreams
> The one they fix, the one you'll know by
>
> Don't you ever ask them why
> If they told you, you will cry
> So just look at them and sigh
> And know they love you

Part 2
Parenting

Relax

Parenting is not about managing your children. It's about managing yourself when you make decisions about handling your children. Just relax. You already know what to do.

I'd like to begin with a cut from a Moody Blues song, "Eyes of the Child":

> With the eyes of the child you must come out and see
> That your world's spinning 'round and through life you will be
> A small part of a hope, of the love that exists
> In the eyes of the child you will see.

We Didn't Need to "Buy the Book"

When I was just a child I overheard a lively discussion between my mom and the other neighborhood moms about a book, *Dr. Spock's Baby and Child Care*. Back then Dr. Spock intended his book to be *the* book, the indispensable guide, the *bible* on how to care for and bring up a child. I guess some people are more tempted to seek guidance than I find myself to be.

When the arrival of our first child Stephen was fast approaching, his mom Karen and I had similar conversations, but we asked ourselves, "Do we really need to seek out the advice of self-proclaimed experts?"

There aren't any guidebooks for childbirth or child rearing in nature. In the animal kingdom, there is plenty of *instinct* that goes into raising healthy offspring. Likewise with people, so we believed. We wouldn't be all that far off if we just followed our instincts.

But we humans do have a few dependable sources for, let's call it, "relative situational guidance." We have examples we can follow. And validate. With personal experience. Our *own* experience. As opposed to reading the words of some self-proclaimed "expert."

We have parents who were likely involved in our upbringing, and if we were fortunate enough, we have grandparents who were also influential in our formative years.

That's exactly what this chapter is all about. The paths that I chose to follow as a parent myself, from the examples set by my grandparents. And from the lessons impressed upon me by my parents' direction and guidance. Ultimately, they both affected the decisions I made as a parent raising my own children. *PARENTING.*

We didn't need to buy Dr. Spock's book. Stephen and Sylvia were wonderful children. And they turned into fine young adults. Everything we ever dreamed of, and more. And we all enjoyed it every step of the way. And yes, we didn't even need to buy the book.

"Let It Be" - Find Your Own Way

RELAX! The ability for young people to relax is important for the development of their sense of self-confidence. This can be nurtured at a very young age, and continually developed as they grow up at home.

And yes, there's a story to go along with this. Just relax!

Early on both Karen and I had discussed what role, if any, television would play in the rearing of our children. So we had decided to limit the selection of programs to about a dozen age-appropriate Disney films that we had on VHS tapes. Films like *Aladdin.* And *The Little Mermaid.* Great stories. Not anything scary or likely to give a child nightmares, right? Relax!

After only a short while we began to notice that certain VHS tapes were requested more often than others. Really, after only a little while longer the focus seemed to whittle down to only two of the twelve films they had to choose from!

Well, we couldn't just relax about that. Could we? No way! We wanted to know *why* that was the case. The children remembered all of the stories anyway, and they knew all of the outcomes. Right? Yet they still asked to watch only two of the films. Over and over and over again.

This is a cause for concern! Isn't it? There just *has* to be something wrong here. Right?

One would think that they would become bored with the repetition and request other films from time to time, but that was *not the case!* Shouldn't we have been concerned? We became convinced there was more to it, so we started observing more closely. Much more closely.

We discovered that when the story was about to arrive at scenes that made them laugh they would actually begin to laugh *before the scene began.*

They were anticipating what was coming and they were certain of the outcome. Not only was that the case, with each repetition of the film they would anticipate what was coming even earlier, and the laughing would begin even sooner! We just *had* to get to the bottom of it! Didn't we?

My gosh! It turns out that their *self-confidence was establishing itself!* Those requests for the same two films, over and over and over again, were in direct correlation with the development of self-confidence. The more they watched the same film the more often they asked for it. Being big believers in the power of a well-developed sense of self-confidence we ultimately decided to comply with their choices. My gut feeling is that as parents sometimes it's our time to learn to relax. Chill, and let instinct and nature take their course Mom and Dad!

The Routine

Nothing builds confidence better than routine: knowing what is going to happen, when it will happen, and how it will happen. Especially with young children. Things like getting up at the same time every morning. When it's time for meals. Homework hours. Bedtime. Having dinner with Grandma every Sunday after church.

Whatever . . .

Do it your own way, but always do it the same way. Not only do routines build confidence, they make things easier for everyone! And the bonus? Children love the *praise* they get when they follow a routine, not even realizing that a big part of the reason for their success is that they have always known exactly what is expected. They always had the routine!

It's Fun to Learn!

Throughout their entire primary education and right through high school, Karen and l always saw learning through the eyes of our children as something *fun*—for them, and for us. I have always believed that teaching children that learning is fun really starts with how we answer their questions. From their earliest age I made it a rule to never talk down to our children. *Never* adjust the answer to what you think the child can understand, just give them the complete unabridged response. They usually understand more than we expect. And it's *fun* for them to understand. Understanding also inspires confidence. It's fun to learn. So just relax!

It's fun for children to ask questions. Confident children ask questions. And when the answers they get challenge them to think, the process moves ahead. They realize they must consider the parts of the answer that make sense to them. And what if some parts of the answer seem to them to be missing? Or what if a part of the answer just doesn't seem to fit in with the parts they *do* understand? That's when they learn to ask follow-up questions! And guess what? It becomes like a domino effect. The more they ask, the more they know. And that equals *fun.* Followed by the more they ask, the more they know. And that equals fun. And so on. That's when they figure out that it's fun to learn.

Choose to focus on the subjects the child is interested in learning about—in school, at home, and at play. This varies by individual. For For our "whole family" experience, variety was the key for Karen and I. Sports and scouts and music and art are great examples. Open doors for your children, all the while doing things together as a family. Encourage them to try everything, being sure to explain the caveats. Those were the times when we introduced the concepts of commitment and selection. Let them try what they think they might like. Select what they do like, and give their commitments to the programs that they select. Most of all, relax! And let instinct and nature take their course. There are, after all, only twenty-four hours in a day. Point them in the right direction but let them find their own way.

What About College?

One of the first conversations Karen and I had with both of our children about college revolved around their choices of study. Then came their choices of where to pursue their higher educations. And finally the investment involved, including how to pay for it.

Choosing a Major

We spend on average 40% of our waking hours working during our prime years. (45 hours per week working out of 112 hours per week awake, allowing 56 hours per week for sleep.) With so much of our lives during our prime devoted to our work, we had better be doing something we enjoy. And if our choice of work is something we are *passionate* about, then we will be amongst the best at what we do, reaping the commensurate rewards.

Relax! We all know what to do. Choose to do what we like to do, and we will do it the best.

College Impressions

Many institutions of higher education offer standard college tours to attract perspective students. And most high school guidance counselors have schedules for recruitment weekends, families are invited to explore the curriculum and to experience some of the lifestyle that college offers. These experiences are quite informative, especially from the perspective of what that particular institution believes are its strong points and what it wants all to see. While these recruitment activities are worthwhile, they should not be the only means of judging what a college has to offer. I'd suggest when you and your student have narrowed down the colleges to a few choices then visit them again to see how they conduct themselves on a different occasion. You might choose, for example, to tour the colleges on your finalist list during, say, their graduation ceremony. I'll admit I'm offering you this advice in hindsight. I wish I'd thought of this before. Not that it would have necessarily made a difference to my student, but I learned an awful lot from the experience. Of course, there's a story to go with this.

My daughter Sylvia's bachelor's degree commencement ceremony from Cornell University, a fine school, was what I would describe as less than spectacular, especially considering the pedigree of that establishment. Many of the parents and their guests were dressed in business suits. We all walked the half mile from where our vehicles were parked to a crowded bus stop, were herded like cattle onto overcrowded standing room only buses and then had another half mile walk to the stadium for the ceremony. All of this on a hot sunny day in May.

The Cornell commencement address was delivered by the University President and was seemingly centered around what I considered to be excessive praise for the accomplishments of the graduates in earning their degrees. No meaningful message, or any assessment of what the value of their degrees could be beyond the money they were going to earn. And to top it all off? The final send off in that address from the president of Cornell University was about taking that degree out into the world, earning millions, and giving half of that money back to the school, followed with a chuckle from the president himself! *Seriously?*

In contrast, I was quite impressed by how the families of the graduates were treated when Sylvia received her master's degree from Duke University in North Carolina. We were treated almost like royalty, with a gracious touch of attention to our comfort. We were given ice water and driven in shaded golf carts directly from our vehicles to the stadium for the ceremonies.

The commencement address was delivered by Major General Martin Dempsey, a former Chairman of the Joint Chiefs of Staff. His speech covered several areas of great concern for those graduates, many of whom were planning on taking key roles in leading our nation into the future, whether those roles were in government, industry, education, or military service. I've always enjoyed sharing what he had to say. It really struck home with all of us. He began with a story about his wife Deanie Dempsey. His message with that story is easy to decipher. Paraphrased, he said:

Your success going forward tomorrow will be based much more upon the people that you choose to associate with, and much less due to any degree, rank, or pedigrees that you now possess from Duke University.

The second excerpt included below requires a little bit more thought about yourself and how you picture your role in the future of our nation. That message is more personal and requires a more thorough understanding of yourself to decipher. Enjoy!

Two excerpts from Major General Martin Dempsey's address to the graduates at the 2014 Duke University Master's Commencement Ceremony:

About Deanie Dempsey

> "My wife of thirty-eight years and mother of our three children, Deanie, is with me here today to celebrate with you. She's the one who keeps me grounded. Following this commencement address, she, along with the editors of the *Chronicle*, will be grading my work.
>
> You know, when I first made Brigadier General twelve years ago, I was, I was a bit—maybe I would describe it as full of myself for making General. And Deanie and I took a trip back to visit some relatives in upstate New York. It happened that I needed gas in the car, and so I pulled into a gas station, and out of the gas station walked one of Deanie's ex-boyfriends to fill the tank full of gas. And so his name was Bobby. Great guy. Turned out he also owned the thing. But he was pumping gas, you know?
>
> So the gas tank was filled, we got back in the car, we're driving away. You know, I'm kind of—I'm kind of flexing and Deanie said, "What are you doing?" And I said, "Well, you know, you've got to feel pretty good about the choice you made those many years ago. You know, I mean, look, you know, Bobby's pumping gas, I'm

a *General*." And she looked over at me and she said, "Listen, BUB, if I'd have married Bobby, he'd have been the General and you'd have been pumping the gas." I'm OK with that. Choose wisely, men and women in the audience."

The Second Excerpt: Major General Martin Dempsey on the Future

"As you prepared to embark on your own careers, you're probably wondering if the Chairman of the Joint Chiefs of Staff is worried about the future. Well, of course I'm worried about the future.

"I worry about big nations becoming more aggressive, about little nations developing weapons of mass destruction, about religious extremism and what it creates, about the collapse of governance along the Mideast and North Africa, about criminal networks that move drugs and illegal immigrants and arms to and across our borders.

"I worry about a pervasive and growing weakness in national and international institutions and structures that have for decades held together our sense of order and well-being.

"And yet when I look carefully and thoughtfully at all of this, I see more opportunity than vulnerability. A few things do seem clear to me:

-We will have to think our way, not bludgeon our way, into the future.

-There will be more options, but also more ambiguity in dealing with the challenges we face.

-You will need to find, fix and remain true to your moral compass, or you'll find yourself paralyzed. You have to find your own way.

"I hope you genuinely believe in the greatness and in the exceptionalism of this country. Encourage it. Criticize it. Participate in it. But above all, believe in it. It's sunset right now in Afghanistan. Thousands of men and women are either completing their day's work or just about to begin it. They do what they do because they trust each other and because they sense that they should give something back for the opportunities that they enjoy in this country. So they put on their rucksacks, they march out of their base camps and into an uncertain future. That's their way of making it matter. I hope you find your own."

Unbelievable—look at the world today, seven years later! Talk about an accurate vision of the future. The Major General gave this speech way back in May of 2014. Wow!

If the quality of the commencement speaker and the messages being delivered are any measure of the quality of the education one can expect from a university, then I think we can all rate Duke University pretty highly here. Just something to think about.

How to Pay for It

The first and most basic expense that my children, Karen and I zeroed in on revolved around *location.* Where would our student be attending college classes? Either they would be within daily commuting distance or living away from home.

Our feeling was if they chose an institution within commuting distance, it would be the same as skipping college altogether and getting a job right out of high school. They'd be offered the opportunity to live at home rent free in exchange for performing a few necessary chores around the home. Mowing the lawn or weeding the gardens for example. And they would be responsible for their own personal maintenance—doing their own laundry, cleaning up after themselves, helping with meal preparation, etc. Either way, if they lived at home for a few years after high school— whether while going to college or getting off to a good start in adulthood by working—we would not charge them rent since those conditions would meet our interest in getting our children off on the right foot.

On the other hand if their choice of where to attend college meant living away from home, there would be room and board expenses to consider. Likewise, in the interest of getting our children off on the right foot, we as parents were willing to cover the basic expenses for room and board. Even though it would be a bigger expense for us as parents, we didn't want the choice of *where* our student chose to attend college to be governed by any issue with their own ability or lack of ability to pay for room and board. We would cover basic room and board, dormitory or sorority house, and the campus meal plan. We would not cover the cost for a private apartment. No credit card for use at their own discretion for "personal" expenses. If they wanted that, then they would have to figure out how to pay for it.

On to the issue of paying tuition expenses, including buying the required books and other learning aids for their chosen curriculum. As parents, this is where we decided to draw the line. We believed the best way to encourage our college student to get the absolute best and most complete education and experience out of their college years would be to make them invest in themselves.

We preached this starting in high school. Scholarships, student loans, financial aid, and (after freshman year) the grants that would become available—that's how they would be expected to cover their own college tuition expenses. We believed this policy would help them help themselves when it came to balancing their lives. We all knew they would be continuously challenged over the next several years by the awesome educational opportunity being offered, while the challenges associated with becoming a young adult—the parties and the social life!—competed for their attention.

We were fortunate. With my family owning two businesses of our own (the marina and the restaurant), and aunts and uncles with businesses of their own, there was ample opportunity for our children to be gainfully employed from a very young age. I am pleased to say they both took advantage of this starting at the tender age of twelve! And throughout high school and college, we didn't make any arrangements for an "emergency fund" available from us to them to be used at their own discretion. If a real emergency came up? Ask for help. And explain every extra cent. And expect to pay it back.

Conclusions

Whether we are seen as having been too easy or too hard on our children while raising them, a few things are very clear:

We all love and respect one another. All four of us have made our own way in this life. All four of us reach out to help when any one of us is in need. We are willing to help others in need as well. We thoroughly enjoyed the years we had together under the same roof living as a family.

To close this chapter, here is my single parenting suggestion for everyone:

We are all born blessed with the knowledge and the wisdom to raise our own families. And we have our own parents who set many examples for us to follow. So relax! And let nature take its course.

Close families raise families who stay close!

My dad Arthur Sable, my grandfather Andy Sable, my grandfather Mike Santangelo, and myself holding my son Stephen. Four generations of loving our children, spending precious time together, and learning by example.

My Grandfather loved to fish! He took my father fishing, so they both took me fishing. Grandpa Andy top left, my Dad top center, and myself kneeling, touching the day's catch of Atlantic bluefish!

This was The Big One that day out on "The Lenny!"

We had a few spots we'd go to for largemouth bass.

A nice northern pike for Mike!

As I got bigger each year so did the northern pike!

Dad continued to take me out on fishing adventures, and vacations with the family always included fishing. A favorite of ours was our annual fishing trip in early May for Northern pike out of Gananoque, Ontario Canada, in the St. Lawrence River, Thousand Islands. Great fishing there!

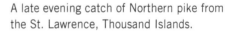

A late evening catch of Northern pike from the St. Lawrence, Thousand Islands.

Dad with the only Muskelunge we ever caught up in the Thousand Islands. Northern pike left, "Muskie" on the right. Skin pattern markings tell the two species apart.

Growing up on Keuka Lake, the children were always swimming. And fishing of course with Dad and their grandfather!

Stephen admires Sylvia's big smallmouth bass caught with her new fishing pole!

I took my own children fishing and they still love fishing! Here they enjoy an early spring brother-sister charter trip on Lake Ontario. Together as adults and having fun! Mom and Dad are so proud! Chances are they'll take their own children fishing someday.

I have to believe the experience my children had growing up in our family and sharing our recreation time together has played a role in the continued stability of their relationship as adults.

Sylvia's seven-pound northern pike

Stephen with his Lake Ontario Brown Trout.

Let's make up the perfect soil for growing those plants we started from seeds in the sunroom in early spring!

Let's fix up that old wagon, Dad. We don't need to buy a new one!

The two of them took their break and planned the late afternoon swim at the lake!

Stephen and Sylvia shared witness to the miracle of seed sprouting into a flower tower!

Their relationship began oh so early in their lives.

They even got Dad his start in construction management by building Lego creations!

Of course they took time out for their own educations!

Pursuing their secondary educations found them just as close while at Cornell University, and still not too far away from Mom and Dad!

As young adults they find themselves very close to those roots that we all had planted together so long ago!

Sylvia's passions continue to this day, from grow lights...

To the greenhouse...

To keeping up with her farm!

Where did she learn how to make the rows so straight?

Sylvia and Eric celebrate their
engagement in spring 2021.

She and her beau Eric have
brought new life to an original
regional farm homestead!

Steve, Sylvia, and Eric helped us get the garden set up with the new barn, spring 2020.

One of Stephen's passions is physical fitness, which he put to the test exploring the Canadian wilderness with me in 2004.

And on the wrestling mat his passion and hard work earned him the Section Five Wrestling Championship in 2006!

Additionally, Stephen is a "people person," just like his great grandfather Michael Santangelo, great uncle Matthew Santangelo, and me, his dad! He's known for his friendly, magnetic personality around Keuka Lake where he bartended throughout his Cornell University years. There was never a dull moment with Stephen behind the bar and he has occasionally made returning guest appearances!

Sylvia has continued to nourish a wanderlust that began early.

At fourteen, Sylvia signed up for a West Coast Women's Empowerment Adventure with Outward Bound. Over ten days of backpacking she prepared for and completed a solo climb up a snow-covered mountaintop, spending the night alone in a home-made shelter erected with a simple tarp and a length of cord!

Today Sylvia is a project manager in global health. Working much of the time from her home base at her farm, she also regularly travels the globe. In her professional role she enables the education of children around the world who are displaced by conflict and detained in refugee camps.

Stephen used his degree from Cornell, his academic and athletic achievements, and his people skills to become a successful process engineer for a respected chemical products manufacturer. He was subsequently invited to join a team of his Cornell fraternity brothers in a unique start-up venture in the food products manufacturing and development industry where became the director of operations.

I am so proud of my family!

Our first family home on Burleigh Drive in Ithaca, where Stephen and Sylvia came home after they were born!

The love and companionship that filled the activities we all did together, the self-confidence and self-esteem we gave one another as we grew close as a family—these laid the foundation for how we developed into happy, well-balanced and productive adults.

I firmly believe that the smiles we wear today are the result of the structure and stability of our family environment.

Chapter 7

Grandparents and Roots

**Part 1
Santangelo**

Pop & Nana
Michael Santangelo &
Rosa DeGiuseppe Santangelo
September 26, 1937

The Santangelo Grandparents

Nana Rose. I used to call her Nana Rose and Green Car Nana.

When the four of us siblings were young and living in Avenel New Jersey she'd visit once or twice a week in her new green Oldsmobile. Pop Santangelo got her a new Oldsmobile every two years. Pop also got his own brand new Oldsmobile every two years. It was part of Pop's compensation package at work: two new Oldsmobiles every two years. Pop knew how to negotiate!

Back to Green Car Nana. Nana Rose visited a lot. Our mom, Julie, had the four of us children in about five years. Dad was just getting back into civilian life after his discharge from the Marines, and Mom needed the help. We only had one car that Dad used for work five days a week at the trucking company and another day each week buffing the office floors at the same place. So Nana was able to help out with the babies and the errands, shopping, etc. Nana was always just a phone call away!

I remember Nana Rose taking us to Woolworth's and to Grant's, two local five and dime department stores. She'd buy lunch at the lunch counter—every department store had one of those back in the day.

Best place around for grilled cheese and tomato soup!

She'd give Julie and me some change so we could go have a horsey ride on the mechanical horse or get bubble gum balls from the machine out in the front lobby. It made it easier for Nana and Mom to get the shopping done. Things were different in those days when it came to child safety and supervision. We were just five and six years old at the time.

Nana Rose was a bargaining machine! We'd go to check out, and every item being rung up was open to negotiation for price as far as Nana Rose was concerned. "What? Are you crazy? Fifty cents for those socks? I'll give you a quarter!"

And she usually got her way.

Oh yes, Nana Rose was old school. I grew up next door to her home in Edison, New Jersey starting in third grade. We had moved into Nana and Pop's old house when they built a new home in the Stephenville Parkway suburb of Edison. I'd stop by to visit with her after walking the two miles home from school every day.

She always had a frozen Milky Way candy bar ready for me when I'd arrive. In fact she kept a treat for each of us. Lisa reminded me of the canned plums in the kitchen cupboard, and Julie remembers the ice cream sandwiches I'll admit to having her treat in addition to my own if she wasn't there that day!

Nana Rose was usually at the stove stirring her homemade pasta sauce. It always smelled so good in her house! She taught me how to season the sauce, cut the garlic, and make the meatballs. Sometimes we'd even stuff these big pasta shells with cheese to eat with the sauce.

She loved her can of Schaefer beer while she made the sauce. Sometimes she had the old-fashioned glass bottles that didn't have the twist tops. She was a small woman with small hands, but somehow she'd pop the bottle lids off with her thumbnail!

Pop used to call right before he left work to come home. It seemed like he was always bringing a guest with him to dinner. In spite of the short notice Nana never complained, and always had enough food ready and a smile on her face.

Nana loved to fix cold cut sandwiches for lunch and watch the soaps with her housekeepers Miss Belle and Miss Pearl.

And Nana always hosted family gatherings at every holiday. Adults went to the dining room table while the kids ate in the TV room. At every holiday meal there was pasta, meatballs, sausages, lasagna, a roast beef, a ham, a turkey, and a pork roast. Of course there were side dishes and casseroles too. Pies and ice cream for dessert. Pop made everyone try everything!

The living room was off-limits and was roped off with these felt covered ropes stretching between two poles like you see at the movie theater. In case a child got through there were clear plastic furniture covers fitted over the plush gold couch, sofa, love seats, and chairs. I never did see anyone in that room. Was it just for display? No, I did know Nana and Pop entertained in that room on occasion. That type of room was standard fare for older Italian households out in Corona and Queens where they had grown up. And there were always clear plastic covers over the furniture. I chuckle when I think about how I never did find out whether or not Nana ever took those covers off when they used that living room.

Circa 1976, when I happened to be visiting my grandparents in Edison in the late spring. Grandpa Mike (Pop Santangelo) had started a conversation about my plans for college. "Have you thought about Villanova? Great school. Just outside of Philly. I know people there." He got on the phone and poof, just like that, we were headed to Villanova for an interview the very next day!

When Michael Santangelo says he "knows people," he means it. Needless to say, after "our" interview, Pop and I headed back home to Edison with my acceptance at Villanova in hand, pending the forwarding of my high school transcripts, which went through without a hitch.

That was Pop. He always had a connection—and a great story to go with it. Pop had a story for any occasion, and stories he'd use to influence people without them even realizing it.

Pop took me to my first baseball games. He was a great fan of the game. We'd go to Yankee Stadium where I saw Micky Mantle, Mel Stottlemeyer, and Joe Peppitone play. But he made me promise never to become a Yankee fan! He said his team was the working man's team—the Brooklyn Dodgers. So I asked, "Why Yankee Stadium, Pop?" He told me we'd go to see the Yankee games because his trucking company owned the box seats behind home plate! Pop was thrifty. Besides that, those seats were outstanding!

Yeah, Pop "knew people" all right. Through his trucking company he was connected with the likes of Jimmy Hoffa and Anthony "Tony the Pro" Provenzano, a capo in the Genovese crime family! But Pop wasn't involved with the bad parts of that business. He was just the head of sales for the trucking company. You know, the part of the company that brings in the money and has some general influence over things.

Yes, Pop knew a lot of people and had a lot of stories to tell. He also had a lot of real friends. He was able to share with the people he liked, and that he did. I learned my people skills from the best!

Pop played a lot of golf, and he was very good at it. I remember going out to dinner at the Metuchen Golf and Country Club. They had one of the finest golf courses in the state of New Jersey, plus a posh clubhouse, bar, pool, and a nice restaurant. Pop was always so proud to introduce his grandchildren to his buddies at the club.

Pop did well enough at work to ensure his family never went without. In his later years his nickname became "Didgyaeat?" He came from a world and a time when putting food on his family's table was the best a man could do. Pop never forgot that when he could afford to feed us right and give us the best.

Pop loved his family, and he loved his *lawn.* He was very particular about his landscaping. He'd pay me to mow the lawn with the riding mower then he'd come home after work and run the push mower back over where I had just cut it to make a diagonal pattern on the front lawn! And Pop made sure to bring out the businessman inside me. He made sure all the neighbors knew I was cutting his lawn. Somehow when they needed help with their own landscaping chores I was the only one they'd call.

Santangelo Trunk

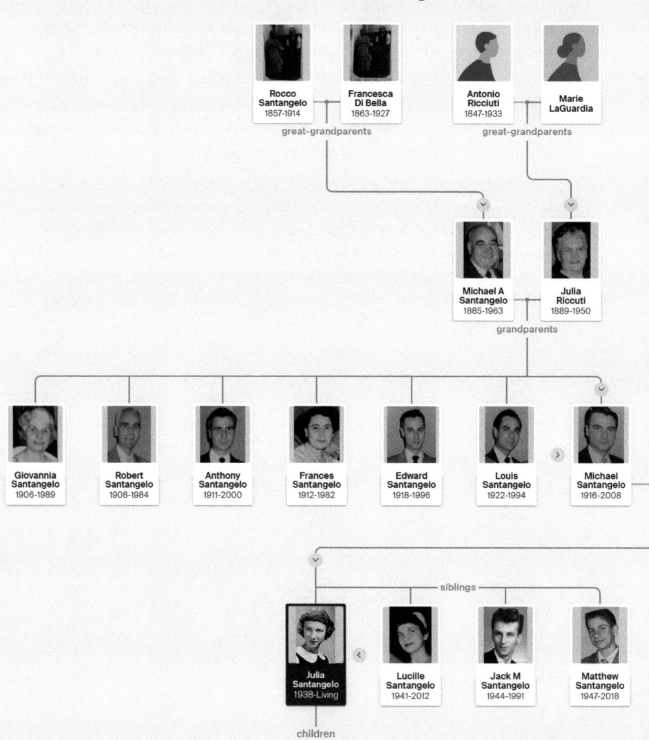

Rocco Santangelo
1857-1914

Francesca Di Bella
1863-1927

Antonio Ricciuti
1847-1933

Marie LaGuardia

great-grandparents

great-grandparents

Michael A Santangelo
1885-1963

Julia Riccuti
1889-1950

grandparents

Giovannia Santangelo
1906-1989

Robert Santangelo
1908-1984

Anthony Santangelo
1911-2000

Frances Santangelo
1912-1982

Edward Santangelo
1918-1996

Louis Santangelo
1922-1994

Michael Santangelo
1916-2008

siblings

Julia Santangelo
1938-Living

Lucille Santangelo
1941-2012

Jack M Santangelo
1944-1991

Matthew Santangelo
1947-2018

children

DeGiuseppe Trunk

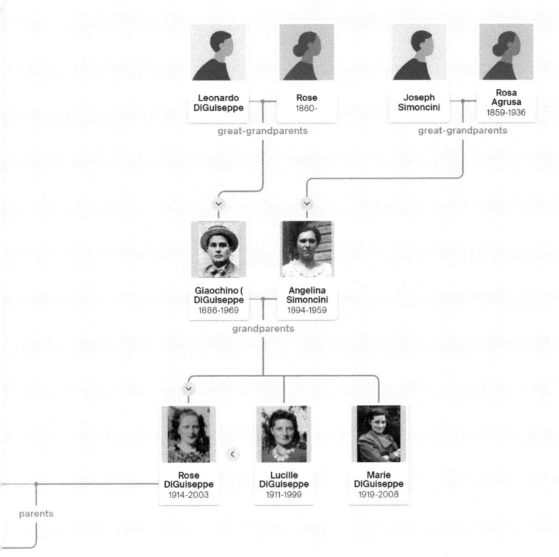

Leonardo DiGuiseppe — Rose 1860-

great-grandparents

Joseph Simoncini — Rosa Agrusa 1859-1936

great-grandparents

Giaochino (DiGuiseppe 1886-1969 — Angelina Simoncini 1894-1959

grandparents

Rose DiGuiseppe 1914-2003

Lucille DiGuiseppe 1911-1999

Marie DiGuiseppe 1919-2008

parents

My Mother

Julia Marie Santangelo/Sable
November 28, 1938

My Two Grandparents

Michael A. Santangelo Jr.
1916–2008

Rosa DeGiuseppe/Santangelo
1914–2003

My Four Great-Grandparents

Michael A. Santangelo Sr.
1885–1963

Gioachino DeGiuseppe
1886–1969

Julia Ricciuti/Santangelo
1889–1950

Angelina Simoncini/DeGiuseppe
1894–1959

My Eight Great-Great-Grandparents

Rocco Santangelo
1857–1914

Leonardo DeGiuseppe

Francesca DiBella/Santangelo
1863–1927

Providenza Lopes

Anthony R. Ricciuti
1846–1933

Joseph Simoncini

Marie LaGuardia/Ricciuti
1856–1892

Rosa Agrusa/Simoncini
1859–1936

Santangelo Roots

Grandpa Mike &
Nana Rose Santangelo

Santangelo Estate, Flushing, NY

Rocco & Francesca Santangelo
Papa Mike's grandparents, the author's great-great grandparents. Rocco, born 1857 and died 1914.
Francesca, born 1863 and died 1927. They had a family with seventeen children! This is the oldest
known Santangelo photo we have found, taken sometime around 1905–1910. This is probably the
oldest picture we will ever find of any of our ancestors.

The Santangelo Family

All siblings with their parents at an anniversary party sometime in the late 1940s or early 1950s, L-R.

Standing
Grandpa Michael Santangelo
1916–2008

Uncle Edward Santangelo
1918–1996

Uncle Louis Santangelo
1922–1994

Uncle Robert Santangelo
1908–1984

Uncle Anthony Santangelo
1911–1992

Seated
Aunt Frances (Francesca) Santangelo (Sapio)
1914–1982

Great Grandma Julia Santangelo (Ricciutti)
(1889–1950)

Great Grandpa Michael Santangelo
1885–1963

Aunt Jennie (Giovannia) Santangelo (Roma)
1906–1989

The DeGiuseppe Family

L-R: Marie, Great Grandpa Jack, Lucy,
Great Grandma Angelina, Rosa

Great Grandpa Gioachino
(Jack) DeGiuseppe
1886–1969

Great Grandma Angelina
DeGiuseppe (Simoncini)
1894–1959

Grandma Rosa DeGiuseppe
(Santangelo)
1914–2003

Lucille DeGiuseppe
(Meystrick)
1911–1999

Marie DeGiuseppe
(Crecca)
1918–2008

We Cousins Remember the Times We Shared

From Mike Sable

Meeting Great Grandpa DeGiuseppe

This was the only time I can remember meeting Great Grandpa DeGiuseppe and his second wife Mary. He gave me a tiny toy car he had that day. I think he had found a small toy for each of us because he knew we were coming to visit. I sat on his lap while he told me a family story about when Papa Mike was dating his daughter Rosa. One day Mike came over and they were making wine in the cellar. (Red wine from grapes that were shipped by train from California to the Italian neighborhoods in New York City.) As the story goes, they were drinking from an older barrel that day and they saw a rat in distress that could not climb out of the old ceramic tub where they crushed the grapes. The rat was jumping as high as it could. Papa Mike got a baseball bat and stood like he was hitting a tee ball off a stand. He swung and killed the rat! I still remember hearing that story, it must have been fifty-seven years ago, on my Great Grandpop's lap.

From Sista Jewel

Nana Santangelo

Two Christmas trees. One—like the living room just for show—usually gold. One with the other ornaments. Always singing in perfect harmony, always singing the wrong words! I used to correct her even though I couldn't sing. High heels and a dress with stockings even just to sit with Pearl and watch "Days of our Lives." Papa Mike's long stories over dinner. Baseball lessons in the yard. And that basement wallpaper that looked like a fake window. I got stuck on the ledge leading to the basement once and to this day I'm afraid of ledges and heights.

From Sista Be

Nana Rose

She used to watch me after school on Fridays while Mom got her big bouffant hairdo done. She'd always make me scrambled egg sandwiches, cut into fourths, for my after-school snack! She'd always have on "Days of Our Lives" and I would watch with her. And you can't forget the cream soda that was down in the garage. I remember all the cousins and I always raiding the soda stash—Nana always had cream soda!

From Sista Lisa

"Green Car" Nana and Papa

- Going after school to Nana's house for after school snacks. The brown cupboard door—I remember exactly where it was. Inside would be canned plums or prunes, which I loved!
- Papa Mike going to his cabinet in the TV room and loading us up with Branch paper notebooks and pens so we could play school.
- Sitting around the table with the painted/wallpaper scene all around us sharing stories—some would last from lunch until dinnertime. We would just bring food out several hours later to eat again. "D'ja eat?"
- Playing "bar" in the basement was always a hit with our cousins.
- The gold living room, which we could only look at but never enter until we were older and then, boy was it a treat! I remember sitting on the fancy couch, crossing my legs and pretending I was rich and famous.
- The fancy dining room with red carpet, I believe—another room off-limits to us kids unless it was a special occasion.
- Later years, going to Nana and Papa's house on Middle Road here in Hammondsport and spending many hours at the pool. We loved having them back near us!
- Most importantly, I remember the love I felt being around them. They both made us feel so important and loved. I forever will miss them.

From Art Sable

Mowing for Papa Mike

Not long after Nana and Pop moved to Hammondsport I began mowing their lawn using their riding mower. It was my first mowing job and I truly enjoyed doing it—entirely because of Pop.

The previous lawn guy had taken five or six hours to complete the job. Me? Just 2.5 hours. The mower was always wide open, even on the steep side hill. As I mowed, I'd occasionally look at Pop standing on his deck with his hands on his head saying something like "Ohhhh my God . . . Jesus . . . Artie!" as he grinned from ear to ear.

Every week I'd come in afterwards for a sandwich. He'd carry on and on about how he didn't understand how I could do it in half the time and how amazed he was.

After the mowing compliments he'd talk about what kind of sandwich I'd like, in great detail—for a long time—with a few 'jeets' thrown in each time. Up to that point in my life, I'd just grab whatever was in my parents' fridge, eat it and move on with my day. There wasn't much glorification of the process and ingredients involved. Pop taught me the intricacies of a great sandwich, focusing on every little detail from the quality of the tomato to the type of cheese to the freshness of the meat. Needless to say, after the lead-up process was over and the time to eat had arrived, they were the *best* sandwiches I've ever had. I loved and cherished those days.

From Jennifer San Angelo

Nana and Pop's

Being at Nana and Pop's with *all* of the cousins. We would play in the basement and dance around under the disco ball near the bar.

Eating ice cream cups and drinking cream soda that never seemed to run out. I remember Uncle Matt would entertain us by eating light bulbs!

From Pam Aini

Edison

My memories of going to Edison were some of the best of my childhood. All of the cousins together playing in the basement. Roller skating by the washer/dryer area and playing at the bar—we all put that to good use when we got older!

I remember the cases of soda and beer in the garage. Cream soda at Nana's was the best! While we were waiting for dinner Papa used to play the dollar game with us. We had to guess the number that was in the serial number more than once and we'd win the dollar! And Nana would always sneak us an ice cream cup—the kind with the wooden stick for a spoon—even if it was just before dinner. But the best part always was sitting at the table eating, talking and laughing.

I miss them and those days. I love getting together now, it's like we're still there!

Family Photos

My Grandpa Michael Santangelo's Parents
(My Great Grandparents, Michael and Julia Santangelo)

Great Grandpa Michael

Great Grandma Julia

Grandpa Mike with his mother Julia

Mike Santangelo (back right), Queens City Championship, 1930–1931

Mike Santangelo

Rosa Santangelo

Mike & Rose Santangelo

Mike and Rose dancing at
The Lakeside Restaurant

Julia, Matthew, Jack, Lucy

Julia (Mama Jul),
Papa Mike,
Auntie Lulu,
and Uncle Matt

Julia, mother Rosa, and Lucy

Julie and her dad

Julie, Matt, and Lucy

Julia Santangelo

My mother

Lucy Santangelo

Jack and Lucy

Jack Santangelo

Matthew Santangelo

DeGiuseppe Family Photos

Great Grandpa Gioachino DeGiuseppe

Great Grandma Angelina DeGiuseppe

Angelina with MJ

Jack with child

Marie, Lucille, Rosa, and their mom,
Angelina DeGiuseppe

Young Ladies:
Marie, Rosa, and Lucille

Lucille DeGiuseppe

Rosa and Lucille, 1925

Marie DeGiuseppe

Rosa DeGiuseppe

Part 2
Sable

Andy & Jeanne (Bruzdowski) Sable
(Pop and Nana)
October 12, 1930

Sable Grandparents

Nana Sable. I used to call her the Stuffed Cabbage Nana, Red Car Nana, and Nana with the Birds.

Nana just loved to wake up to hear the birds chirping outside her window every morning. "Thank you, dear Lord, for another wonderful day" was her prayer on awakening each and every morning. She always recognized her little statue of Saint Francis of Assisi during those moments; it set the tone for her day. She'd open up the windows to let fresh air into the bedrooms and praise the Lord for this beautiful world and all of the blessings of just being alive to experience it all.

Nana was very "old school" when it came to her role in the family. It was especially important to her that her daughters, Jeannie and Judy, cook the traditional holiday meals along with her when the family visited over the holidays. Every year she prepared the same original family recipes the same way, almost always by memory. Those memorized recipes set the stage for a lively debate each holiday while Nana cooked with her daughters. Stuffed Cabbage, stuffed peppers, kielbasa and other sausages, the tomato and cabbage sauce, and sauerkraut were some of the wonderful aromas in the air when our family arrived.

There was a special older Buick parked behind the house in Nixon Park, Edison, New Jersey where Nana and Papa lived when I was very young. It was from a model year in the late 1940s or the early 1950s. Papa told us it was Nana's old car and that it didn't run anymore. It had what looked like exhaust pipe headers exiting on each side of the hood. I thought my Nana was a hotrod driver! But nothing could have been further from the truth. She was a very gentle, sincere person with no desire to compete for anything. By her example, she taught me that kindness, patience, and tolerance were true virtues to live by.

And we can never forget the home Nana and Papa built in the woods in the mountains at Forest Lakes in Andover, New Jersey. They had a great old cocker spaniel named Duchess. That doggie had the softest coat I've ever petted!

Forest Lakes House, as we called it, was where my siblings and I first experienced nature in a country setting. Papa had built a rock retaining wall along a small hill garden bordering the path from the driveway to the main entrance. Chipmunks and squirrels competed for the seeds that fell from several bird feeders Nana had Papa placed throughout the garden. We'd even see snakes sunning themselves on that rocky wall. And the lake! We'd swim and go fishing at the lake. Papa had a little rowboat for fishing and touring around the islands. And in the winter there was always plenty of snow and hills for snowmen, snow forts, sledding and tobogganing!

Papa Sable was what they called an "Old Salt" back in the day. Papa loved the ocean, the bays and the rivers. And Papa loved fishing. He had a small wooden boat in the yard at the Edison (Nixon Park) home with the name "Judy" painted on the side. It had an Elgin outboard motor that never ran, so we'd always end up renting a boat when we went to the shore to fish.

Papa, my dad and me would get up really early to go fishing for fluke, weakfish, ling, and the smaller bluefish called snapper blues, usually in Sandy Hook Bay, sometimes down in the Manasquan outlet, and also further south in Barnegat Bay.

We also went after the Jersey blue crabs in Barnegat Bay. Those were memorable trips—I'd have trouble falling asleep the night before because I'd be so excited to go! We'd head home to Edison in the late afternoon after crabbing, sometimes going to Papa's house and sometimes to our house.

Wherever the family gathered, the women were ready for a picnic feast. We'd bring home the blue crabs in our wooden bushel baskets and they would steam them. I'll always remember the sight of our oldest Polish and Slavic relatives with missing teeth. They'd go after the crabmeat, still half in the shell, with whatever teeth they still had, nibbling away at the crabmeat as fast as their teeth could go!

There'd also be an open fire pit going. Corn on the cob, kielbasa, sauerkraut, sometimes clams too! The men would eat the clams raw and the women steamed theirs, dipping them in butter and lemon.

Then there was the "speck," as they called it. Basically a chunk of pork belly fat skewered on a stick just cut from a tree in the yard. There was this wonderful Polish bread with a hard crust, an airy center and sourdough flavor. I was just a kid, but I still remember that bread fifty years later!

The adults gave each of us a stick with a little chunk of speck on the end of it. We'd hold it over the flames and it would heat up and eventually catch fire. Then we'd pull the speck out of the flame, hold it above a piece of the bread, and let the fat drip onto the bread. We'd eat it just like that! Very rich meaty flavor with the airy texture and sourdough, all together with that hard, chewy crust. Amazing!

Pop had a career in electronics. He was involved with the government's development of radar technology during World War II and later had a role developing television. He taught me about components like tubes, capacitors, resistors, transformers, and the functions they performed. Papa had a cool workshop that he kept locked, but if we asked he'd take us in and show us the electronic inventions he was working on. Pop was a secretive kind of man, probably a result of the work he had done with the government during the war.

Papa loved his Cutty Sark scotch whiskey and his Dutch Masters cigars. When we'd go fishing he'd light up a cigar if the fish weren't biting and guess what? They'd start biting! The little kids called Papa "Buzz Buzz" because he'd catch them if they got close and tickle them! You always knew when that was coming because he'd get this playful look on his face and say, "buzz buzz, buzz buzz…"

The Sable Family Tree

Sable Trunk

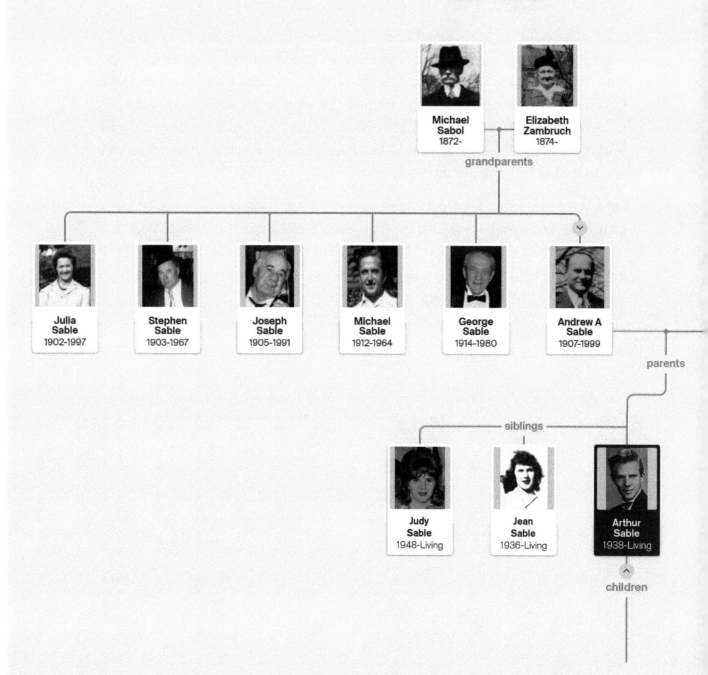

Michael Sabol 1872-

Elizabeth Zambruch 1874-

grandparents

Julia Sable 1902-1997

Stephen Sable 1903-1967

Joseph Sable 1905-1991

Michael Sable 1912-1964

George Sable 1914-1980

Andrew A Sable 1907-1999

parents

siblings

Judy Sable 1948-Living

Jean Sable 1936-Living

Arthur Sable 1938-Living

children

Bruzdowski Trunk

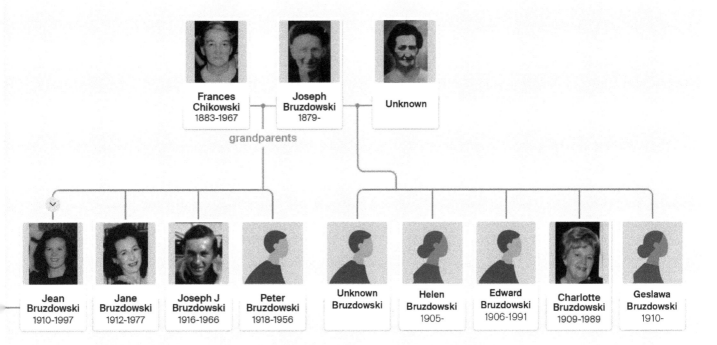

Frances Chikowski 1883-1967 — **Joseph Bruzdowski** 1879- — **Unknown**

grandparents

Jean Bruzdowski 1910-1997

Jane Bruzdowski 1912-1977

Joseph J Bruzdowski 1916-1966

Peter Bruzdowski 1918-1956

Unknown Bruzdowski

Helen Bruzdowski 1905-

Edward Bruzdowski 1906-1991

Charlotte Bruzdowski 1909-1989

Geslawa Bruzdowski 1910-

My Father

Arthur A. Sable
August 15, 1938

My Two Grandparents

Andrew Sable
(Grandpa Andy)
1907–1999

Genevieve Bruzdowski/Sable
(Grandma Jeanne)
1910–1997

My Four Great Grandparents

Michael Sabol
1872–

Elizabeth Zambruch/Sabol
1876–

Joseph S. Bruzdowski Sr.
1879–1947

Franciszka Czajkowska/Bruzdowski
("Grandma X")
1883–1967

The Sable Family Roots
From Eastern Europe to the United States

Home and bungalow of Mike Sabol
723 Mary Street
Perth Amboy, New Jersey

Five Sable Brothers

Grandpa Andrew, Michael, George, Stephen, and Joseph at Uncle George's birthday celebration, April 8, 1953

The Sable Family

Great Grandpa Michael Sabol
1872–

Great Grandma Elizabeth (Lizzie) Zambruch/Sabol
1876–

Grandpa Andrew Sable
1907–1999

Uncle Michael Sable
1912–1964

Uncle Stephen Sable
1903–1967

Uncle George Sable
1914–1980

Uncle Joe Sable
1905–1991

Aunt Julia (Thomas) Thomas
1902–1997

Mike Sabol's Story

My great-grandfather Michael Sabol was a soldier in the Hungarian Calvary before he emigrated from his native Hungary shortly after the turn of the century. After much research, we believe that Michael was born in Zeliezovce, modern day Slovakia, on August 18, 1870. Upon immigration it was recorded as Zseliz, which would phonetically match up with the information on his Declaration of Intention for Naturalization form. At the time, the city of Zseliz may have been in Hungary or Slovakia, depending on the ever-evolving border between the Slovak and Hungarian peoples of the time. The proximity of Zseliz to the modern Hungarian border makes the debate of official nationality one of little substantive value.

Michael Sabol emigrated to the United States from the Port of Bremen, Germany on the vessel Grosser Kurfurst. There is some question about the year of emigration. The handwriting could be taken as 1900 or 1906. Based on the most recent birth dates obtained for Michael Sabol's children, 1906 is most likely correct. At the time he was described as a white male, tan complexion, 5'7" tall, with blue eyes and weighing 165 pounds. He had a wife, Lizzie (Elizabeth), born in the same city.

He filed a document for "Declaration of Intention for Naturalization" (United States Citizenship), in the Middlesex County Court, some years after his arrival in the United States. The document is dated June 23, 1919. At the time of this declaration his residence was at 723 Mary Street, Perth Amboy, New Jersey.

No. *11074*

Pops first citizen papers

UNITED STATES OF AMERICA

DECLARATION OF INTENTION

☞ Invalid for all purposes seven years after the date hereof

State of New Jersey,

County of Middlesex, ss:

In the _____ Court
of _____ Middlesex County, N. J.

_____, aged _____ years,
occupation _____ *Labr* _____ do declare on oath that my personal
description is: Color _____ *White* _____, complexion _____ *Fair* _____, height _____ *5* feet *7* inches,
weight _____ *165* pounds, color of hair _____ *Brn* _____, color of eyes _____ *Blue* _____
other visible distinctive marks _____ *None* _____
I was born in _____ *Zemplen Hungary* _____
on the _____ day of _____ *August* _____ anno Domini 1 *870* I now reside
at _____ *723 Mary St Perth Amboy N J* _____
(Give number, street, city or town, and State)
I emigrated to the United States of America from _____ *Bremen Germany* _____
on the vessel _____ *Grosser Kurfurst* _____; my last
(If the alien arrived otherwise than by vessel, the character of conveyance or name of transportation company should be given)
foreign residence was _____ *Zemplen Hungary* _____ I am _____ married; the name
of my wife is _____ *Lizzie* _____; she was born at _____ *Hungary* _____
and now resides at _____ *Perth Amboy N J* _____
It is my bona fide intention to renounce forever all allegiance and fidelity to any foreign
prince, potentate, state, or sovereignty, and particularly to _____
_____, of whom I am now a subject;
I arrived at the port of _____ *New York* _____ in the
State of _____ *May* _____ anno Domini 1 *900*; I am not an anarchist; I am not a
polygamist nor a believer in the practice of polygamy; and it is my intention in good faith
to become a citizen of the United States of America and to permanently reside therein:
SO HELP ME GOD.

_____ *Mike Sabol* _____
(Original signature of declarant)

Subscribed and sworn to before me in the office of the Clerk of
said Court this _____ day of _____ *June* _____, anno Domini 191 *9*

_____ Clerk of the _____ Court.
By _____, _____ Deputy Clerk.

Mysteries abound regarding the birth city of Michael Sabol and the origins of The Sable family.
Clues in the document include the city of birth and the name of the vessel he arrived on.

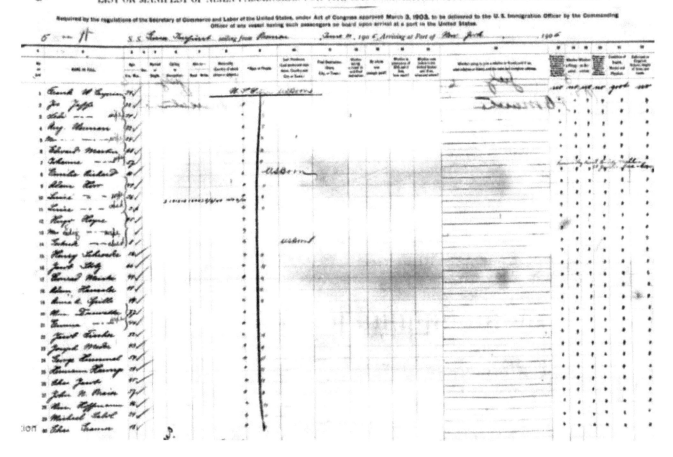

Family history from stories handed down

Mike lived in Carbondale, Pennsylvania from the time of his arrival at Ellis Island until about 1915, working as a coal miner. Mike and Lizzie had six children, five sons and a daughter. He later became a roofing tile layer for the clay tile roofs above the cathedrals in Perth Amboy, New Jersey. He died after a long and arduous battle with black lung disease.

Out of Mike Sabol's six children, Pop Andy Sable and his brother Uncle Stephen Sable owned a hardware store and radio repair business in Perth Amboy, New Jersey. Stephen ran the hardware store and my grandfather Andy ran the radio repair. Pop later took a job with ITT and then went on to work for RCA.

The Bruzdowski Family Roots

From Krakow, Poland to the United States

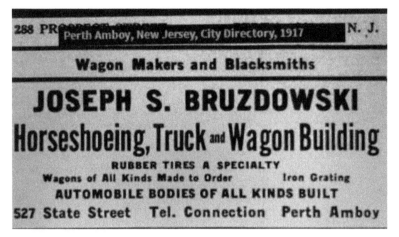

In 1917 Joe Bruzdowski Sr. owned and operated a specialty business located at 527 State Street, Perth Amboy

Grandma Bruzdowski's home circa 1945
520 Johnstone Street
Perth Amboy, New Jersey

The Bruzdowski Family

Great Grandpa Joseph Bruzdowski
1879–1947

Great Grandma Francis Czajkowska/Bruzdowski
1883–1967

Grandma Jeanne (Genevieve) Bruzdowski/Sable
1910–1997

Aunt Jane V. Bruzdowski
1913–1977

Uncle Joseph Bruzdowski
1916–1966

Joseph Bruzdowski Jr. served in the Pacific during the Second World War and was shot in the head landing on the beaches at The Marshall Islands, leaving him a paraplegic. He was fitted with a steel plate to replace a portion of his skull which allowed him to survive and return home to his family. His siblings referred to him affectionately as Soldier Joe.

Aunt Charlotte (Tessie) Bruzdowski
1909–1989
From Joseph's first lineage

Uncle Peter Bruzdowski
1918–1956
(No photo available)

Peter was born with cerebral palsy and remained seriously disabled for the entire thirty-eight years of his life. He was able to work doing odd jobs for a nearby tavern to help support himself. My aunt Jeannie Martowitcz lovingly described him as a "kind and gentle soul."

Bruzdowski Family Photos

Frances Bruzdowski (center) with her daughters and some of the grandchildren

Tess, Jane, and Jeanne are holding the babies, top row.

The Bruzdowski Family Mysteries

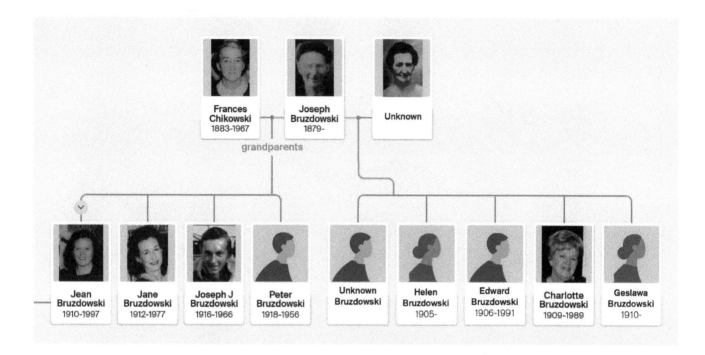

Frances Chikowski 1883-1967 · **Joseph Bruzdowski** 1879- · **Unknown**

grandparents

Jean Bruzdowski 1910-1997 · **Jane Bruzdowski** 1912-1977 · **Joseph J Bruzdowski** 1916-1966 · **Peter Bruzdowski** 1918-1956 · **Unknown Bruzdowski** · **Helen Bruzdowski** 1905- · **Edward Bruzdowski** 1906-1991 · **Charlotte Bruzdowski** 1909-1989 · **Geslawa Bruzdowski** 1910-

What do we know about Great Grandpa Joseph Bruzdowski's "two families?"

Questions, questions, questions! Did the mother of Joseph's "first family" of five children, two boys and three girls (below), pass away in 1910? Was Geslawa born before or after Joseph's first wife passed away? Who was Geslawa's mother?

When did my great grandfather Joseph Bruzdowski marry my great grandmother Franciszka Czajkowska? Was it right after the death of his first wife, also thought to be in 1910?

My Great Grandma Francis gave birth to my grandmother Jeanne (Genevieve) Bruzdowski, in 1910. That was a very eventful year. Joseph and Francis then went on to have a family of four children together.

Joseph Bruzdowski and the "first" Mrs. Bruzdowski. We do not know her name.

My great grandmother Francis Bruzdowski, 1947 & 1967

Julie Sable, my mom, tells a story about when the first wife of Joseph Bruzdowski passed, that Joseph's brother Frank Bruzdowski promoted the idea that his brother Joseph should marry his wife's unmarried sister Francis, who was living with them at the time. The intent was for Francis to raise Joseph's motherless children. This story has corroborating evidence in the form of an obituary found recently. The obituary for Francis (Chikowski) Bruzdowksi mentions a sister named Mary Bruzdowski. This would only be possible if Mary was married to Frank Bruzdowski.

In addition there is the issue in the spelling discrepancy of Francis' maiden name. We can easily explain the spelling of Chikowski/Czajkowska as the phonetically correct, and Americanized version (Chikowski) of the Polish spelling (Czajkowska). Chikowski would be utilized henceforth for documentation discovered for both Mary and Francis. Joseph and Francis went on to have four children of their own, including my Grandma Jeanne, their first child. We know from the Sable and Bruzdowski family stories that in addition to her own children, our great grandmother Francis played a role in raising Helen, Edward, and Charlotte (Tessie) as their stepmother. I have heard over the years that there was a competition of sorts between my grandmother Jeanne and my great aunt Tessie for the favor of Great Grandpa Joseph and Great Grandma Francis.

Fond Memories

I still have vivid memories of when I first met Helen, Edward, and Tessie. We met again several times at my Sable grandparents' home in the Edison, New Jersey housing development of Nixon Park for holiday gatherings and christening celebrations.

There was an accordion-style door separating the front door, upstairs, and stairwell from the downstairs living quarters where my grandparents resided. That accordion door would open and Aunt Helen, Uncle Edward, or Aunt Tessie, sometimes all three, would arrive with Great Grandmother Francis in tow. I remember how she struggled to communicate with me in English, but she always smiled so wide and warm as she greeted me with huge hugs and very wet and loving kisses exclaiming, "Oohh, hello! You're my little Artie's Boy!" Let me tell you something, you don't forget face-to-face greetings like that from your Great Grandmother. I know I never will.

We knew Great Grandma Francis as "Grandma X" because, as the story goes, when she arrived at Ellis Island she signed her name with a mark, an "X," due to her inability to read and write. I remember as a first grade student being stunned to learn this fact. So I asked her about it. In her broken English, Grandma Francis explained that when she was my age there was no school for her to go to. You don't forget face-to-face answers like that from your great grandmother either—and I'm sure I never will.

The Nine Bruzdowski Family Children

I remember very clearly when I spent a week with Grandma and Grandpa at Forest Lakes, somewhere around 1969. A whole week, just the three of us, weekend to weekend.

One evening we were looking through old photo albums in the basement. Grandma was busy licking these little adhesive corner pieces that held the photos in place as Pop tried to tell her where each photo should go. I got to question both of them, at length and in depth, about their lives growing up. And about the family—who was married to who, who were the oldest and youngest, all of that sort of thing. I always took an interest in that. A lot of what I remember is based on the stories they told me that week.

In addition, and more significantly, the information below has been compiled from Ancestry.com, family stories, census records, military service records, birth records and certificates, death certificates and obituaries, Mass cards, immigration and citizenship documents, and stories my eldest relatives told when I asked them questions during visits.

I was told by Pop Sable in the late 1960s that my Grandmother Jeanne was the oldest child of Great Grandpa Joseph Bruzdowski and his second wife Francis Czajkowska (Chikowski).

Examine the dates of birth and death for Joseph's nine children (below). It appears that Aunt Tessie was actually Grandmother Jeanne's half-sister. We are not sure of the bloodline for Geslawa (pronounced Ges lava), but I do know that I never met her, and that Grandmother Jeanne never spoke of her to me.

Who was "Geslawa"?

(Pronounced Jes-la-va)

Geslawa shows up on the genealogical chart and family tree as my father's half-aunt on the Bruzdowski side that also includes Aunts Helen and Charlotte (Tessie), Uncle Edward, and the "unknown" uncle. So the shared DNA with our family would be from our Great Grandfather Joseph Bruzdowski.

Obviously, there are several possibilities regarding her bloodline and also many possibilities for why we have not heard of her until now. Three of many scenarios that might serve to fill in the blanks:

1) When our Great Grandfather Joseph Bruzdowski's first wife passed away perhaps she died during childbirth. Perhaps the child died as well, which might explain why our Grandmother Jeanne never spoke of her.

2) Might Geslawa have an entirely different mother than either of Joseph's families? Suppose Joseph's first wife passed, and he had a relationship with another woman who wound up pregnant at the same time as our Great Grandmother Francis Bruzdowski was pregnant with our Grandmother Jeanne—might that woman have chosen to raise her child on her own?

3) Suppose that Joseph's first wife passed after giving birth to Geswala in early 1910. That might add the possibility that Geslawa survived and was raised by someone else because Francis was taking over raising Joseph's children in addition to having a newborn of her own.

Any of the scenarios above—and probably quite a few others—would account for both Geslawa and Jeanne being born in 1910.

Who was the "Unknown" child?

The Ancestry.com website tree indicates that Joseph had a total of four sons between the two families. (See above—first family, first originally listed as "Private"— no other information.)

The "Unknown" child of Joseph Bruzdowski shows up on the genealogical chart as a brother of Helen, Edward, Tessie, and Geslawa Bruzdowski—Joseph's first family.

Census records indicate an additional male, employed as a metal fabricator, was also living in Joseph's household. (We know that Joseph operated a metal fabrication and specialty shop.) This additional male may have been Joseph's fourth and eldest son, including sons Edward, Joseph Jr., and Peter.

We Cousins Remember the Times We Shared

From Sista Jewel

Sable Grandparents

I have fake birds now since Nana Sable always had them on the plastic plants inside the front foyer in the Forest Lakes house. I also remember the walks to the lake climbing boulders that seemed a mile high but today as adults look so small. And the time lightning blew up the TV we were watching in the basement.

From Mike Sable

Sable Grandparents, Nixon Park Edison, New Jersey home

Remember the "Secret Workshop" with the Cathode Ray Tube round screen TV? When we visited on the holidays we'd see Grandma Bruzdowski and get her loving and very wet kisses. We'd also see second cousins Richie and Bobbie, Aunt Tessie, and Uncle Roy and his accordion! Sometimes we'd see "Coach," the old Scoutmaster who would always have these little spring-controlled puppet toys for us to play with!

From Lynn Williams

I have been thinking of some of our best times especially at Forest Lakes. Remember the fishing trips at Main Beach with Pop-Pop helping us catch a billion sunnies? Remember when Gram would always take us swimming and we used to think it was so cool if we made it to the raft? Remember the Castro convertible bed at Forest Lakes that Gram always made so comfortable for us? Remember walking around the lake and stopping at each beach and playing in the sand?

From Lee Heigis

Then there were the more benign but precious memories of Forest Lakes hanging out in the finished basement and never being able to go near Pop's desk! We would all sleep together on that one pull-out couch. I think we could fit four and the rest of us took the floor. Remember Nana's cubby hole under the stairs? She was secretly a hoarder and stuffed all her things in there out of Pop's sight. We went fishing in the rowboat to all the secret coves on the lake. There were snow forts, ice rinks, and old Uncle Joe Sable was there too. Most nights, after a nice family reunion, there was a little too much cognac or brandy! Pop loved his brandy and those sweet-smelling cigars. I think it was cherry tobacco, but I'm not sure. I just know whenever someone is smoking it, I get taken back to Forest Lakes all over again.

From Mike Sable

Stories from a week at Forest Lakes

In around 1969 I spent a whole week with Grandma and Grandpa at Forest Lakes, just the three of us. I got to ask both of them, separately, about their lives growing up. They told me a lot of the old family stories I still remember.

That week Pop taught me all about radio, television, and radar. I now understand what capacitors, resistors, transformers, and cathode ray tubes are, and the functions that they perform. Pop took that technology very seriously and even kept a lot of the files and diagrams about radar, radio, and early TV sets locked up in his workshop in the basement.

I made stuffed cabbage and stuffed green peppers in tomato sauce with Grandma, and she taught me how to form a meatloaf!

And the freedom to roam was like nothing I had ever experienced. Grandma and Grandpa would tell me what time to be home, and I was on my way.

They let me walk the mile or so to the lake with my entry badge for the main beach and clubhouse. I'd bring a thermos of Kool-Aid and a sandwich in a brown paper bag, a beach towel or two, and my fishing gear. I was about ten years old that summer.

I remember "sailing" Grandpa's little wooden rowboat on the lake by myself! I rigged up a sail with some sticks, one oar, and two beach towels, with some light rope. Using the other oar as a rudder, I sailed from the beach all the way across the lake to the dam and back.

Grandma would come into my room every morning at seven o'clock, singing a song about the morning and the birds and the sunshine. She'd gently wake me up and open the window to let in the fresh morning mountain air—always such a happy and positive note to start out the day!

From Cousin Lori

Memories of Grandpa

Fishing at Forest Lakes, no hooks—we used safety pins bent backwards with a stick and some string! Caught some mad sunnies. Grandpa cooking in the backyard at Forest Lakes. Walks around the Rotunda. Sitting in the igloo in his bathing suit on Easter Sunday. Many, many long talks at the kitchen table in Forest Lakes.

Memories of Grandma

Sitting on the Indian swing in Millrift with the babies. Working together with Gram and Pop at Stewarts in Branchville. Whenever it got slow Pop would light up his cigars and sure enough, in came the customers. Grandma's apple cake and her chicken soup with the spare rib bones floating on top! I could go on and on. They were the best grandparents and I miss them every day.

From Ian Earle

(Ian is my second cousin, my cousin Lori's son. Ian grew up next door to Grandma and Grandpa Sable, a short walk through the woods, in Mill Rift.)

My memory of Grandma is playing a memory game, which I still have, on the weekends. I remember Grandma's clothesline and her hanging clothes out to dry.

I used to go over to their house on Tuesday nights to watch "Rescue 911" with Gram. I ate Honey Maid graham crackers from her brown cookie jar. I also remember many walks to the Indian Swing. She used to sing "You Are My Sunshine" to me.

For Grandpa, I remember playing whiffle ball in the side yard and him making paper airplanes in his office. I remember my dad going over there and indulging in his favorite blackberry brandy. I used to ride my quad to their house to get on the bus.

From Mike Sable

Remember the cubbyhole space under the split-level stairwell at Forest Lakes? That was a cool fort! A place where we could talk about things that our parents didn't want us talking about. Remember sneaking under there with all of Gramma's stuff, and talking about the Beatles, the Doors and the Monkees? We'd all sleep downstairs with the old TV that eventually got hit by lightning in a thunderstorm. We were sneaky and watched "The Ed Sullivan Show." Remember Rowan and Martin's "Laugh-In" and "You bet your sweet Bipee!" Television censorship. The 60s in general—our parents tried to limit what we were exposed to. We got away with plenty though!

Family Photos

Great Grandpa Mike Sabol

Great Grandma Lizzie Sabol

Grandpa
Andy Sable

Grandma
Jeanne Sable

Grandpa Andy and Grandma Jeanne

Sable family photo
Jean & Andy with Judy, Art, and Jeannie

Grandma Jeanne with daughter
Jeannie and son Arthur

Bon voyage 1954
Andy, Jeannie, Judy, and Art

Arthur Sable
My father

Jeannie Sable

Judy Sable

Great Grandpa Mike Sabol and Great Grandma
Elizabeth with granddaughter Jeannie and grandson
Arthur

Mickey, Pop Andy, Steve, and my dad, Arthur

Mickey, Mike Sabol, and Andy

Joe, Andy, Steve and Mickey Sable enjoying a few beers!

The Bruzdowski girls were very prolific! Tess, Jane, and Jeanne (Genevieve) with their children in their arms!

Aunt Tessie, Grandma Jeanne, and Great Grandma Frances welcome Judy and her son Ronald.
Four generations!

Grandpa Andy and the ladies!
Grandma Jeanne, Aunt Julia, unknown, and Florence.

Grandpa Andy laughing with brother George at George's second wedding

Grandma and Grandpa Sable always have something to smile about!

Joe and Andy belt out a tune!

Great Uncle Joe Sable visiting Keuka Lake, mid 1970s

Chapter 8

Family Stories

Introduction

This chapter includes stories from my extended family of aunts, uncles, cousins, in-laws, stepchildren, and some of our family friends. As in Chapter 5, my family members and friends are characters in these stories. Personalities are revealed in these reminiscences, bringing the events to life for everyone to enjoy again. In this chapter I've included stories and excerpts as told to me directly via email at my request.

I hope in the future there will be a copy of *Legacy* at family gatherings, and this chapter may inspire thought and joyful conversation.

Family Ties

Family. Tradition. Relationships. New experiences that we share. Exchanging memories of the times we've spent together.

All of these flow back and forth, like rivers forever crossing the generations. This is what forms us. And this is what ties us.

Yes, these times are part of what makes you and I who we are today, and foretells who we shall become tomorrow.

We Sables grew up with five families of aunts, uncles, and cousins of the same generation, plus or minus a few years.

Our "Immediate Family" Tree

SABLE

• My parents Arthur and Julia (Santangelo) Sable

• Mike Sable (the author)

• Julie Ullrich (Ray)

• Be Sable

• Lisa Cole (Andrew)

• Andy (Tiffany)

• Artie (Melissa)

My Children

• Stephen Sable

• Sylvia Sable and husband Eric Engdahl

• Their mother Karen (Krivanek) Mann

My Wife

• Maria (Felese) Sable,
  her parents Anthony and Pasqua
  (Ricarddi) Felese

My Stepchildren & Grandchildren

• David Demarest, wife Sarah,
  daughters Maddie, Ava, and Clara

• Dana (Demarest) Haggerty,
  husband Brian, and daughter Harper

My Brothers-in-Law

• Mike Felese, partner Trish,
  granddaughter Angelina

• Tom Felese, daughters Elena
  and Olivia Felese

FARRIS Cousins

- Uncle Joe and Aunt Lucy (Santangelo)
  - Denise
  - Pam
  - Michele

MARTOWITCZ Cousins

- Uncle Ed and Aunt Jean (Sable)
  - Lori
  - Lynne
  - Lee Anne
  - Jim

BARANKOVICH Cousins

- Uncle Ron and Aunt Judy (Sable)
  - Ron
  - John
  - Melissa
  - Stephanie

SANTANGELO Cousins

- Uncle Jack and Aunt Barbara (Fromme)
  - John
  - Lori
  - Jennifer

SANTANGELO Cousins

- Uncle Matt and Aunt Janet (Riedel)
  - Kim
  - Heather

The Sables

The six siblings: Mike, Lisa, Andy, Be, Art, Julie.

We Sables all love to tease MJ (Momma Jule) about her unique way of speaking. She has a gift for inventing her own word pronunciation and sentence structure. Add to that her Long Island dialect and strong accent and this will inspire a chuckle from anyone who knows her well. I'd like to take this opportunity to give her unique way of speaking a name, designating it a language all its own:

"MJ Speak"

The MusliNs use SherMan Williams paint when they paint with fawks and spoons and sell pawrtrets ta Julia Robbits an the utha queese.

Awrti an da boyce ah heah exkaping skoowell again!

Awe jeeze! If yous guys don't believe me ask the Menintights, they know everything!

And be schaw to drink lots of waater for ya diabetis when ya get ta ITLY, NOT vodker an arrange juice!

Lisser betta watch out fawr Covit cause she went to Walmarts ta get some sawsage and peppahs fawr Dad, but Govena Coomo had used scissas to cut holes in ha meisk!

Nana doesn't werry about ha canca so much now. She werries instead that Sylvia is headin' ta Afriker again!

So that's the story. Let's put are thinkin' caps on, and yous all betta rent a "Uhaul It" ta take ta Roanokie college for Mike . . . Andy . . . I mean Awrti!

LOL MJ! We Luv Ha!

Eating the Catch

For Miles, Macklen, and Mazlo

We have to remember the first time you guys ate fish that we caught at the dock at Keuka Lake. Maria and I were fishing a couple of weeks back and you guys joined us on the Idlehurst dock. We caught several fish: perch, rock bass, smallmouth bass, sunfish, etc. I was telling Maria how good the perch were to eat. You guys heard that and wanted to try some, and Mommy said okay. So we brought three fish to the lower apartment where you were staying for the summer.

It was time to clean the fish and prepare them to cook. It may have been the first time it occurred to you guys that in order to cook and eat those fish, we would have to gut them first. Miles, you and Macklen were old enough to realize the time had come. Uncle Mike got out the knife, and while you guys were looking at the fish Macklen pointed to one of them and said, "You do THAT ONE first!" Miles agreed.

At eighteen years old reading this, you now understand the position Macklen and Miles were taking. (Mazlo—you may not have been old enough to vocalize, but we're sure you also agreed!)

The fish were served broiled with butter. Boy, were they tasty!

Felese, Demarest, and Haggerty

Dana and the Night at The Hickey

When I first began dating my wife Maria I was staying at a hotel not far from her home in Olean. My company had arranged for the hotel suite to serve as my home for the duration of my project with the Olean City School District, which was expected to last two years, until early 2012.

Maria and I had already been through the earlier stage of dating when we went out for dinner four nights a week or so.

It wasn't very long before we discovered we shared a common interest in great wine, extraordinary cooking, and fine dining.

We also knew we could prepare our favorite dishes better ourselves than what was being served up at the local eateries.

Unfortunately the hotel suite kitchen was not adequate for creating the kinds of meals we enjoyed preparing for ourselves. We were both very good chefs. And once I sampled Maria's daughter Dana's cooking, it was obvious that as a chef she was cut and sewn from the same roll of fabric as her mom and I were!

As a result we soon found ourselves enjoying cooking together at Maria's home practically every night.

During this time in our relationship Maria's daughter Dana had just graduated college and was starting her first professional position in the working world. Until recently Dana had been living at home with Maria while finishing up her master's degree at St. Bonaventure University. So Dana was, of course, always welcome to join Maria and I for dinner and was often our guest. And it was common for the three of us to enjoy a television show or a movie while relaxing after dinner.

The particular evening I'm recounting here followed as described above, and after dinner the three of us had settled into our comfortable chairs in the living room.

Maria and Dana were discussing that evening's entertainment options when I began to notice I was feeling a bit more tired than usual—as I recall it was only about 9:00 p.m.

I decided to excuse myself for an early retirement to my hotel suite for the evening, explaining the activities of the day had taken their toll and I was going to need to get a good night's rest to be at my best the next day. With my apologies we said our good nights and I headed out to my pickup truck for the short ride down the street to the hotel.

I was just about to fire up the truck when my phone rang. Who could this be? Turns out it was my musician friend Jeff.

A recent acquaintance, Jeff was a local disk jockey who ran his own DJ business catering to weddings and private gatherings. Jeff was also a talented guitarist and bass player with an excellent voice known locally for his high singing voice.

Months earlier I had jammed with Jeff a few times, before I met my Maria. I used to occasionally stop in for a beer at a college bar known as The Hickey. This place had a biker-style motif. Only about a mile from the hotel I called home, The Hickey was also right across the street from St. Bonaventure University, hence its reputation as a college bar.

Jeff was calling from The Hickey because he was scheduled to play a three-hour, three-set gig there that evening with a list of material that most definitely required accompaniment. Unfortunately his regular duet playing partner had canceled due to illness.

Jeff was wondering if I would join him and play guitar for a few songs in the last set while he played the bass and sang. He had another guitarist playing who had offered to fill in and play a few tunes but needed to leave early and couldn't stay for the last set.

I thought about it for a moment and told him I'd be there. I headed over to the hotel, changed clothes, grabbed my guitar, and was off to the Hickey!

Near the end of the night we were really cruising right along. It was obvious that we were doing well with the crowd. We'd just had a request for the Neil Young tune

"Old Man." Jeff and I looked over at one another, discussing whether we both knew it and in which key to play it. The crowd gathered close and was watching quietly, surprised that we were going to play it together for the first time right then and there.

"Old Man" was a favorite of Diane Luck, the wife of Norman Luck. Norman was one of the most significant influences in my musical life, especially when it came to improvisation. As a result I had literally performed that tune hundreds of times, in several positions on the guitar, playing several of my own arrangements, (with a pick or simply thumb and fingers). I'd even performed it in several different keys. It was definitely a great choice for a performance by these two musicians who had never played the song together before!

Jeff's voice was doing a great job of imitating Neil in the original key, and the arrangement I was picking was very close to that of the original recording (with a few minor improvements to the rhythm!) Every eye in the place was on the two of us and not a word could be heard from the crowd.

It was a very satisfying experience to pull off this performance so flawlessly. I was really enjoying that final solo guitar run of "Old Man," picking my way up the neck to those last five notes of the final chord: one two, one two three... As I glanced up to view the crowd (who had worked their way up to within 10 feet of us) my eyes locked with a very familiar pair, wide open and glued to my own. It was Dana, out with a group of her college friends and enjoying the live music at the Hickey!

With a quick nod and grin of surprise she turned and rejoined her friends. I never heard another word from her about it until I brought the subject up later that week at dinner with the three of us at her mom's home.

Apparently Dana had not mentioned our running into one another that night to her mom. Nor did she tell her that this guy (Me!) who earlier was "too tired" to stay and watch a movie at the house that night was actually out late playing star at a college bar!

I figured honesty would be the best policy in this instance and brought up the subject myself during that next dinner at the house. I simply explained to Maria exactly how the situation had come about. Dana joined in, mentioning that she didn't even know I played the guitar – and well enough to impress her and her friends.

It's always amazed me that without any discussion between the two of us, Dana had kept the events at The Hickey that night to herself. Her silence allowed me to show the both of them that I was truly interested in a healthy and honest relationship with her mother, and for that matter with Dana as well.

Meeting the Feleses

When Dana married Brian—or "Haggs," as he is affectionately known—I finally got to meet Maria's brothers Tom and Mike and their families. Due to my ALS I was not able to make the trip for the wedding, but we did plan a get-together for the following day at our home in Pulteney along with a dinner at Mom's Waterfront Restaurant.

Maria's youngest brother Mike Felese, his Partner Trish, and Trish's granddaughter Angelina, who is like a daughter to the two of them, were coming from their home in Syracuse. They arrived at our home in Pulteney for our introductions and a short visit before we headed to the Waterfront Restaurant for dinner. Over the past year and a half they have made regular trips to visit Maria and I here in Pulteney, about every two months or so. We always enjoy catching up, cooking, and having a meal together. Maria's brother Mike and I share an interest in sports and history. I find our conversations about Mr. Anthony Felese, their dad, so enlightening and historically significant. He served in an artillery battalion in World War Two, landing at Normandy and advancing across Europe to fight at the Battle of The Bulge. Mike has a good deal of knowledge about the ordeal our soldiers endured and how that battle affected the rest of their lives. Mike often brings artifacts, photos, and documents left by his dad when he visits. The evidence from his dad's experience and the accounts from the Battle of The Bulge offer a unique perspective into the Felese Family dynamics. Mike and Trish have since relocated to Cortland which is a little bit closer to us. We continue with our visits on a regular basis. I've gained a lot of insight into the Felese family, and I'm certain that we all enjoy catching up with one another (and the cooking) when they visit!

Tom Felese, the elder of Maria's younger brothers, and his daughters Elena and Olivia hail from Denver, Colorado where Tom owns and operates his Italian restaurant The Cherry Tomato. We had a wonderful time discussing food, meal preparation, and the restaurant business over our meal at the Waterfront Restaurant.

And the entire group enjoyed cooking together at our home in Pulteney before the three of them had to fly back to Denver. Maria and I have a huge vegetable garden, and from August to November every year Maria is a canning machine. We enjoyed a wonderful meal with sausages and pasta with our homemade sauce from Maria's canning cupboard. It was such a pleasure for the five of us to share that time preparing the meal together, not to mention the amazing sauce from our garden tomatoes! Even though we only had a three-day visit, in that short time we really developed a bond that is described so well in the following writings. I am truly blessed to have had the opportunity to share that time with them.

The following stories are compiled memories from the first introduction of the Felese and Sable families at and after Dana's wedding in August of 2019.

Excerpt from Elena Felese

> We hadn't seen my aunt Maria since 2006, the years flying by and eventually totaling up to 13. It had been too long, I felt like we'd missed out on so much, but the nights spent catching up and telling stories old and new were what really brought us all together again.
>
> Maria had gotten remarried. We unfortunately missed the wedding but could see through the Facebook photos and occasional phone calls we had with her that she was in a very happy marriage. Her husband, Mike, is a very kind, educated, and free-spirited person.
>
> It was last October when Mike was diagnosed with ALS. I had never really known much about the disease other than that it's terminal. We of course sent Maria messages and tried to be there for her

through the process, but it was so important to us that we meet her husband and welcome him into our family as he would for us.

When we walked through the door and rounded the corner, we saw Mike, sitting in his favorite chair with his oxygen mask on. The moment he saw us a giant grin spread on his face, and his arms opened to us. Mike has a contagious smile and overall such a positive presence, even in light of his situation. We sat and spoke with our uncle for hours listening to his many stories about his youth and his career. He quickly became one of the most interesting people I've met, each story had us all tied in.

Maria and Mike liked to spend their weekends harvesting their giant garden or canning salsa, jam, peppers, or even my grandma's famous marinara sauce. They are the type of couple many people see as what they'd want to be after settling down—happy, content, and growing old together.

He'd had a "celebration of life" a month prior. He told me, "Hey, why wouldn't I want to be at my own funeral? With all that food there, and all the people I love."

I'd never heard of anything like that, but hearing it said by Mike, with no resentment or anger in his voice made me see how strong and admirable he really is. He told us, "I wanted everyone to know that I'm okay with what's happening, and I wanted for them to be at peace with it as well."

Mike had grown up next to Keuka Lake and had spent so many days on sailboats that he basically grew up on the water. Throughout the day, he noticed I would look out on the water, studying the people in boats. I'd never been on one and I was very curious.

Mike was used to being on boats almost every day of his life. But he hadn't been on the water since his diagnosis. He looked over at my sister and I at one point and insisted we all go out on the water.

My aunt drove us all down to the marina, and as I was grabbing Mike's walker from the trunk the sun hit Mike's face and a big smile appeared, his eyes lit up, and I knew once we got on the boat, he was home.

We spent hours exploring, looking at the lake houses, Mike pointing out his old hangout spots from when he was young. We steered by this old dive bar, and Mike, while laughing, explained how that bar was a spot for teenagers to get a beer illegally back in the 70s.

We headed over to his family's restaurant, which sits right on the shore of the lake. The restaurant is managed by his sister and owned by his mom who's eighty-four years old and still running this busy restaurant!

Mike said, "We've always had a family table in the back that we've used since I was a kid. No one else sits there but family, and that's where we're all going to be seated tonight." I sat next to my aunt Maria and my sister and enjoyed meeting and talking to all of Mike's sisters and his mom. After a huge meal, we finally headed home.

Even though we only spent a week or so together in New York, I will never forget the impact this visit left on our lives.

The Farris Clan

My "second parents" and family of sisters that I grew up with, next door to the Harbor Lights Marina, our family business: Uncle Joe, Aunt Lucy (aka Lulu), Denise, Pam, and Michele.

The following is compiled from stories told and email correspondence about growing up together as remembered by Denise Horan, Pam Aini, Michele Wendlandt, and Mike Sable, and as recounted through email exchanges between January, 2021 and April, 2021.

Uncle Joe and
Aunt Lucy

My "sister cousins" from the Farris family.
Back: Pam and my wife Maria.
Front: Michele and Denise.
Girls' Weekend!

Denise (Farris) Horan

One of our favorite memories is when the Sables all came to Charlotte to visit us around 1971-72 and our parents went out for dinner and left us with the babysitter, plain Jane. Mike gathered us all together to plan a wild hide-and-seek party in the house. It was so fun, but we wrecked the place and when our parents got home, plain Jane was sitting on the couch crying and told them she could not control us!

Sorry Mike, but they knew you were mad at them for getting a sitter so you got blamed. It was such a great time. We always talked about how much we loved to get together with our cousins. We always asked to visit you at Christmas and to go on vacation with you every year.

It is ironic that we eventually ended up all together more like siblings than cousins. How lucky we are. I still love my visits home to see everyone! And I even love our recent virtual get togethers. At least we can see each other that way!

Pam (Farris) Aini

A fond memory that comes to mind every time we have a big snowfall is the first snow day we had after moving to Hammondsport. Cousin Mike built us the absolute coolest jumps for our sleds!! We flew down the marina driveway over the jump and around a curve especially built so we couldn't fly into the lake. So much fun! I think we bugged Mike every snowfall after that to build it again.

Michele (Farris) Wendlandt

Many of the best memories are the great times we had at the marina, no specific stories, just times spent with family and cousins and having bon fires, listening to Mike play the guitar and Uncle Norman play the fiddle, chasing and catching fireflies, playing hide and seek, running across the marina stones with no shoes on.

Tell people about growing up on the lake in our family "commune" and they are in awe. I'm pretty certain we did not appreciate it as much as kids as we do now, but I do know that we loved having built-in entertainment and friends all the time.

We'll always love and cherish how close we all were and still are. And we already see the tradition renewing itself again in our own children remembering the more recent times that we were together with all the cousins and just how important our family gatherings remain.

Remember when the lake froze, we'd send Michele down the hill on a sled from Aunt Jule's house and right out onto the icy lake. Our mothers used to go nuts!

That is why Michele lived in a life jacket winter, spring, summer and fall! She'd even wear it over her winter coat!

The Philadelphia apartment

The earliest memories I have of visiting my Uncle Joe, Aunt Lucy, and my cousins Denise and Pam (Michele had not been born yet), was when we traveled to see them at their home in the suburbs outside of Philadelphia, Pennsylvania. Actually it was a half house apartment. (Duplex was the term back in the day.)

It was about a two-hour drive from our home in Avenel, New Jersey. I recall as a child I was always nervous when we had to go over two very large bridges to make this trip—the Raritan Bay Parkway Bridge and the Walt Whitman Bridge at the

Delaware River. They seemed so tall and intimidating to me! When we arrived at Lulu and Uncle Joe's I recall going right over to the model that my Uncle Joe had been working on for some months. Apparently we had been there before, but I only remembered that model of the square rigged sailing ship, the Cutty Sark, from our previous visit. It was a very large and complicated scale model of the ship with tiny details down to the cannon balls and the crow's nest basket. Uncle Joe was painting each part and every detail, preparing subassemblies, and adding those to the basic ship's hull and the deck. There was even cordage rigging for the masts to tie and install! I was truly impressed with my uncle's patience and attention to detail and the joy he was getting from slowly watching this ship come to life! What looked to me initially like an impossible project came together over the course of about a year and a half. I learned that setting and then achieving a goal like building this model required a master plan with lots of smaller goals to complete along the way.

We stayed overnight and my dad and Uncle Joe went fishing the next morning in Delaware Bay for porgies. They came home with quite a catch! The duplex dwelling had a basement utility area with a large sink and a block counter where I watched Uncle Joe and my Dad clean and pack the fish for the freezer. All in all it was a great experience for such a little guy just getting introduced to fishing!

Uncle Joe

The Grady White Runabout

Our family made two trips to Charlotte while my Uncle Joe, Aunt Lucy, and my cousins Denise, Pam, and Michele lived there. One year my Uncle Joe trailered his wooden Grady White runabout boat to Lake Norman for a day and to Lake Wylie for another day. Both times we set up for picnics at lakefront parks. The families stayed ashore and played at the playgrounds and my sister Julie and I fished from the shore while Uncle Joe took us all out in smaller groups for lake tours in the boat. Uncle Joe asked me if I wanted to drive the boat! I was about eleven years old at the time and I remember what a thrill it was to get to drive the boat.

The Ferris ladies on the Grady White Runabout

The men and women parted ways on our second visit to Charlotte. Uncle Joe, my dad and I trailered the boat three hours down into South Carolina to a pair of man-made reservoirs created by what is known as the Santee-Cooper Dam. There are two large, shallow lakes, Lakes Marion and Moultrie, connected by a short waterway.

The lakes had only been created and flooded by the dam within the previous twenty years or so. The dam was finally completed to fill the lakes during the spring spawning season for the saltwater striped bass. Apparently a large number of the stripers as we called them were migrating upstream to lay their eggs and got trapped there when the dam was shut. They adapted to the freshwater environment and were able to reproduce, creating what at the time was the only population of freshwater striped bass in the world. That's what we were there to catch—freshwater stripers!

The funny story from this trip? You've got to laugh when you consider that we would all own a marina and a sales dealership for boats and boat services just a few years later! Why laugh? Let me tell you the story.

We were so excited when we arrived early that first morning and checked into our cabin on the canal. We immediately made our way to the bait shop where the launch was located and stocked up on the locally popular equipment for going after the stripers. We launched the boat, parked the car and began driving the boat out through a couple of miles of the canal and then into Lake Marion.

When Uncle Joe tried to throttle up to enter the lake the engine began to speed up, but then bogged down and the boat would only reach maybe five miles an hour or so. Then I looked back at that 40hp Evinrude Lark and noticed the water up over the floor at the back of the boat!

We had forgotten to install the drainplug in the boat before we launched it!

We scrambled to shove the plug into place to keep the boat from sinking and were able to get back to the ramp to drain the boat. How many times, years later, did we laugh watching other "rookie" boaters make the same mistake when launching at our very own marina?

The Marina: The Biggest Decision Our Family Ever Made

Since the mid-1960s it seemed as though whenever the Sable and the Farris families were together, whether for a holiday, a vacation, or even just a short weekend get together, the conversation amongst the adults always came around to the subject of a small business that the two families could operate together. And where Art and Joe could go fishing after work. Every day. (Just kidding about the fishing part! I think...)

My Mom and my Aunt Lucy were sisters who were close in age and had grown up as friends as well as sisters. My Dad and my Uncle Joe were friends from fishing, as well as brothers-in-law. They both lived for their families. They loved fishing, and took us on vacation adventures camping. They enjoyed time in the outdoors and escaping the competition of the workplace.

Art and Joe both had very good jobs in corporate America then, but they robbed them of family time. These were the type of jobs that demanded their own personal commitment to remain within the company's set of values. To dress like the boss did. To maintain a vision of their "rise through the ranks." To always be seeking more responsibility. Not just to "keep up with the Joneses," but to *surpass* the Joneses. That's what their companies wanted from them—to win the rat race, not just run in it! Without exception. But neither of them truly saw that for themselves. Or respected it.

As the only male child among the cousins, and also the eldest of the seven of us, I often found myself with the adults, listening in on the discussions they had about their work, the children, and how life in the sixties in the suburbs was affecting the social and moral growth of the families in a very negative way.

For both Dad and Uncle Joe, in their early thirties at the time, it seemed like they needed to get out of that rat race. NOW. Or to risk getting more entrenched in what truly was a race of rats. To nowhere. While running with the rats they were losing their most important connections with their wives and children.

Aunt Lucy and Mom were very good mothers, but they were getting caught up in societal pressure to fully conform to the suburban housewife model. The social norm. Their children were also suffering through the racial tensions and the violence of the times, in the suburbs where those battles were being waged.

And the peer pressure. Living in Edison, New Jersey we had finally made it to the point where we could afford a second car for Mom. I can actually remember a time when it mattered to me which car Mom drove when she'd drop me off at Scouts or to practice with my band. I wanted to be seen in the newer luxury car, not the old station wagon! How pathetic is that? I was old enough to be affected by the environment where I was being raised in what I now realize was a very negative way. Our parents recognized that. I'm forever grateful to them for getting us out of there!

Mom and Dad and my aunt and uncle, only in their thirties, were loaded with the responsibility of raising families with four and three children respectively. Yet they felt like they needed to strike out on their own, make their own way in the world, and make their own decisions. To take a risk. To take control over their lives once again. To decide for themselves how they would raise their children. Ultimately, they hoped to enjoy their own lives more, while also setting the best examples for their children.

So they grappled with this important decision for several years—*what* to do, and *where* to relocate the two families to run a small business of their own. To escape the rat race, and to remove the children from the racial and social turmoil of the times. Well, they did it! The decision was made in 1972. They took the risk and jumped in. We bought the marina right after "The Flood of '72," Hurricane Agnes. Let's just say the property had been "compromised" by the Hurricane Agnes floodwaters.

Our first season at the Marina

The shop was in awful shape

The flood damage was real

The shoreline was a mess

Early on in our new adventure in the boat business the Corning, New York newspaper reported, "They loved boats and boating, so they bought a marina." A featured human interest story, nothing more. We didn't write the title! Yet we were told that many local people reading the article interpreted it as bragging, as if we were wealthy and we wanted everyone to know it. Wealthy? What were these people thinking!

It wasn't like that at all. Our families had purchased the marina property using every last penny they could squeeze from every hard-earned cent they had. They sold their homes and liquidated every asset. And they mortgaged the marina to the maximum in order to provide the start-up capital needed to open the new business. What initially resulted from that courageous move made by our two families is that we were in jeopardy of losing our homes and everything that we had if we were not successful. That's the way it really was. And we knew it. So we picked up our tools and got to work.

The Boat Shows

We sold a few new boats at several shows over that first winter season, bringing in some dollars to reinvest.

We worked into the spring getting the boatyard in order

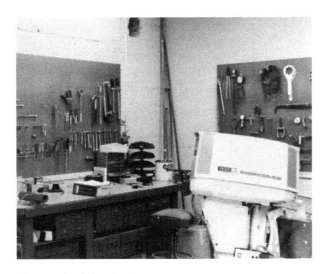

We organized the shop

And we added a small store

We even installed new docks the following spring!

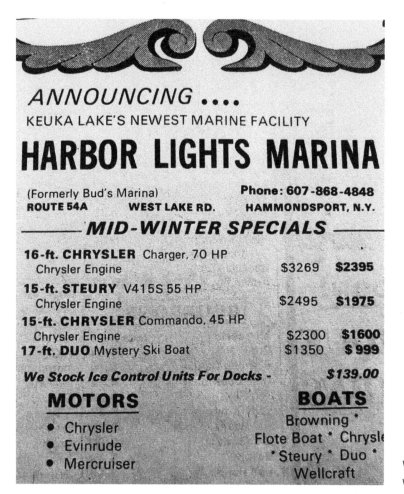

We let people know what we did and what we sold.

It didn't matter how young we children were at this time. That risk we lived under of losing everything and becoming homeless came through loud and clear, believe me. At work at the Marina every day. And at home every evening at the dinner table. The risk of losing everything was palpable (not necessarily palatable). We tasted it in every lick of the thousands of envelopes that we stuffed and sealed for the twice annual newsletter we sent out to our growing list of customers around Keuka Lake.

That bold move our young thirty-something parents made back in 1972 successfully removed us from the racial and social turmoil of the suburbs. Not only that, the move also taught each of us, even the children, about good decision making. About accepting good new ideas from one another. And about the hard work that was necessary to make our new family business venture successful.

And as far as having some of the local people misunderstanding the background of how and why we had come to own the marina? Well, we all got a good lesson in developing a thick skin when it comes to facing off with the uninformed opinions of others.

Introduction to Norman Luck

Circa 1975. By our third season together at Harbor Lights, our two families, the Sables and the Farrises, had settled into the new life we were living as the owners and operators of the Harbor Lights Marina on tranquil Keuka Lake in the center of the Finger Lakes region of West New York. (That's kind of like West Virginia as opposed to Virginia.) We consider ourselves a separate state up here. Certainly NOT related to the likes of New York City and Long Island!

Uncle Joe Farris had lost his father Joe Sr. to a heart attack three years prior. His mom had decided to make a new home for herself as a neighbor to the marina on the lake. She had her son (my Uncle Joe) and his family right next door. We Sables also became part of a new extended family for her.

That Summer of '75 Grandma Farris invited her daughter Diane Luck, her husband Norman, and their four children for a couple of weeks of R & R at the lake. They fell in love with the area and, long story short, they decided not to leave! That's how I met Norman Luck, an original hippie from the sixties.

Norman was a graduate of the Juilliard School of Music and an accomplished pianist and violin player. With his musical ability and the influences of the music of the 1960s, his style and creativity were like nothing I had ever heard before! As an aspiring string musician myself on the guitar, we immediately bonded playing the music of Bob Dylan, Neil Young, Willie Nelson, and other folk and rock artists. And we both loved to improvise! It wasn't but a few years of jamming and working out our favorite covers and we had become an entertaining duo known around the bars and restaurants of Keuka Lake! We'd cruise the lake all summer long playing music under the stars on a boat called The Garvey—some of the best years of my life!

Norman Luck and Mike Sable

Tales from The Garvey

The beloved Garvey was a 1957 example of a twenty-seven-foot butt planked, shallow draft, three-inch-thick solid cedar commercial fishing boat. A very durable lightweight craft that was cheap to build and economical to operate. It was built and worked in Barnegat Bay, New Jersey. It was powered by a flat head six-cylinder Chrysler Crown Block inboard motor with an exhaust stack rising from its central engine bay. It was a truly unique craft to find on the waters of the Finger Lakes. Uncle Joe and I purchased The Garvey in 1978 from the Cole family who had brought the boat from New Jersey to Keuka Lake.

The Garvey had two bunks and a toilet in a forward bunkhouse and down below. It sported a spoked mahogany wheel and a huge brass ship's bell. The unique scent rising up from its hull reminded us of the ocean salts and the clams it had once collected daily.

In its prime, The Garvey had been a hardcore working boat of the bay. It was built by and had belonged to clam diggers. The diggers would fill burlap sacks with the clams they dug out on the mud flats of the bay at low tide. They would hang the bags from dedicated pilings that stood alone out in the mud flats. At high tide when the flats were flooded The Garvey, which only drew three feet of water, would make its way from piling to piling collecting the sacks of clams and bringing them to market.

In retirement The Garvey found a new purpose. Its large open workspace surrounding the engine bay could hold a nice group of people, while the back deck accommodated a cooler full of food and wine, a portable grill, and a large, galvanized tub filled with ice that cried out for a keg of beer! Add Uncle Norman and his fiddle, Aunt Diane, my wife Diane, myself with my guitar, and just a few of our friends. We'd tour the lake from bar to bar, with a restaurant added in here and there, playing for free drinks and picking up new friends!

The Garvey had a spirit of its own, and no doubt found its own way back to the dock on many nights. We'd often find ourselves mesmerized under the northern lights which were prominent in the Finger Lakes region during the late 70s and early 80s. And I remember on many occasions awakening at sunrise to a soothing rocking and the quiet lap of gentle waves from the morning breeze, tucked away safely in the port side bunk, with the boat tied perfectly to the pier. The Garvey had brought us home, tied itself up, and tucked us in safely for the night...

The beloved Garvey

The Trips to Chicago

Uncle Joe and I made what I would later call our annual pilgrimage to Chicago to attend IMTEC — the International Marine Trades Exhibit and Conference, held at the enormous convention center known as McCormick Place. We attended together every year from 1978 through 1983. Those years will put these stories into historical context.

My Uncle and I really had a chance to bond each year for the four days we'd spend together traveling and attending the convention. Besides checking out the next year's competing products against the brands we sold we'd scout out the newest accessories and predict trends for products to stock for the coming summer season.

By this time the families had expanded the business by purchasing the local bar next door known as The Lakeside Hotel. We began with just the bar room. In just two years we had grown into what became the busiest restaurant on Keuka Lake! Mom, Dad, and my aunt and uncle quickly realized just how different running the restaurant was from running the marina. They made a wise decision to stay partners in both establishments, but to have each couple concentrate on just one business apiece. Mom and Dad ran the restaurant and Joe and Lucy the marina. With my background at the marina I stayed on with Uncle Joe and worked there. That's how we ended up at IMTEC each year!

Touring the exhibits by day and meeting with our suppliers was only part of the gig in Chicago each year. Uncle Joe and I really enjoyed our time together at dinner and out on the town afterwards too. As the beef capitol of the world, Chicago was known for great steak. At a restaurant called The Black Hawk we were seated alongside a glass wall, and right on the other side we could see whole sides of beef hanging to dry age at a precise temperature and humidity. They were covered with a greenish gray mold. For each order the restaurant butchers would go in and select a cut of meat, scraping off the mold and sampling the taste, tenderness, and aroma of the meat before choosing. They told us when they were selecting our cuts so we could watch! It was a very entertaining experience. As for the quality of the steak? I was served a cut of prime rib medium-rare and the waiter delivered it *without a knife!* And let me tell you, I didn't need one. After dinner we had cocktails at The Playboy

Club—that company was founded in Chicago. It was an interesting experience, but a little bit too sophisticated for a simple country guy like me!

Beyond that I think we both enjoyed observing the people attending IMTEC from around the globe. Checking out what the people around our ages from other countries were like, and comparing that to what we saw back at home on good ol' Keuka Lake.

I think those Chicago trips are when Uncle Joe first set his sights on the Datsun 280ZX, a sports car from the company now known as Nissan. He kept saying how the styling was so similar to the Jaguar XKE from the 1960s. And wouldn't you know it, a year later Uncle Joe had one parked at the marina! After goading me into learning to alpine ski one winter we'd drive "The Z" over to Bristol Mountain for our winter entertainment. We made quite a pair, the two of us from Pulteney, pulling up in that 280ZX with our skis strapped to the roof, stepping out in our work boots.

My "Secondary" Education

With guidance from Mom, Dad, Aunt Lucy and Uncle Joe

Early in my time in the boat business I became a mechanic. Our boat sales and service business were more than doubling each year in the early and mid 1970s. We needed an extra mechanic at the marina shop in the spring and summer, but not over the winter months. That would be perfect for me while I was in high school! I had started out pumping gas to the boats for a few years at a wage of 50 cents, then 75 cents, and finally $1.00 an hour. I wanted to earn more money than that for a car and to take out a girlfriend when I turned sixteen.

So I went to the guidance office at school and explained my plans. I told them I would have to get a mechanic's certification from the engine and boat manufacturers and that I would need to have time off from school to do that. My grades at school were right in the top of my class, so the guidance office and my teachers had no objections to me taking my schoolwork with me to complete in the evenings at the hotel where I was staying while attending the mechanic certification schools. Our older part-time college age mechanic was going to attend the schools too, so we had the driving arranged. By the time I was seventeen I was a certified mechanic for Chrysler and Evinrude outboards and Mercruiser outdrives. To top it off my regular GPA at high school actually bumped up a notch each time I was away. Must've been because I wasn't out partying with my buddies back home every night!

Working the marina full time with my Uncle Joe after graduating high school, I was the main guy installing the motors, controls, and instruments in our new boats. It was a natural progression. I earned the title of master rigger at age twenty and Uncle Joe had also begun taking me to work the boat shows with him selling the boats and motors.

I was always eager to advance, wanting to learn as much as I could. As a married young adult, Dad and Uncle Joe decided to send me to night school classes in Rochester, New York to attend the series of Dale Carnegie courses entitled "How to Win Friends and Influence People," which included classes in public speaking and remembering important details about people I had just been introduced to. Details like remembering people's names—how important is that when trying to gain the trust and confidence of new acquaintances?

I was well on my way to becoming a "people person," a role that I have continued to fulfill my entire life, no matter what my occupation or official job title was.

I went on to become the sales manager at McPherson Sailing Products in Ithaca, New York where we sold and outfitted 40ft.+ racing yachts. I later owned my own business as a mechanical contractor for construction projects, Eagle Mechanicals. I had a small vineyard and winery that I operated on the West Side Hill overlooking our beloved Keuka Lake. I became a field manager for a large construction management firm, and eventually a founding partner in a construction management company specializing in the construction of schools in New York state.

All of this grew from the examples set for me by my mom and dad, and my aunt and uncle so many years ago, when we all held one another so tightly and with our eyes wide open made that leap of faith and bought the marina!

The Martowitcz Crew

My Dad's older sister, my Aunt Jeannie (Sable) Martowitcz , has four children. Two daughters, Lori and Lynn, were born before I came into the world. They are my only elder cousins on either side of the family. I looked up to them, even though they were only one and two years older than me, to expand my "wilder side!"

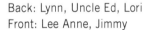

Back: Lynn, Uncle Ed, Lori
Front: Lee Anne, Jimmy

Lynn, Aunt Jeannie, and
Lee Anne, Whitehouse Era

Aunt Jeannie

While I was writing this book, my Aunt Jeannie, my dad's eldest sister, ninety years old at the time, visited me from the Delaware Water Gap in southeast Pennsylvania. My Cousin Lee Anne drove her here and back for a four-hour visit—thank you Lee Anne!

Aunt Jeannie is very sharp at ninety and still has her wits about her. She has been a huge contributor to Stephen's and my efforts to document the Sable/Sabol and Bruzdowski family histories. She always knew more about the family than my dad, and she has a better memory to boot!

Stephen has located distant relatives that we didn't know we had through his genealogical research and Ancestry.com. He has done extraordinary work filling in the extended Sable/Sabol family tree.

I enjoyed trying to work out theories on the migrations of branches of our family throughout Europe before emigrating to America—looking at *why* certain moves may have been made, prompted by social and political changes revealed by regional history. The trades and talents that our ancestors brought from the Old World likely affected their subsequent moves when spreading out from their ports of entry.

One big question Aunt Jeannie cleared up involves the Bruzdowski branch of our family tree. Stephen had originally learned from Ancestry.com that Great Grandfather Joseph Bruzdowski was in fact a widower, having had a first wife who passed away before our Great Grandmother Frances (Czajkowska) Bruzdowski.

The following email exchanges look back on our time spent together as cousins. The Sables were from a more suburban background in the late 1960s, while the Martowitcz family lived a more country lifestyle at the time. Hopefully these memories inspire conversations in our elder years, with our children and grandchildren crowding around to listen to our family stories. As remembered by Lori Serra, Lynn Williams, Lee Heigis, Aunt Jeannie Martowitcz, second cousin Ian Earle, and myself, recounted between January, 2021 and April, 2021.

The Hopelawn Era

My earliest memories of the Martowitcz home were here. "Three cheers for Costa's Ice Cream, the best of them all!" That was the jingle for the company Uncle Ed worked for. Great ice cream too! There were many aquariums in the basement at your Hopelawn New Jersey home which was set up like a man cave bar, with the tanks built into the wall behind the bar. Uncle Ed used to keep each type of fish in a tank with its own kind. There were neons, zebras, angelfish, and guppies, to name a few. Uncle Ed gave me my first aquarium when I was just eight years old and I've had aquariums ever since. Now I have a 210 gallon corner style aquarium with about sixty African cichlids, all but three of them bred right here in this tank. It's right next to my chair in my home in Pulteney. So colorful and so peaceful to watch—your dad had an influence on me! Back in the Hopelawn days I remember "I Love Lucy" and "The Honeymooners" were our favorite programs on TV.

I remember the mosquito trucks spraying insecticide all over town in Hopelawn and Lori following behind on her bike in the smoke!

Visits to Nixon Park

The oldest home that I remember where Pop and Nana Sable lived. The old 1940s Buick and the witches in the barn behind Grandma's house in Nixon Park, Edison are etched in my mind forever! So is Pop's round screen TV in his secret workshop. Trick-or-treating in that neighborhood without getting lost. We actually did that without adult supervision in those days. When we visited on the holidays we'd see Grandma Brudzowski and get her loving but very wet kisses, we'd see Uncle Kaz, second cousins Richie and Bobbie, Uncle Roy and his accordion, and the stack of magazines we found in his apartment closet upstairs in Nixon Park.

Cousin Lori (Martowitcz) Serra

How about the crabbing trips to Buoy 62 to grab the "big ones!" Grampa used to say, "Don't get as many way out here, but the ones you get are extra large." The trip out to the buoy was intimidating and scary to me, but we always trusted that dear man with our lives!

Cousin Lynn (Martowitcz) Williams

Cousin Lee Anne (Martowitcz) Heigis

Forest Lakes Era

Some of our best times were especially at Forest Lakes, the North Jersey country home of our Sable grandparents.

Remember the fishing trips at the Main Beach with Pop-Pop helping us catch a billion sunnies? Remember when Gram would always take us swimming and we used to think it was so cool if we made it to the raft! Remember the Castro convertible bed at Forest Lakes that Gram always made so comfortable for us? Remember walking around the lake and stopping at each beach and playing in the sand? Remember catching fireflies at Stephenville Parkway in Edison and putting them in plastic soda bottles? Remember many years later (twenty-five years?) the time Mike came to Stewarts in Matamoras and Lynn walked right past him not even realizing that it was Mike?

Whitehouse Era

My first experience with chickens was when we visited you all in Whitehouse, New Jersey at your new home! Your dad walked us some distance out into the field to the coop. You told me you guys would eat some of the roosters. When I asked about it you told me your dad would chop off the chicken's head and then they would run around with no head for a while! I remember Uncle Ed was having trouble protecting the chickens from the weasels. Today I have eight hens in a coop attached to the new barn we just finished. They're good girls, and we get eight eggs every day just like clockwork. Playing in the brook and catching crayfish were always highlights for me when we visited. We couldn't do that in Edison because it was too suburban and there just weren't any brooks near our home.

"Gilligan's Island," "Dark Shadows," and "I Dream of Jeannie" would be on the TV. We made several visits to the Round Valley Reservoir while it filled over the course of two years. I found that whole subject very interesting and your dad knew a lot about it. He always answered my questions. And I remember Lori breeding the guinea pigs in the garage—the whole garage was a guinea pig factory! Around this time I first remember hearing the adults talking about opening the Stewart's Root Beer and the restaurant in Branchville.

Lori, Lee Anne, and Lynn with Sneakers' puppies!

Whatever was so fascinating about the cubbyhole spaces under the split-level stairwells at Whitehouse and Forest Lakes? Cool forts! A place where we could talk about things our parents didn't want us talking about. Remember sneaking and talking about the Beatles, the Doors and the Monkees! How about Nancy Sinatra and "These Boots Were Made For Walkin'"? We were sneaky and watched Jim Morrison on "The Ed Sullivan Show." Remember "Rowan and Martin's Laugh-In" and "You bet your sweet Bipee!" Television censorship, mandatory school bussing for integrating the races, Vietnam protests, the 60s in general. Our parents tried to limit what we were exposed to. We got away with plenty though!

Lee Anne told us that the Sables were worried we were listening to the Doors... Now what's so wrong with Jim Morrison and "The Celebration of the Lizard?"

Matamoras and Mill Rift

From Lori

Oh, the memories! How about the time Mike got lost in the dark going from Ray and Lori's log cabin to Grandma's?

I was driving through Corning, New York one day and while allowing a group of pedestrians to cross the street, I recognize Cousin Jim! (He was at college in Mansfield at the time.) And how about my couple of unannounced visits with my Boy Scouts at the Stewart's Restaurant in Matamoras PA? Twenty-five years had flown past—basically 1977-2002!

Those times after our canoe trips from way up north in Callicoon... It took us three days by canoe to get to Port Jervis. Every one of us was ravenous and the soups surely hit the spot! Those were fun moments on busy Sunday lunchtimes when we finally recognized each other!

From Lee Anne

So many memories—no words to express how wonderful those memories are. I am so grateful for all the time we spent fishing in Whitehouse and just how much we always enjoyed each other's company. Yes, there are tears rolling here. They are good tears, happy and reflective of blessed memories. I'm truly grateful to have shared so much growing up together!

Sharing these memories for your book has given us all the opportunity to stop and re-member how blessed and wonderful our lives have been.

Lee Anne looking a bit like her sister Lynn

All families have their share of difficulties and challenges, but we have been fortunate to have shared the love and support through it all from the beautiful folks around us. We are the lucky ones. It is not an exaggeration that we can say half the time our parents never even knew where we were, like the time we wound up in the storm drains to-gether (underneath the whole neighborhood in Edison, New Jersey).

We can always remember our adventurous spirits, and perhaps reading our stories will inspire our children to look up to us and challenge themselves with some amount of adventure and daring growing up as we did.

Later in life we have all benefited from our adventurous spirits! It's what gave us the courage to leave home at the right time and make our lives what they have become today! There certainly were times when we ignored the voice of reason from our parents. The bottom line is that the love and support was truly always there when we needed it. When we sometimes ran low on answers for life's problems, we knew we could find what we were looking for in one another.

It's a wonderful thing that amongst our children, Sylvia and Jenny are friends. They have such a nice relationship. Jenny is very careful about who she lets in, and with Sylvia it was effortless.

Remember the saying, "cousins are like brothers and sisters that just live in different houses."

We were lucky to have grown up in the 70s. It was a wild and crazy time, but we were still really kind and caring human beings, just having a great time being young. Rock on, old hippies!

Lee Anne Heigis

Cousins San Angelo

San Angelo (also written Santangelo) — Uncle Jack, Aunt Barbara, John, Lori, and Jennifer

The following memories of us cousins growing up together were shared by Mike Sable, John, Lori, and Jennifer San Angelo through conversation while visiting and through several email exchanges and text messages sent between August, 2020 and May, 2021.

Here is a popular period of memories going back to the earlier years after the Sables had relocated from Edison, New Jersey to Keuka Lake in the Finger Lakes region of West New York:

> A great memory from the cousins spending time together is when we stayed together and slept above Aunt Julie's restaurant and bar where my dad lived (Uncle Jack at The Lakeside Restaurant). At night, after the bar and restaurant closed, we'd help the crew do the shutdown and cleanup. It was fun finding loose change on the ground.
>
> Every morning we'd go to Aunt Julie's for breakfast with all our cousins. The table overflowed with pancakes, bacon, eggs, orange juice, toast, jam, cereal, fresh fruit and sausage. It was so special to be able to enjoy the family all together in one place eating breakfast and talking. No one ever felt they were too young to sit at the same table. The bond is strong and special, not like many families who barely have time to eat dinner together.
>
> Every day was special. After breakfast, we'd go for a dip in the lake and a boat ride with Lisa or Betty Jean.

Dinner was always at the restaurant and all the cousins pushed tables together to be next to each other. No one was ever left out. Aunt Julie made sure that we stayed close and knew that family is everything.

We also have fond memories of going to Cousin Mike's home. He taught us how he grew grapes for the wineries, the grocery store, and his own wine cellar—Chateau Krivanek Sable. Different grapes are grown for making wine or just for eating, and Mike grew both types—in fact he grew eight varieties!

The winery under his home produced an average of about 250 cases of wine each year from 1992 through 2005.

My cousin John San Angelo and I became close in 1977 when he helped me build a '69 Camaro Z28. The full story is told in Chapter 9, Part 3, "The Mechanic and His Fast Cars." Johnny and I hadn't spent a lot of time together prior to this. We were several years apart in age. But our shared interest with this project formed a bond between us that we share to this day.

Cousin John as a young boy   A similar '69 Camaro Z28

In October of 2019 I was in the process of selling my beloved powerboat, a classic 1988 Correct Craft Barefoot Nautique, with the 454 straight inboard V-8 engine. I had purchased the boat from Cousin John several years before that. John only sold me the boat because he knew I would treat it right!

So when the ALS signaled the end of my boating days, I made sure to let John know that it had gone to the perfect new owner.

Saying goodbye to my Barefoot Nautique

Memories of my Uncle Jack

The first memory I will share is from a visit our family made to the home that Uncle Jack and his family had purchased in South Central New Jersey. I was pretty young, but I seem to remember Grandpa Mike saying Uncle Jack's new house was "on the way to the Pine Barrens." Sounds kind of ominous, don't you think? Like something out of *The Godfather*. The Pine Barrens are near the Jersey shore, where the ground is easy to dig, you know what I mean? (Not that it had anything to do with my Uncle Jack. Just something I remember from that first trip to his home.)

I believe my cousin Jennifer's christening was the occasion for our visit. It was a very nice day, maybe in

My Godfather Uncle Jack and Godmother Aunt Lucy

late spring or early summer. The neighborhood was a newer suburban development with single family homes and the backyard where the picnic party was held had a fence around it, like all of the other homes.

I know there were other children at that picnic too, probably from my Aunt Barbara's side of the family. They must have been because there was a girl there about my age who I didn't know, and through the course of the morning I guess you could say she and I caught each other's eye! Just after noon all of the children were playing in the grass. It was a very nice lawn with a clover here and there, the short type with the little white flowers. I got my first bee sting that afternoon. (Does Aunt Barbara have any Bactine, Mom?)

But there was still hope on the horizon. The younger children were still busy hunting for those elusive lucky four leaf clovers. As for me? I'd rather make my own luck. I tied together a nice bundle of the prettiest flowers from Aunt Barbara's gardens, presented them to the young mystery lady, and introduced myself. I guess I was just born that way. That afternoon went just fine for me!

Uncle Jack had a pretty good sized German shepherd. We Sable siblings had never had a dog of our own, and for the early part of the day we were afraid of the dog. Uncle Jack noticed, and took the time to introduce us to him. Eventually we began to relax once we realized how well trained the dog was. I remember that about my Uncle Jack—he was very gentle with children and he had a big heart with pets.

A few years later Uncle Jack took in a homeless kitten that he named Boots. I don't remember exactly why, but he couldn't keep the cat. He thought about the four of us without a pet, and somehow he talked my mom into letting us keep Boots, who became the first four-legged member of our family. Uncle Jack was also behind our taking in one of our favorite pets—an orange and reddish-brown tiger cat named Rusty that we adopted and brought with us to Hammondsport when we left New Jersey. Yes, my Uncle Jack had a big heart.

Uncle Jack told us about his job as a crane operator and engineer that day. I believe he said he had a certification in rigging to operate the cranes that loaded freight onto ships. I remember my father speaking with Uncle Jack about his work because Dad worked in the containerized shipping industry at SeaLand. They both were talking about the long climb up to the cab at the top of the crane. It took more than twenty minutes just to get into the cab and get ready to work. So all the children gathered around Uncle Jack to hear about his work—and you know the question most of them had about his job, way up in the sky, all by himself for the whole shift? "Uncle Jack, what do you do if you have to go to the potty?"

Years later my uncle was also living up here in the Finger Lakes not far away in Bath, West New York. At the time I needed a car just to get around in while I was working on one of my fast cars. He loaned my wife and I a 1965 Ford Mustang! Nothing really fast or fancy, just good old nostalgia. What a cool car to drive around town, it was like going back in time. Uncle Jack had a soft spot for everyone family. Whenever anyone needed something he would be there for us. He held family above all else.

The Barankovichs

Barankovich — Uncle Ron, Aunt Judy, Ron, John, Melissa, Stephanie.
(Later to include Uncle Jerry and the combined Arzi/Barankovich Family.)

The Barankovich visit at MJ's house shortly after my ALS diagnosis in late 2018.

Memories of Many Visits

Most of the memories I have of my Barankovich cousins when I was a kid were when all three sets of cousins—Martowitcz, Sable, and Barankovich—got together at family events at Nixon Park, Forest Lakes, the Martowitcz's Whitehouse home, and our Edison home.

In this book, Chapter 7, Part 2, "Sable Family Photos," there is a photograph taken at Nixon Park of Grandma Bruzdowski holding her newborn great grandson Ronald Barankovich. I remember that family gathering clearly! I had those memories on my mind when I began working on Chapter 7, and when that photo emerged *later,* well that was proof enough for me that my memory was pretty sharp!

I also remember a visit to Whitehouse, possibly for Cousin Jim's christening. Uncle Ron had recently purchased a small wooden outboard powered runabout. He was in the process of restoring it and had to meet a deadline either to show it or to launch it for some reason. But he absolutely needed to get the waterline painted on his boat *that weekend,* so he trailered the boat to the party and showed it to interested family members, including my dad and Grandpa Sable of course! He then opened the trunk of his car loaded with paint and supplies and proceeded to lay out the masking tape for the tricolored red white and blue waterline. I stayed and watched him for the entire project and asked a lot of questions. He took the time to answer every one of them.

And I have a clear memory of a visit to the Barankovich home in Hopbottom, Pennsylvania. I believe that visit was for a christening for either Melissa or Stephanie. I remember Uncle Ron's brother Uncle Roy playing the accordion. I believe that it was Grandpa Sable got that part of the party started later in the day, with help from a couple of highballs—Uncle Roy was playing polkas and people were dancing dances from the Old Country! I was fascinated with the accordion and how it was like playing a few instruments at once and keeping them all in time with one another.

That day in Hopbottom was also my first close encounter with cows, face to face with only barbed wire between us! I'll admit I was intimidated by the size of the creatures, even though I knew they weren't going to bite me. I felt a little bit embarrassed for being nervous while all of the younger cousins were so relaxed.

My Uncle Ron always seemed to have a special place for me in his heart. His eldest son Ron was several years younger than me, and looking back today, I think he was eagerly anticipating the time when young Ron would reach the age that I was when we lived in Edison, around ten or eleven years old. Back then I had a "hobby room" next to my bedroom, the only two rooms fashioned out of the attic in that Stephenville Parkway ranch house. Uncle Ron thought that it was pretty cool that I had a space of my own in a house full of sisters!

I was at the age when I was building the "Revell" brand glue together plastic model kits, mostly of the 60s muscle cars. Uncle Ron had given me a few of the models as Christmas gifts that year and visited with me several times to see how it was coming along. In the beginning I was excited to see the final projects completed, and couldn't wait to finish them. As a result I'd end up with a completed model pretty much constructed of plain white plastic with the kit decals applied, but entirely lacking the colorful impact and drama of the model pictured on the cover of the box! The parts of those models had of course been painted first before assembling them and applying the decals.

I was explaining this problem to Uncle Ron one day and he told me something very simple about model building, and yet something that is so *profound*. It's almost a philosophy that I've carried with me ever since and applied to how I've lived my entire life. And I can still quote his exact words to this day. He said, "Mike, the fun thing with building a model is in *taking your time*. Take a step back and slow down. Think of how you want the model to look when you are finished. Think about that each and every step of the way. Paint each piece before you add it to the construction. You will not only end up with a better-looking model when you finish. You will have more thoroughly enjoyed the process every step of the way."

Years later I was living in the home that I'd designed and built for my own family and where I was raising my children in Pulteney, New York overlooking Keuka Lake. I glanced out the windows one day and saw a 1970s era Corvette coming up my driveway. I went out to find my Uncle Ron behind the wheel who I had not seen in a number of years! He was touring the area and had stopped to see my mom and dad. When he learned that I lived just a half a mile away in a home that I had designed myself he didn't hesitate to stop by for a visit. I got to show him the home which I was still in the process of completing. In a way, it was a larger version of the models I had built with his guidance. And in fact I was doing exactly as he had recommended years earlier with the model building—taking my time and thinking about how I wanted it to look, and enjoying the entire construction process along the way!

In recent years it had come to my attention that my cousin Ron was working for a company that I often did business with for the school construction projects I was managing. We had discussed this on several occasions at family gatherings. As it happened, I was living out in Cortland, New York at the time managing a rather large school construction project in a small country school district in South Otselic. It didn't occur to me that the Otselic Valley area fell under my cousin Ron's territory in his capacity working on building HVAC systems, including those at the Otselic Valley schools!

One morning I left my office at the job site and headed across the parking area to the school when I saw a gentleman strolling towards me. I looked closely and I thought, "Oh man! Does this guy look like me a couple of years ago or what?" Right about then this huge grin breaks out on his face—it was my cousin Ron Barankovich! He was there working on the building's new HVAC system. It's a small world.

And I'd like to think I was as good looking when I was younger as he was that day strolling across that parking lot. It was awful good to run into him like that—we've laughed about that impromptu meeting every time we see one another!

Look alike? That's me down front, Cousin Ron center back.

Santangelo Theatre

Santangelo (SanAngelo) — Uncle Matt, Aunt Janet, Kim, Heather

Heather Passarelli, the younger of my Uncle Matt's daughters, heard that I was writing this book and volunteered to write a short piece describing her best memories of the times she had spent visiting her Sable cousins at Keuka Lake.

Heather made the most of those visits. Not only was the Keuka Lake destination the home of her Aunt Julie and Uncle Art and her six Sable cousins, it was also the home of her Aunt Lucy and Uncle Joe and three Farris cousins.

But don't stop there! Her Santangelo grandparents, Mike and Rose, lived up here until they passed, as well as Heather's father Matthew. So whenever Heather made a trip up here she always had a jam-packed schedule for visiting.

Why Santangelo Theatre, you may ask? Gotta go back to 1967 or thereabouts to find out where I got that from.Aunt Janet, Uncle Matt, Kim, and Heather lived in the apartment complex overlooking the drive-in theatre on New Dover Road in Edison, New Jersey—free movies on the big screen!

Since she wrote this short piece specially for this spot in the book, it appears basically unchanged:

Looking Back to 1995

> My husband and I were just talking about his first visit to meet my family on our trip to upstate New York. You invited us to your house and showed us the vineyards and shared with us the wine making process. I was so impressed with your knowledge, and you even had young Steven and Sylvia impress us with their knowledge of grapes and wines. You truly made it a memorable experience (the free wine was also a bonus)!
>
> We then went to Lisa's house nearby and she let us crash in her basement (honestly, not the last time she took us in on a visit).

Forever in my heart: My best memories are of the nights (yes, more than one) that I would come from Florida to visit and we would end up back at my Dad's really late. Or should I say til early in the morning? You would play the guitar and would even let me sing along (although you shouldn't have). My Dad would keep the food (who doesn't need meatballs in the middle of the night?) and drinks flowing and you would provide the amazing music. I will treasure these times forever!

All My Love,
Heather Passarelli

Uncle Matt with Mom and Aunt Lucy.

The Golf Course in December

A few years later Uncle Matt set up a really big surprise for his mom and dad. Pop and Nana Santangelo had not seen their son, my Uncle Jack, in over a year and it was the Christmas season. I remember I was living with my Uncle Matt that winter up on Lake Mohawk in North Jersey. Matt and Jack knew how sad their parents were to not see a child of theirs for over a year, and it was the holidays to boot! They had to do something.

So we set up a holiday dinner at Uncle Matt's house which had the lake out front, and with the 10th green of the Lake Mohawk Country Club set just outside the dining room window. It was December and of course most of the fairway and the green were covered in snow. We had secretly brought Jack home from Florida for a holiday surprise for Mike and Rose! And what a setup we had arranged.

We had Jack hide in the basement when Pop and Nana arrived. He could hear what was going on upstairs, and just as we had planned he slipped out the basement door when he heard us sit down at the dining room table for cocktails before dinner.

Jack had taken a golf club and a fluorescent orange golf ball out with him and hid in the trees just off the fairway awaiting a signal from us. Uncle Matt got up from the table and went to the window pointing out to the green. Uncle Jack tossed that bright orange ball onto the green when Matt pointed, just as planned. Uncle Matt blurted out, "Would you look at that! Some idiot is out there playing golf in this weather!" as the ball stopped just short of the flag.

Well you know how much Pop loved golf—he wasn't letting that comment (or the golfer) go undefended. No way! In a flash Pop was up and pressed against the window. "Look Rose, he's got an orange ball!" Of course Nana commented about that "orange ball." (You can imagine if you knew Nana Rose!)

Uncle Matt led Nana to the window too. When the three of them were at the window, just as planned, Uncle Jack strolled out onto the green with the golf club, heading straight for the ball. That's when all the yelling started – joyful yelps of surprise and bewilderment. Nana and Pop just couldn't believe their eyes! One of the best and most heartwarming pranks I've ever witnessed.

That was Uncle Matt! Family forever. No matter what.

My nephew Ryan, my niece Jennifer, Crazy Uncle Matt, my children Stephen and Sylvia

The Gillman and the Garvey

This era coincides with a Carlos Castenada literary gift from my dear friend Jim Zimar: my introduction to "A Separate Reality," speaking both literally and figuratively. Together through a number of winter and summer seasons we let our creative spirits lead us, playing guitar and enjoying fine wine and other libations out on the Keuka Lake ice by winter, and in the summer aboard a mysterious craft known as "The Garvey." The beloved Garvey had a spirit of its own and found its own way back to the dock on many nights. We'd often find ourselves mesmerized by the Gillman under the northern lights which were prominent around the Finger Lakes in the late 70s and early 80s.

I'll always remember Jim's first taste of Gerwurztraminer (Clos Du Bois) at my apartment at the lake with my wife Diane and I—we had just been introduced to the wine ourselves by my friend David Utter upon his return from California. Not a vintage or two later when Jim was working at Bully Hill Vineyards, I sampled his own home crafted wine (White Siebel, if I'm not mistaken) from a cluster of carboys in his closet at his house on The Hill. This was at the start of Jim's illustrious career as a Finger Lakes winemaker, and later he would help his family out with their own business, the Steuben Brewery.

After having been apart and living our own lives for about fifteen years, Jim and I fell right back into our friendship soon after my return to the Hammondsport area from Ithaca. During the years apart we had both become fathers of sons who themselves would later become close friends throughout their school years in Hammondsport. That bond, much like that of their fathers, continues to this day! Frank was the pitcher and Stephen his catcher in the great game of baseball. And just as it has been with their fathers, this tossing of the ball back and forth is a part of the balance that guides us as we navigate this life with our moral and spiritual compass.

From James Zimar, Poetry

February 24, 2021

> Three pre-smog, big-block sedans
> leapfrog along the lake.
> A car with dealer plates.
>
> Snowmobiles and frozen beards on a night
>   of surreal, record cold.
>
> Seeing with clarity inside a hollow tree
>   by single, shared ember's glow.
>
> The same old guitar in the same old case
>   you gave.
>
> The same few, old chords despite
>   your best efforts to teach me to play.
>
> We searched by Garvey for the Gillman
>   and I found my Wife.
>
> We are seldom in proximity, yet
>   somehow always close
>   in a way that does not prioritize
>   wheres and whens.
>
> Thank you for these and more
> Kindred Friend

With Love,

Jim

Chapter 9

Mike Sable:
The Man and His Passions

Passion One:
Mike's Family in Photos

The Wedding Photos

December 27, 2015

The Sables
Standing: Art, Andy, Mike, Maria, Lisa, Be, Julie
Seated: Mother Julia and Father Arthur

Maria's Children
Back: Brian & Dana (Demarest) Haggerty, Mike, Maria, Dave & Sarah (Rice) Demarest
Front: Dave & Sarah's children Ava, Maddie, Clara

Mike's Children
Stephen Sable, Mike, Maria, Sylvia Sable

Meet The Family!

(Above and below) The author with his wife Maria, 2016

The author and wife Maria enjoy a local craft brew, 2019

National Honor Society 1976
Mike Sable (far upper right) at 17 - big hair!

Mike Sable at 21, circa 1980

Mike Sable, 2017
Partner at Campus Construction
Management Group

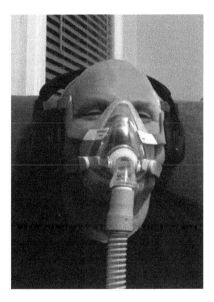

What will they think of next?

Mike's Years

Halloween Costumes

The Gambler playing with the
Queen of Hearts, 2012

The Yellow Flag Lady
and her Cowboy, 2015

Construction Managers
Mike and Maria, 2016

Howard Stern and the Iron Chef, 2013

Osama Bin Laden and
Cat Woman, 2014

Mike as "God" with his "Holy Cowgirl" Maria, 2017

The Pulteney House Gardens, 2020

Steve and Eric preparing the gardens, spring 2020

Sylvia building raised beds

Eric laying Mike's stone steps

Sylvia plants the beds

By summer the gardens were transformed

Fitz guards the harvest

Finally became CEO!

The Sable family often gathered in the garden
for happy hour during covid.

Sylvia harvesting swiss chard

One weekend's harvest

And Maria fills the cupboard!

Eric, Sylvia, Mike, and Maria
Hiking at Bushkill Falls while visiting Milford, Pennsylvania 2016

Sylvia and Eric on their newly purchased farm, 2020

Sylvia and Eric getting married on their farm, July 31, 2021

Sylvia "at home" in the Adirondacks

Eric and Sylvia at the Moulin Rouge in Paris, 2020

Eric and Sylvia at The Louvre

Dreaming up dinner!

Eric Engdahl, so relaxed!

Eric Engdahl with his architecture license

Eric inspects the view from a project in New York City

Sylvia bathing in the Ganges

Sylvia dressed for a prayer ceremony at Radha Kund in India

Dana & Brian's Wedding, August 2019

Mr. and Mrs. Brian & Dana Haggerty

Sylvia, Maria, and Stephen Sable

Maria's daughter Dana
(Demarest) Haggerty

"Hags," our Brian Haggerty

Dave, Courtney, Stephen, Brian (groom), Dana (bride), Sylvia, Eric

Dana & Brian
Finger Lakes Winery Visits, 2017

Harper out for a drive, 2021

Dave & Sarah Demarest and Family

Sarah, Maria, and Dave at Lake Norman, NC, 2016

Ava and mom Sarah share a moment

And Maddie said, "I'll have one of each, please!"

Ava with the biggest tomato plant she ever saw! 2016

Ava at home schooling, 2020

Maddie the gymnast!

Clara all made up! 2020

Clara plays in the Carolina snow, 2021

Serious Bills Fans!

Dave and Sarah with Brandon Spikes

Must be in Charlotte dressed like that!

Sunday is Buffalo Bills Day at the Demarest home!

Granddaughters on Valentine's Day 2021

L-R: Maddie, Ava, and Clara Demarest, Harper Haggerty

Brother Dave and Sister Dana

What a cute child!
Maria, (right), takes a bite of her grandma's pizza

Mike & Maria, Sarah & Dave Demarest, Dana & Brian Haggerty
Heron Hill Winery, 2018

We Love Pets!

Barley

Fitz's baby photo

Fitz standing guard

Sylvia's "Orphan Augie," sleeping like a human!

200-gallon Lake Malawi aquarium

Mixed African Cichlids

8 ISA Brown chickens = 8 eggs a day!

Size matters!

Charter Fishing

Lake Ontario

April 10, 2021

Eric's northern pike

Jenny's brown trout

Danielle's northern pike

Stephen's brown trout

Robert Mench's northern pike
(Stephen & Sylvia's cousin)

Sylvia's northern pike

Passion Two:
The Guitarist

It was the sixties and I was just seven years old, but I already had my eyes on the ladies and needed a way to get their attention. It didn't take long for me to figure it out—pick up an instrument, learn a few hit AM radio songs and that's all it took!

With the long hairstyles, boots, and the Nehru jackets, I'll tell you one thing: it didn't go over well with Mom and Dad.

But the young ladies at school were a different story entirely!

I was introduced to the "New Age" of music in my bedroom after bedtime, which was 8:00 p.m. in the Sable household during the week and 9:00 p.m. on the weekends.

The following stories tell how my friends and I found our path to real music and real musical instruments—real enough to perform a few of the popular songs of the day before an audience of our peers.

Real equipment + real practice = real music!

Over a period of fifty-three years, 1965-2018, I had the pleasure of owning, holding and playing a number of the very best stringed musical instruments. Real, high-quality instruments—not the five and dime lookalikes that can't be tuned or played.

But the truth is that in my youth I, too, was subject to the typical parental experiment of the cheap toy instruments from the five and dime. What to do?

That was how many parents decided whether or not our interest in playing music was serious, or just a passing fancy, before making any real investment in a quality musical instrument. Can't blame them for that.

Staying up late

First order of business was to have a plan—learn about music in a quiet, private location with no one else there to judge.

Learn about the music popular on the radio. The songs our parents liked to listen to while driving. From the radio to albums, Eddy Arnold to the Beatles! Songs that our parents knew and approved of. Particularly the lineups played daily from 9:00 a.m. to 1:00 a.m. on the radio and some of the music accompanying entertainment-oriented television programs.

My own setup

Staying up late after bedtime to familiarize myself with the music my parents listened to became a regular thing for me. Our house in Edison was an elongated ranch with a hallway on one end leading through a series of bathrooms, bedrooms, closets, and anchored by the master bedroom with an en suite master bathroom.

Now for the good part! I was the only male child, living with three sisters and our mom and dad. So for my privacy we took a portion of the walk-up attic and finished the space to create a private bedroom and bathroom for me at the opposite end of the house! Perfect! Was I the spoiled only son or what?

Now for the music

And we can't forget amplification! I certainly could not afford the latest stereophonic equipment in my bedroom as a child. But learning about the recording process from my grandfather and father got me experimenting with what could be done within my budget.

I had collected the old speaker units from televisions, radios, stereos, musical amplifiers, and any speaker I could find in the junkyard, and if they tested out okay, I would mount them in sturdy shoe and cigar boxes.

With a roll of speaker wire supplied by my grandfather strung around my bedroom I was able to enjoy what might have been the first "surround sound" system in my neighborhood. At a relatively low volume, every night I drifted off to sleep to the sounds of Neil Diamond, Paul Mauriat, and Herman's Hermits, with host DJ "Cousin

Brucey" on "77 WABC" out of New York City—very cool for an eight-year-old!

I could stay up as late as I wanted to, listening to AM radio late into the night on my homemade surround sound system. I remember staying awake for live AM radio broadcasts like Herman's Hermits in concert, and even the first fight Cassius Clay (now Muhammad Ali) fought after serving his prison sentence for draft evasion, beating Joe Frazier to become the heavyweight champion of the world.

My friends and I would gather by day and practice, working out the vocal parts to popular songs. We worked hard on learning the lyrics and singing, and we sounded pretty good!

An unexpected bonus came with our efforts—the effect our singing had on the younger children. The minute we began singing as a group of two or three, the wild younger siblings stopped what they were doing and just stared at us, as if hypnotized.

Soon the moms would be humming along and even singing with us. They were plainly enjoying the break from chasing the younger children around, and proud of how the quality of our singing was coming along.

Next? Getting real band equipment

We needed real instruments and gear to play real music. And at ages six to eight with no income of our own, this meant what you'd call kissing up—setting an example of good behavior for our younger siblings.

Any safe, acceptable behavior that we six- to eight-year-old musician wannabes could inspire now became a tool to civilize our monster younger siblings, intended to give our mothers a break. If our efforts were noticed we would be heroes for rescuing our mothers, giving them short breaks from those barbarian infant hoards! And it worked.

Another way to win the good favor of our parents was by helping our dads with chores. Back in the day that meant dealing with the trash, the recycling and yard work. Shoveling snow and keeping the garage clean and in order are time honored classics too.

So my buddies and I had actually conspired to take on some responsibility helping out our mothers and fathers in whatever ways we could. And even though we were really after our parents' help to purchase real musical instruments, we ended up with the bonus of spending a little bit of quality time with Mom and Dad.

Next? When a "gifting holiday" approached, such as a birthday, Hanukkah, Christmas, etc., we'd plan on having a band practice a few weeks before. The moms loved the break from their regular play date schedule with the little monsters. And the real bonus in our eyes? Our parents' memories of how we had been so helpful recently were still fresh in their minds when they went gift shopping!

Band Practice

More like a recital or a performance than a band practice, we'd get together to perform a few hit radio songs. We worked hard correcting our pitch issues when singing them on our own, and we sounded pretty good when we got together. Once we had the vocals down pretty well, we decided to start adding instrumental parts into the mix on our toy plastic instruments. This is when we launched our little plan...

The accompaniment (noise) from the out of tune toy plastic instruments we were playing sounded terrible! The attention from the little kids disappeared, and they started yelping and running around again. The moms couldn't sing along anymore, and Christmas was only a few weeks away.

And then we overheard the moms talking. And it sounded like our plan had worked!

"Mary, don't you think it's time for a real drum set for Tommy? We're getting a new electric guitar for Brian for Christmas. And I heard they've got a guy giving lessons over at that new music shop and he's been doing a great job with David on the piano..."

Yesss! Music lessons included. We were on our way!

Band One: The Gruesome Threesome

Ages 8, 9, and 11

The Gruesome Threesome, our first garage band! 1968
Mike Sable, rhythm guitar, Joe Monek, drums, Anthony Fiorentino, guitar and vocals.

We practiced and performed in Mom and Dad's garage at 30 Stephenville Parkway, Edison, New Jersey. We were nine and ten years old!

Our repertoire included hit rock songs like "Gloria," "In A Gadda Da Vida," "Sunshine My Love," "House of the Rising Sun," "Light My Fire," "Downtown," and "Wipeout."

We just played to an open garage door at first. This was in a 30mph speed limit zone in a residential neighborhood where it seemed as though children lived in every household. It didn't take long for young people our own age to come gather around to listen, and a host of young ladies wanting to dance.

My First Guitars

The first real quality instruments I played as a young boy were of course gifts from my mom and dad.

Later in my life as I became an accomplished guitarist I enjoyed owning a number of truly fine instruments of my own selection. Each of these fine and specialized instruments allowed me accurate introductions into playing the special styles of music that had originally influenced their design.

As my technique developed and my abilities matured my interests in music styles wandered. I always reserved a place in my heart for a sound, a specific pattern of picking and strumming that eventually became a distinct style of my own.

My First Electric Guitar

Mike's first electric guitar: a copy of a Gibson ES 335 by Univox.

My Univox was a quality copy of the semi-acoustic guitar that musicians like Chuck Berry played through the 50s and 60s.

Out to the Garage!

In grade school I acquired an acoustic guitar, an electric guitar, and an amplifier! My buddies were equally successful with guitars, drum sets, and keyboards. Some of these musical instruments and accessories were gifts from our parents, but we began purchasing many items on our own with money from part time jobs, and trading with one another and the music store.

Through high school we all had jobs. I also played lead guitar in our high school jazz band! Most of our continued growth with contemporary music came through jam sessions and playing parties on weekends in the summertime.

Many of the friends I jammed with who also played in the high school jazz band moonlighted with small time local bands on Friday and Saturday nights at the local clubs and bars. We were never questioned about being under eighteen back in the seventies!

Soon there were replacements for the original equipment, more musicians to play with and new styles of music. Playing in the bars and clubs around the Finger Lakes in the summer season came with a collection of new instruments. Soon there were a couple of banjos, a bass guitar, a dobro, a synthesizer, a steel guitar, a saxophone, and lots of new musicians. But I'm getting ahead of myself—let's go back to New Jersey and junior high school, and then we'll cover the move in 1972-73 from Jersey to the Finger Lakes.

Band Two: The Syndicate

Ages 10, 11, a three-piece band

- Mike Sable - guitar and bass
- Brian Segner - guitar and bass
- David Bourne - keyboards and vocals

We practiced at the local Lutheran church. David, our keyboard player, got us in there because his dad was the pastor.

By this point obviously we'd met David who wrote music and played the keyboards—both an upright piano and an electronic keyboard with synthesized sound effects and amplification. David also wrote music, lyrics, and sang.

We were able to continue on briefly without a drummer, since Joe, our drummer had moved outside of the range of his "Mom Mobile" transportation service for bringing his drum kit to practice.

My sense of timing and rhythm covered some of the bass lines, and I also played the role of keeping time with my strumming on the guitar.

We played primarily church sponsored youth group gatherings and events. David's dad was not only pastor of the church but also a scout leader and a youth league baseball and basketball coach. And he held a sponsorship role within the Girl Scouts, who had also chosen to have their meetings and gatherings at the church.

Our repertoire expanded to include Creedence Clearwater Revival, The Rolling Stones, The Moody Blues, and some early Chicago tunes.

Band Three: The Syndicate Plus One

Ages 11, 12, and 13, a four-piece band

- Mike Sable - guitar and bass
- Brian Segner - guitar and bass
- David Bourne - keyboards, bass, and vocals
- Bobby Napoleano - percussion

We practiced in the basement at the home of our newest member, Bobby the drummer, since moving his entire drum kit for each practice wasn't practical. Plus, his basement offered the best sound insulation for the amplified volumes that became necessary with the addition of percussion.

We continued playing events at the Lutheran church, and were able to add local family backyard parties, Bar Mitzvah and Bat Mitzvah celebrations, Eagle Scout awards banquets, junior high school dances and graduation events, etc. We got our gigs by word of mouth through our peers and their parents.

If there were young ladies dancing without partners, we'd cover for a fellow band member. We always had a list of songs that could be performed by three pieces. One by one, we could dance with the girls who had begun to "follow" our performances.

Every young lady our age then had the Carole King album *Tapestry*, and we made sure to add a good portion of those tunes to our song list!

After junior high school, with my move to the Finger Lakes and Brian moving to Tom's River, the group disbanded.

Two of the major influences on my music style with improvisation, and a budding knack toward mastering timing and rhythm, were Ron Parker and Norman Luck.

Ron Parker

I wrote earlier about our parents buying us our first real musical instruments, the first we owned that could actually be tuned and played in specific keys. Instruments that added to the quality of our performances, which previously had been vocal recitals designed to grab the attention of our siblings and parents.

To let them know we were serious about wanting to be musicians, and to learn the skills required, we needed to take lessons and learn how to read music.

After spending a year learning to read music—a true asset—but also struggling along through "Home on the Range"-type songs, one by one we all quit the lessons at the music stores. We could read music and play what we were reading off the sheet music, but we weren't learning the songs we wanted to play.

Our parents were disappointed to say the least. And our progress noticeably stalled.

Then we found the answer in a man named Ron Parker. As advertised, he'd give me a weekly lesson in our own home for just five dollars an hour.

My highly anticipated first lesson with Ron began when a 1940s Indian motorcycle pulled up outside our suburban home. The long blond locks of its helmet-less rider flowed in the breeze, lapping at the acoustic guitar in a soft case strapped to the sissy bar behind the seat.

My mom sounded concerned. This was the summer of 1968, and we were a middle class white suburban Catholic Republican family living in a neighborhood filled with similar families. What would the neighbors think?

But we invited Ron in and he graciously accepted a cup of coffee as we sized each other up. Me, a nine-year-old suburban musician wannabe, and Ron, a seasoned professional musician cruising around the suburbs giving guitar lessons for five dollars an hour—my mom watched intently the entire time.

Ron reached over and took out his instrument, a pretty nice semi acoustic archtop jazz guitar, custom built for a left-handed player. He quickly touched up the tuning and ripped off a couple of impressive licks, left-handed. Then he picked up my right-handed Univox and did the same thing—a quick tuning and a couple of impressive licks, but right-handed!

I asked him about playing right-handed and left-handed equally well. Ron chuckled. He picked up his own left-handed guitar and proceeded to play it upside down (right-handed) just as well, and then did the same with my right-handed built Univox, playing it upside down as if it was a custom built left-hand model.

I can't explain how utterly in awe I was to witness the most amazing display of equal ambidextrous abilities I've ever seen!

Not only that. We would devote half of the lesson time to chromatic scale exercises, and as long as I had practiced and improved with those, his lesson policy would be to ask me what song I wanted to learn to play that week! I distinctly remember answering him, "Who'll Stop the Rain by Creedence Clearwater Revival!"

Ron pulled out a pad of blank staff paper, and as fast as he could write it down the music score was there before me and he said, "Let's jam, Mike!"

And that's the way it went until the winter of 1972–73 when our family prepared to move to the Finger Lakes.

Sometime after I had begun showing marked improvement and enthusiasm with my guitar playing, my mom asked him, "Ron, how can you make a living riding around the suburbs and giving guitar lessons for a mere five dollars an hour?"

Ron's reply surprised us, but with his talent did prove to be the truth. Ron explained that the lessons he was giving were a hobby for him, a source of relaxation by day. He earned his living playing "first chair lead guitar" in the pit orchestra of the original Broadway production of the smash hit musical *Hair*.

Who could have known? A very cool guy and a great influence as I learned to play the guitar.

Norman Luck

The Summer of '75 Grandma Farris invited her daughter Diane Luck, her husband Norman, and their four children for a couple of weeks of R and R at Keuka Lake. They fell in love with the area and, long story short, they decided not to leave! That's how I met Norman Luck, an original hippie from the sixties.

Norman was a graduate of the prestigious Juilliard School of Music and an accomplished pianist and violinist. With his musical ability and the influences of the music of the 1960s, his style and creativity were like nothing I had ever heard before! As an aspiring string musician myself we bonded immediately. We began playing the music of Bob Dylan, Neil Young, Willie Nelson, and other folk and rock artists. And we both loved to improvise! After just a few years of jamming and working out our favorite covers we had become an entertaining duo known around the bars and restaurants of Keuka Lake. We'd cruise the lake all summer long playing music under the stars on a boat called The Garvey. Some of the best years of my life!

Read more about Norman Luck, playing the Finger Lakes, and cruising on the Garvey in Chapter 8.

My Favorite Guitars

1976–1981 Gibson Les Paul Custom Black Beauty with three Gold Humbucking pickups

1977–1981 Martin Sigma Dreadnought

1976–1981 Ovation 12-String

1975–1977 Fender Telecaster

2008–present Palmer Dreadnought
Acoustic Electric

2012–2015 Fender Stratocaster

2013–2015 Alvarez Jumbo Maple
bodied Cutaway

My Favorite Amplifiers

From the 70s and 80s

Fender Dual Reverb 100w Amplifier head (above),
with (2) Ampeg v4 (4x12") bottom cabinets (below)

From 2012 to present day

Bugera Vintage V22

Vox AC15

At the end of my playing days in August of 2018, the three guitars below were the guitars I held dear and still played:

The Martin D–18 "Diane"

I bought the Martin new in 1978. At that time Martin had a few issues with consistent quality. At the House of Guitars in Rochester, New York I had my choice of at least a dozen new D18s. This was one of the best examples of a quality Martin from that era and the primary guitar that I played with Norman Luck. Its rich deep tones (strung medium round) held up well with Norman's violin as we made our way around the Finger Lakes, often playing acoustically. I named the Martin Diane in honor of my first wife who was always there with Norman and I when we played out. Diane had an extraordinary voice and sometimes sang along with us. She was especially known for her rendition of George Gershwin's "Summertime." The Martin was the guitar that I played when I first wrote and performed most of my original music.

The Gretsch Electromatic "Karen"

I purchased the Gretsch for its mellow jazzy tones when strung with medium flatwound strings, as I had adopted a more jazz influenced style at the time. I named the guitar for my second wife Karen, which was fitting because during the early years of our marriage as young parents our tastes in music included Bob James, George Benson, and Earl Klugh. We listened to jazz while strolling the Plantations at Cornell University with our son Stephen in the stroller, and during the many long drives with our children to visit their grandparents in New Jersey and Florida. With its semi-acoustic design it was the perfect instrument to play later in my life when my career in construction management often found me temporarily housed in hotel suites and town houses. I could hear it just fine and the neighbors never knew I was even playing!

The Taylor 918e "Maria"

I purchased the Taylor after nearly forty-eight years of playing because from the moment I held it I made it sing. The richest and cleanest tones I've ever heard came from this concert hall jumbo bodied piece of rosewood perfection! The deep bass and smooth mid tones evoked by my recently matured finger picking styles told me that this was the one. (Much like my choice of Maria for my third wife.) The Taylor was always ready when I felt that special yearning inside to express itself. Yes, I named the Taylor Maria. How could I not?

And of course there's a story to go with these three guitars named for my three wives.

I was living in a town house in Cortland at the time. I also owned and had been playing an Alvarez Jumbo cutaway guitar in those days.

Since it was only a short ride from Cortland to Ithaca I had brought both the Martin and the Gretsch over from my Pulteney house to bring them to Ithaca Guitar Works to have them gone through completely by their factory-trained luthiers and make any necessary repairs or adjustments. When I dropped off the Martin and the Gretsch I couldn't help but look over the wall of guitars for sale.

After I had played quite a few of the nicest guitars on the wall a small crowd had gathered to listen to the music and tones coming from each of the instruments.

I finally got to the Taylor lineup. I noticed the crowd of onlookers had gotten a bit larger, and even the store staff had joined!

(I had been playing with a pickup to this point to amplify the sound because I hadn't yet unveiled my recently mastered finger picking style in public.)

The last guitar left on the wall, the top of the line for the Taylors in many aspects, was the 918e. The 918e is not necessarily designed for being played with a pick. It's not even equipped with a pick guard to protect the face of the instrument.

So I went for it. I chose the song "Sunny," a Bobby Hebb original jazz tune that would put the "concert hall" billing of the 9 Series Taylor to the test. (It was also a song I'd been playing since 1970—seriously.) I put down the pick and stretched out my fingers.

My thumb started picking the bass line. My first, second, and third fingers added the middle rhythm strumming, and I finally completed my arrangement by adding the melody.

The guitar came alive! It excelled, articulating one of my favorite tunes. Sunny. Always a joy to play. Another tune I'd first played along with Ron Parker. Sunny is known as a jazz tune originally written and performed by Bobby Hebb in the 1960s.

Occasionally I looked up and noticed the smiles on the faces in the audience. Not a word was spoken!

I didn't realize my playing in the shop had become an impromptu live performance. Right there in downtown Ithaca at Ithaca Guitar Works no less. A performance for an audience of other guitarists and guitar enthusiasts.

It didn't occur to me what was happening until I had finished the song and looked up to the appreciative applause and smiling faces gathered around asking for more!

Once I held that guitar in my hands and finger picked the opening bass line I was lost in another world. A world where all I needed to do was to think what I wanted to hear. And then my hands held this perfect instrument and began finger picking and finger strumming, while I listened to what I was imagining, in every way exactly how I wanted it to sound. I was in the zone.

Providence, or Personal Projection?

I knew right then that I had to have this Taylor 918e always at my side. I made the necessary arrangements to hold this guitar, putting down a deposit while I got the funds together. I was to return in three weeks to pick up the Martin D18, the Gretsch Electromatic, and the Taylor 918e.

Three weeks later I returned to Ithaca Guitar Works as scheduled to pick up my guitars. I carefully strapped the Taylor 918e in its case into the front passenger seat beside me and strapped the Martin D18 and the Gretsch Electromatic in their cases into place in the two rear seats of my pickup truck.

It might have been my imagination, but I really thought I heard complaints from the back seats about the "new kid on the block" getting to ride shotgun!

I'm sure when I returned to my townhouse in Cortland I really did hear some complaining. You see, I waited for a bit to let the guitars acclimate to the temperature in the room. Then I opened up all four cases (the Alvarez was there as well). But the only guitar I played that evening was the Taylor. The other three were there but could only watch as the Taylor and I really got to know one another!

Passion Three:
The Mechanic and His Fast Cars

The '69 Camaro Z28

I was born a mechanic. I'm a troubleshooting kind of guy, with my own ideas for how to improve the performance of what is readily available to everyone else on the market. And I possess the knowledge, training, technique with tools, and the patience necessary to make any modifications that I could dream up to maximize performance. And imagination I have!

I bought a 1969 Camaro Z28 in 1977, right after graduating high school. It was fast but it needed some work, both mechanical and body work. The original "Hugger Orange" paint was worn, and some metal in the doors and the floor needed replacing. I wanted all metal body work done welded. The engine had been modified, but with me knowing the difference between just adding performance parts, and actually having a workable balance and design strategy when adding those parts—well, I didn't trust that the car and the engine that I had just purchased for a mere $1,500. possessed *either* balance *or* strategy, nor had it been assembled with any true mechanical ability, or even with *safety* in mind.

Besides that, the very first time I took my friend Neil Perkins for a ride on the West Lake Road outside my home we had, shall we say, an "issue." An issue that could have ended in tragedy. The synchros of the transmission were worn, which I knew from having driven the car earlier that day. I went to show Neil the car's acceleration. When I hit second gear at about 7000 rpm the worn synchros, and/or the clutch—who knew anything about the clutch condition? Well, the clutch came apart. It blew through the bell housing and the floor of the car *right between the two of us* and lodged in the ceiling liner *denting the roof of the car!* It could have badly injured or even killed the both of us. My bad for driving that hard without having seen the mechanicals of the car torn down and inspecting them first. That was all I had to see.

With my background and certifications in mechanics from the boat business, it really wasn't much of a jump for me to put my knowledge and skills to work getting this car back in order. Plus I would have the boat repair shop at my disposal soon enough to build an engine and drivetrain—it was going to remain pretty well empty all winter long. Perfect!

In the meantime we had an empty barn across the street that was fine for the disassembly of the car and storage of the parts and the spare car(s). Hunting for the parts would begin *today.*

My young cousin John Santangelo and I pulled out the motor, what was left of the bell housing and clutch components, and the transmission. We stripped out the interior and then sent the car out to have the metal replacement and body work taken care of by a pro.

Then John and I began searching out the parts we needed for a reliable drag racing engine and drivetrain package. John and I were several years apart in age and hadn't spent a lot of time together before this. But our mutual interest in this project formed a bond between us that we share to this day. We both still love nice, well-built machines—boats, bikes, cars, etc. We both still love high performance. And we both still love to see a great project idea come together!

After checking out the classified ads and scouting around the countryside garages I ended up with almost *two whole extra* "parts cars" worth of high-performance parts that I bought mostly from two guys up in Avon who were both Camaro gearheads! I also got quite a few high-performance parts from another guy in Farmington who raced small block stock cars of some sort. The three of these guys each had a collection of Camaro parts for '67-'69 Camaros in their garages, and I purchased quite a bit from each of them over the course of that winter. (In addition to the original car I'd purchased for $1,500. mind you!)

Get a load of this list of what I had accumulated after a couple of months just to start with:

- A 4-bolt main bearing 327 bore (fresh .015 over) Chevy small block.
- A Borg Warner T-10 transmission.
- (2) Muncie M22 close ratio transmissions.
- A pair of nice *aluminum* 202 big valve heads for the 327 small block (minus the entire valve train though).
- A 12 bolt rear axel with 3 decent gear sets - 4.11, 4.88, and 5.13, plus (2) blow-proof bell housings, all from a racing stock car.
- A nice used Edelbrock intake Manifold.
- A high-performance Holley aluminum intake manifold.
- 1 Edelbrock and 2 Holley Carbs with a couple of lift plates.
- A front end clip off of a '69 Z28 in great shape!
- A *rusty* '69 Camaro SS with a "tired" 396 under the hood. (With a decent black interior, all of the exterior hardware and trim—a good spare parts car.)
- A used Z28 hood that I really wanted to have (and needed)!
- 2 *new* '69 Camaro rear quarter panels.
- A Z28 steering box and gear!
- A brand-new billet racing-duty crankshaft for a 283 Chevy. (Combine that with the 327 bore block and there's my "over square" 4 bolt main 302 Chevy!)
- A high mileage '69 Camaro with a totaled front end, but with a decent 350 with good heads and dressed in chrome, a body with a fairly solid floor, and the two decent doors I needed as well.
- An auto trans for the 350.
- Enough decent metal in the floor panels and a great trunk lid between the two cars—all of the body parts I would need.
- A valid VIN registration number! (Not a Z28 VIN number though. Too bad!)

Once we had found and purchased what I wanted and then some, we proceeded with the disassembly and the reassembly of the original engine—I wanted to know what we were *really* working with every step of the way.

Back to the Project

After having the body work completed (and professionally painted by the brother of my high school friend Rich Jaquier), we went to work getting the engine and transmission back into the car. We were excited. But bodywork delays had left us out of sync with the shop availability and the work came to a stall. It was already past April. We had spent a frustrating day at the marina trying to get the engine fired up, and we realized we would have to put the concept of a Z28 Drag Strip Project Car to rest again, but only temporarily.

My affair with the Z28 Strip/Street concept car didn't end with that car not running on that day. More modifications would have been required to improve the handling of that car to the level it should have been. For example: I suspected the car I had originally purchased contained the incorrect steering gear ratio because of its slow steering response. Turns out that original car had begun its life as a Rally Sport model, not as a Z28! The numbers on the car revealed that. Oh well, what did I expect from a car I had purchased for a mere $1,500?

So it was back to the drawing board for authentic Z28 style handling and performance! But this time I got it right. For me at least. And with a non-matching numbers car.

Remember, I still had quite an assortment of parts that I had accumulated.

Below is the story of "A Tale of Two Cars" so to speak, and the creation of my own version of a Z28! Actually by the time I was done more than two cars' worth of parts had gone into the project. I sold what I didn't need, including the original $1,500 car, to help pay for the new parts that I still needed to buy. By the time I was done I had sunk about $7,500 into my own Strip/Street Project Car.

It really didn't matter to me anymore that I hadn't started with an authentic numbers matching Z28, once I had decided to build myself a car specifically for the drag strip. Very little of the car that I ended up with was factory original specification Z28 anyway, except for the correct Z28 steering gear and the handsome tags, stripes, and emblems on this finished car freshly painted with an original Z28 paint color!

See for yourself—
looks like a Z28.

For starters, the engine in this "Z28" sported an awesome 12.5:1 compression ratio! That meant filling up with Sunoco 260 *plus* octane booster please. (Or fuel up at the airport!) And it meant *high revving horsepower!* We set the ride height low with a soft rear suspension for great tire grip. The small block up front helped with the traction too. Avoiding excessive wheel spin was a breeze compared with other cars with this kind of horsepower! Even with *me* driving, this bulletproof machine could run the quarter mile in just over eleven seconds! (And much better than that with a better driver—I really didn't have much experience.)

With the safe redline of this well-balanced package estimated at 10,000 rpm before valve float, the top highway speed was probably about 145 mph! I Got that from a chart, but it's hard to be sure. With modifications to the gears, the speedometer was not accurate any longer anyway.

'69 "Z28" Strip/Street Project.
A well-balanced small block.

Drag Strip Surprise!

The engine in this neck snapper started with the 302 CID small block Chevy, strip modified complete. I built it with the 202 aluminum heads and set up an entirely new valve train for a roller cam with the correct lifters, pushrods, valve springs, and roller rocker arms too—all matched for the highest RPM usable for the overall engine and drive train goals I had in mind. I had the heads milled, the block milled, and added the correct connecting rods and high-performance matched pistons and rings for an awesome 12.5:1 compression ratio. This was a 4 bolt main block. I installed the finest racing duty crankshaft and bearings, and I blueprinted, ported, and balanced the entire engine myself. It was built right.

For the 12-bolt rear end I had the 4.11's (street), the 4.88's (1/4 mile and street), and 5.13 (1/8 mile drag racing only). I kept the rear end gears always ready to swap out! For the transmission I settled on the M22 "Rock Crusher" close ratio 4 speed transmission shifted by Hurst. The M22 was bolted behind a blow-proof bell housing stuffed with an ultra-high-performance clutch and pressure plate. (Let's not forget about that required roll cage I had made up in Guyanoga!)

Under the hood the powerhouse was dolled up with chrome covers and braided stainless hoses. It was *clean and shiny!*

All in all this "Z28" was a real thriller at the strip and on the street! It was always fun to check the oil and the coolant levels when fueling up in town. People would gather around and check out what's under the hood. I met a lot of fellow gearheads that way—I'd do it all again.

Check it out

The '79 Bertone/Lancia

After the Z28 and the drag strip experience, I got interested in the dynamics and the balance of automobile handling. I sold the Z28 and went shopping for a car that I could afford with the design attributes that I consider necessary for excellent handling. Namely, those attributes would be: rack and pinion steering, acceleration (as it affects the cornering performance), braking (and brake cooling), 50/50 weight distribution (ideally mid-engine design), front and rear independent suspension, low unsprung weight, and fully adjustable dampening and recoil at all four wheels.

One day a friend of mine from high school, Mike Heise and I went to Rochester, New York and we stopped at Pacesetter Motors (the Ferrari dealer). I saw a new, 1979, Bertone-bodied, targa topped, mid-engine Italian Fiat powered sports car, in my price range! I just had to have this car. I had never even driven it, but before I knew it that day, I had purchased it! I just knew that with this car's design and credentials I could make it perform exactly the way that I wanted it to. With my ingenuity with making the required modifications, simply leaving it just as I had purchased it was *never* my intention!

My '79 Bertone/Lancia

I drove the car for about 8,000 miles. Although it was the best balanced and the finest handling car I'd ever driven, it was incredibly *slow*. So over the winter of 1981–1982 I took the car apart. I researched what I thought I needed and sourced the parts directly from Italy. I chose to re-power the car with an all-out race engine that I would build myself, modeled after the engines used by Bayless Racing Midwest and several Lancia Beta/Scorpion Racing Team cars that were currently competing in Europe.

So, I needed to replace the stock 1.5L SOHC Fiat X1/9 engine with a more powerful engine of similar size, weight and configuration. I felt that *doubling or even tripling* the stock engine output would be appropriate. Lancia is a part of the Fiat family of Italian cars with a solid racing background and a reputation for having a sizable list of high-performance parts readily available. It would make sense, therefore, to begin my performance upgrade working with the Lancia engine and drivetrain platform. I found a good start by studying the Lancia Scorpion engine designs behind the Beta series of DOHC engines—just what I was looking for! The Scorpion was a slightly larger and more powerful version of the mid-engine Bertone/Fiat x1/9. The more powerful engines and drivetrains share many of the same parts and employ the same installation configurations.

The Lancia Scorpion,
seed of my high-performance engine.

The brand new DOHC 16 valve head prior to my modification.

I started with a new 4 valve per cylinder, DOHC, fully ported, milled aluminum racing head. I took on adding a performance upgraded cam box with a set of 245-degree duration camshafts and the appropriate valve springs. Combined with a matching 2.2L Lancia milled aluminum block that I fitted with racing specification rods, bearings, crankshaft, pistons and rings this lightweight powerhouse sported an 11.2:1 compression ratio. I continued the upgrade by blueprinting and balancing the entire engine. I chose 4 Weber carburetors to feed the fuel for the estimated 200 horsepower through a custom aluminum intake manifold set. The 5-speed transaxle and 15" wheels netted a top speed of 140+ mph at a redline of 9000 rpm! A roll bar cage with cross chest safety belts was also welded in place.

Mike's own version of this custom built 2.2L DOHC 16v all-out Lancia race engine.

The stock rear trunk space had to be sacrificed in order to accommodate the new Italian built "long tube" tuned header and exhaust system.

Note that I also chose a different exhaust camshaft box to rotate the distributor position forward.

The center body/chassis with the racing roll cage welded in.

The modified vehicle was still a great sports car for the street. The trunk up front accommodated the targa roof along with the spare tire and wheel.

The trunk space became a part of the engine compartment. The removal of structural body components necessitated the installation of welded metal tube replicating chassis function. The new design allowed for stiffer suspension adjustments that improved handling performance.

I had a taste for enjoying the best of the best in my reckless young adulthood, and this car was the best of its type and style I could have ever dreamed about driving, much less owning! I thoroughly enjoyed every aspect of this automobile over the course of the next 8,000 miles.

But in keeping with the reckless part of that time of my life, I ended up wrecking this truly beloved and special one of a kind Bertone/Lancia Italian sports car on the West Lake Road at Keuka Lake, going 105 mph.

It was raining, midnight, and there was a spot on the road where water had puddled. I spun out and up a steep bank and struck a utility pole, which acted as a ramp and launched the car through the air. I was told by the Sheriff that did the investigation that the car and I had traveled *270 feet* (90 yards) *AIRBORNE* before coming to rest on the targa roof.

I highly recommend roll bars like the one I installed on that fast little car when I added the race engine. And I recommend the racing harness too! I walked away from that wreck, albeit with a large black and blue "X" across my chest (from the belt harness) which I had for two-and-a-half months afterwards. I was very lucky. (I wonder sometimes if the ALS is payback from God!)

The Research for my own Lancia 2.2L all out racing engine!

The Abarth Prototipo

The engines used in these race cars and the modifications to fit the Bertone X1/9 platform inspired the 2.2L 16 valve DOHC high performance Lancia race car and engine that I built.

The Fiat/Bertone Abarth X1/9 Prototipo

These Abarth race cars were fitted out with all the necessary required competition equipment including racing seatbelts and a roll-bar cage.

The chassis for the race cars was reinforced with welded metal tube and Mario Colucci modified the engine compartment so that it was possible to put in a 2-liter Lancia DOHC Montecarlo unit. I copied what I saw in photos of the race cars for my own design.

Basically I cut out the wall between the engine bay and the trunk (part of the monocoque) and replaced the span with three triangle structures of welded tubes anchored with borrowed Ford Escort engine mounts. The strut mounts to the monocoque were unaffected by this modification. I believe the tubes that replaced the portion of the trunk wall that was removed, along with the roll cage that I had fabricated locally, allowed for both stiffer suspension dampening and recoil. The roll cage certainly stiffened the midsection of the car! So I took advantage of that with stiffer struts all around when I moved up to the heavier 15" wheels and tires.

I also studied what the race cars in Europe and the U.S. were doing with the DOHC engines that powered their cars. In Europe the first engines used in the race cars displaced 1756 cc and had the Abarth DOHC 8 valve cylinder head fed by twin Weber 44 IDFs. They were able to push out over 170 bhp at 8000 rpm.

In the first race, the power delivery to the rear wheels overheated the transmission, and the car ended its race shortly after it started.

After some testing and a few races the cars were equipped with a DOHC 16 valve cylinder head on the 1756cc Abarth Type 232 engine normally mounted in the 124 Abarth Rally Group 4 cars. These engines, also fed by two Weber 44IDF carburetors, were able to push out 190bhp at 8000 rpm.

The transmission also had problems in the car's second outing. During the event, the X 1/9 was so fast that it was fighting for the lead, and on the second stage it broke the third and fourth gears. But on June 29-30, 1974, on just its third outing, the X 1/9 won the 'Rally delle Alpi Orientali.' Clearly, at this time, the X1/9 was capable of competing for the World Rally Championship.

By the time that "tough luck" first season had come to a close the Fiat Abarth X1/9 Prototipo had proven that it was a fast and stable handling competitor but needed some beefing up in the transmission. Not intending to actually race the car I was building, I was willing to avoid spending any more time and money working with the transmission, something that admittedly I had no experience with.

At the Tour de France Abarth entered three cars, each equipped with a different engine: One was an 8 valve Type 232 DOHC 1756cc engine, another a Type 232 DOHC engine also displacing 1756cc but topped with the Abarth 16 valve cylinder head. These both were fed by twin Weber 44 IDFs, and the power outputs ranged from 170 to 190bhp at 8000rpm respectively. The third car was equipped with a 'Type 232G' 16-valve engine of 1839cc fed by Kugelfisher fuel injection and putting out 210 bhp at 8000rpm.

During the race, the (under) 2L X1/9 Prototipo demonstrated that it was a very competitive car and was so fast that it could compete with the Porsche 911 Carrera 3L.

Since I had the capability for the larger 2.2L, I decided to go with the bigger displacement. I also upgraded the intake to (4) Weber 28 carburetors. I played around cautiously with the camshaft timing a bit over the first few hundred miles of break-in. I saw significant improvement in performance at each level of advance. (And I never heard a valve touch a piston!) I figure that my engine must have been producing over 180 bhp, but I didn't have any real effective way of measuring that at the time. I do know that I was more than satisfied with the performance when I declared that stage of my project complete!

The 1968 Pontiac GTO Royal Bobcat

Last up: My 1968 Pontiac GTO that included the optional Royal Bobcat Pontiac 428 cu. in. engine and the Hurst automatic lock out shifter (as an aftermarket kit conversion). Dynamite car! Motor Trend's "Car of The Year" in 1968. And I saw no need to modify this vehicle. A real cruiser, and easy on the eyes to boot!

Performance (Royal 428 cid)

I bought the car from its third owner, in really nice body and mechanical condition, in early summer 1983, after wrecking the Bertone/Lancia Italian sports car.

Back to the '68 GTO! This car was heavy built and *solid,* and could top 150 mph with the tall 3.55 rear axle. And on the right road it reached its top speed in a hurry! It was a good enough highway cruiser for me to get a ticket for "110 in a 55" on the empty newly constructed Route 84, near the Hawley exit in Southeast Pennsylvania.

I was running alongside a 440 cu. in. Barracuda from about the same vintage. The guy in the Barracuda and I kept glancing over at each other with big grins on our faces as we took the cars from 55 to 110 mph in 5 mph increments. I think we'd probably have continued on up to see which one of us was faster if it hadn't been for that state trooper parked and shooting radar on the bridge over the highway at that Hawley exit.

Yes, the speed limit was 55 back then, even on that long, lonely stretch of brand-new smooth highway! I tried to explain to the officer that we were just two guys with classic muscle cars testing them out on a perfectly empty, safe and straight section of highway, but he wasn't hearing any of it. I never did find out what happened with the guy in the Barracuda—he didn't pull over for the trooper. I lost my license for six months for that one! He kept the throttle down and I watched as he disappeared into the distance. But even as fast as he was I still doubt he could outrun the trooper's radio!

'68 Pontiac GTO

Times change, and people change too. These three very special automobiles bore witness to but a single chapter in the long and storied life I have had the blessing of living. For all it's worth, I have no regrets. After owning and driving three awesome automobiles like these, I finally realized that what I really needed was a pickup truck. And not long after that a minivan!

Passion Four:
Wilderness Man

The author "suited up" for a day of portage canoeing through the lakes and swamps of The Canadian Wildlife Preserve "Woodland Caribou" in August of 2004.

I served as the Scoutmaster of BSA Troop 18 in Hammondsport, West New York from 1998 through 2006. During my tenure Troop 18 was blessed with the assistance of several qualified adults holding positions within the troop leadership. Like me, they valued the importance of scouting's outdoors program in both the social and environmentally responsible development of healthy young individuals.

The Boy Scouts of America offers "High Adventures" through their programs at Philmont Scout Ranch, Boundary Waters Canoe Base, Sea Base, and now Space Base. These BSA High Adventures offer physically challenging experiences that embody the core values and interests taught in the scouting program. For the experienced scout who has been successful with rank advancement, High Adventures are a logical next step for experiencing the physical demands and the mental challenges that come with advancing through the scouting program, particularly when combined with filling junior leadership positions available within the troop setting.

Why then did Troop 18 of Hammondsport choose to design their own High Adventures?

Consider that scout who has demonstrated ability with scouting skills. That scout who *has* achieved rank advancement. That scout who *has* demonstrated leadership responsibility within the troop setting. Place that scout in a *real-life* situation where leadership skills would be tested, where making a real-life decision really matters—where others' lives are affected as well.

At the BSA High Adventures camps, BSA provides the guides. That is mandatory. Someone in charge knows and can control the outcome of any situation that arises. No doubt, the BSA High Adventures can be physically demanding. But when measured for the test of using scouting taught skills in real-life situations to make a real difference, the BSA High Adventure experience falls short.

Take Philmont for example. The same trails have been travelled for many years. You can't *really* get lost, so you can't really put your orienteering skills to the test. The animals know what humans are. They know that you are coming, and they know that you have food with you! And just like the bears that live in Adirondack Park, there's nothing natural about how wildlife behaves in those scenes any longer. Nice places to visit, sure. But the pressure is off! There's nothing about the conditions on the BSA Adventures that will actually test the applications of the scouting skills in real-life situations—except maybe the *very* real test of your state of physical fitness.

Now I don't mean to scoff at the Philmont, Boundary Waters, or Sea Base Adventures. Our Troop 18 has sent scouts on all three Adventures and with positive results. The scouts who complete these experiences have a lot to be proud of, and they also enjoyed the experience immensely.

But at the time, our Troop 18 was blessed with a number of scouts who had already achieved significant rank advancements and been elected to junior positions of leadership well before the age of sixteen. Some had recently been to both Philmont and Sea Base.

And these same scouts had concentrated on pursuing merit badges that would allow them to participate in more advanced scouting activities such as canoeing, which required a swimming merit badge in order to participate in at our local scout camps. (Not to mention that our Troop 18 is headquartered on Keuka Lake and we own our own canoes and trailer.)

These same scouts had also pursued first aid, lifesaving, rowing, sailing, pioneering, and orienteering. These scouts had their eyes on the skills necessary to receive the ranks and the awards required to safely participate in the most advanced scouting programs.

And they brought with them a group of equally experienced parents who enthusiastically participated in what amounted to the most active scouting program in our region—Troop 18. (See Chapter 4, "Giving Back to The Community.")

From our perspective, when it came to High Adventure, we were looking for a bit more from our scouts, and a bit more from ourselves, when we chose to challenge ourselves in the real-life environments of our passions.

Our home-built Troop 18 trailer converts from handling up to nine canoes into a mountain bike trailer that will carry up to twenty-six bikes.

Troop 18 High Adventures: A History

Our local Boy Scout Troop 18 of Hammondsport, West New York has had a long history of our own brand of High Adventures.

Every year starting in April or May we could be found conducting the training for that year's High Adventure activities. And every year in August we'd depart for a ten- to fourteen-day outing designed specifically for our most fit and our most experienced scouts, leaders, and parents.

Asserting and exerting ourselves mentally and physically to both explore and excel at our chosen passions were our goals. And we chose to accomplish those goals by putting our scout training, education, and experience to the test by living out those passions in *real-life* settings.

That's the very essence of what drove us to plan our own brand of High Adventures, designed specifically to meet our own exacting standards. Just as in the past these second-generation Troop 18 High Adventures would be scheduled for early August.

Some of the places we visited, and the activities we included between the years 2000 and 2006 were:

Mountain Biking

Across the wilds of the Northern Tier of Pennsylvania, Journey #1. 2000

The Scouts take a photo break on a logging road typical of 90% of The Adventure. We averaged thirty miles per day.

Backpacking and Canoeing

In the Adirondacks in northern New York State, 2001

Mountain Biking

Across the wilds of the Northern Tier of Pennsylvania, Journey #2. 2002.

Canoeing The Lakes

Of The Allagash Wilderness Waterway in north central Maine, 2003

Lunch break on the big lakes of
the Allagash Wilderness Waterway!

Portage Canoeing

Through the northwest section of the Woodland Caribou Wilderness Preserve in
Northern Ontario, Canada at the eastern Manitoba border, 2004

Portage! Hauling the canoes
and all of our equipment after
first locating the next lake, and
then breaking a trail to it!

Mountain Biking

In The Presidential Mountain Range of Northern New Hampshire, 2005

Running riverbeds sometimes allowed us clear passage from point A to point B.

Climbing Mount Washington

In The Presidential Mountain Range of Northern New Hampshire, 2005

The weather that day was perfect as we climbed to the summit of Mount Washington!

Whitewater Canoeing

The Allagash River from North Central Maine to the confluence with the St. John's River in New Brunswick, Canada, 2006

We held our paddles still and silently watched, while the river swept us so closely past this awesome wild animal, completely relaxed and dining on river grass in the untamed Allagash Wilderness.

For all of us, these had to be authentic real-life adventures. We didn't want to experience wildlife that was so used to being around people that their natural life patterns were altered. We wanted to experience real wild animals, in their natural habitat, behaving as they should.

A bald eagle stands guard as we pass beneath his home in the unspoiled wilderness.

A bull moose checks us out in the wooded New Hampshire Presidential Mountain Range.

And we didn't want to be guided. We wanted to face the genuine possibility of really getting lost. We wanted to be challenged to identify exactly where we were, to figure out where we needed to go next and how to get there. We also wanted our scouts to learn that being lost is only a temporary condition, and only lasts until you figure out where you are.

Hmm... According to these hand drawn Ojibway maps... A chuckling Stephen Sable!

Whitewater canoe training for The Allagash at Skinner's Falls during the May high water on the Delaware River.

Our Troop 18 High Adventures were trips of my own design, to places none of us had ever been to before. With my Assistant Scoutmasters and including our most experienced Eagle and Life Scouts we really tested what we had learned through scouting. We pushed it to the maximum, and then some! We witnessed the struggles and the triumphs of our adult leaders and scouts alike while resolving the challenges that arose *together* as a unit. For the duration of these adventures, when it came to applying our skills, the scouts and adults all stood on equal footing.

Part of the fun that came with each High Adventure was the training! Always be prepared. Our Troop 18 required all candidates to complete a rigorous training regimen as an integral part of the group effort for each High Adventure.

We were always prepared. The scouts choosing to participate were among the most qualified in Troop 18 with swimming, lifesaving, first aid, pioneering, and orienteering accolades under their belts. The parents and troop leaders participating in the High Adventures included EMTs, firemen, a local conservation officer, a camp ranger, a Red Cross lifeguard trainer, a registered nurse—people with appropriate training and experience to take on such challenging adventures.

Our District BSA Administration tried to tell us it was a no-go and they couldn't cover us! (I think some of their resistance was because BSA's Regional Council wanted all of our business at their own guided High Adventure Camps.) But when it came down to it, we more than exceeded their high bar for a tour permit. Based on that we ultimately won out over their objections each time and were issued the tour permits, albeit upon appeal.

Yes, our Thunderbird District and the Five Rivers Council definitely looked on Troop 18 and Mike Sable as "The Maverick Troop" led by the "Maverick Scout Master." And we all loved every minute of it! From then on we were in charge of planning and overseeing High Adventures we created for ourselves.

FEATURED HIGH ADVENTURE

Awed and Humbled: The Woodland Caribou Expedition, 2004

Overview

Through some contacts I had made while researching locations where we could see wildlife in its natural habitat, I learned of a dwindling herd of woodland caribou in the central Canadian wilderness. These caribou were losing the battle for their food source—a rare moss species that inhabits specific areas just south of the Arctic Circle.

Woodland caribou
(file photo)

Logging taking place just south of the caribou habitat was driving the whitetail deer population north, and the shy and subordinate woodland caribou could not compete for the moss. This particular battle for survival was taking place in the Central Canadian Wildlife Preserve aptly known as Woodland Caribou. In exchange for being granted the privilege of exploring this untamed wilderness preserve we were asked to record sightings of the elusive and endangered herd for the Canadian wildlife authorities.

This adventure took us into some territory where humans had not traveled in 150 years.

We were humbled. The training we had endured had not fully prepared us for the realities of creating new portage landings, breaking new portage trails through untamed territory, and then portaging our canoes and all of our gear under tough conditions. More often than not, judging from the unspoiled terrain, we were the first explorers passing through these parts in quite some time.

Early in the Adventure:
A typical attempt to find an acceptable portage landing—aka a 12-canoe traffic jam!

First, find a spot to land the canoes. Second, find the next lake. Third, send out the scouts to plan a route. Fourth clear any obstacles. Fifth, record the location of the portage for future use! (Should another group pass this way over the next couple of years they will appreciate a thoughtful previous explorer.) Sixth, put on our dry packs, pickup our canoes and get to the next lake.

We spent a few days thinking about how to make the portages a little more efficient with twelve canoes and twenty-five occupants vying for position. We all shared the same goal, so we knew there had to be a solution.

Often our first landings were intimidating to say the least!

We portaged from lake to lake, crossing islands, steering through wooded areas, and trudging through swamps.

Additionally, the schedule we had so carefully planned did not reflect the time required for these extra "steps" up.

Try carrying a canoe through a wooded area and you'll see why we struggled to complete the route we had originally planned on!

We quickly realized we had vastly underestimated the time and effort it would take to locate the best routes and break new portage trails in this untamed wilderness.

I think "Ojibway Joe" meant to say we'd packed too heavily for what we were about to encounter! He was correct.

I remember when "Ojibway Joe," one of the drivers for our outfitter in Red Lake, dropped us off at our departure point. He looked us and our gear up and down, shook his head a little and said with a grin, "You people all look the same..."

How It Really Was

The Canadian wildlife authorities prohibited the use of soaps, insect repellent, or any kind of activity that could disturb or alter the natural activity of the wildlife. Air traffic overhead was prohibited except by special permission. We packed our bags and completed the adventure strictly according to the rules.

Even the precious moss covering the ground was protected, and rightfully so. I've never seen or felt any moss as beautiful or soft as these rare, slow growing knee-high mosses were. And it was a critical food source for the wildlife, particularly the caribou.

Some of the moss beds were knee deep—we were told it takes fifty years for these moss varieties to grow this high!

The caribou habitat contains the components that allow these rare and slow growing moss species to flourish.

We needed to avoid walking across the growths of these protected species.

Leave No Trace Camping

Everything we brought into that Preserve had to come back out with us or be burned. This was truly a Leave No Trace policy experience! The food products we chose came packaged as self-contained complete MREs (Meals Ready to Eat). We added boiling water, waited ten minutes, ate the meal and then burned the packaging. By journey's end we had accumulated a total of a single five-gallon drywall container of trash from the twenty-five people in our group over twelve days! That is remarkable and a testimony to what can be accomplished with great Leave No Trace planning.

The Woodland Caribou High Adventure unfolded in an isolated location with limited access. No one would come to bail us out if conditions became uncomfortable.

Arrivals at the portage locations involved waiting in line, and for the first few days everyone's patience was tested. Fortunately many of the scouts (like Steve Sable above) had brought along their fishing poles!

Every day we tackled unforeseen obstacles which required us to make continuous adjustments to our overall schedule, ultimately forcing us to consider alternate routes for completing our itinerary. We resolved these issues with input from both the scouts and the adult leadership by making substantial adjustments to the routes we had originally planned on.

Out of the portage lineup delays an even better idea soon evolved. Instead of using this time fishing we could also take advantage to maintain and organize our personal gear. We were all learning an awful lot about managing our time better on this High Adventure. Most importantly, we all learned how to make the most out of challenging conditions and to learn from our mistakes.

Creativity and ingenuity were always welcomed (and often copied) on this adventure!

This was an extremely remote, isolated location with limited access. We carried a satellite radio in case of an emergency, and I even carried antibiotics just in case they were needed.

In every regard, this was the most challenging environment that I have ever experienced.

And what about testing our skills with navigating as a group while constantly being thwarted by unforeseen conditions?

Well, those 150-year-old hand drawn Ojibway Indian maps we carried were often not accurate. And GPS would have been of little assistance anyway with the multitude of topographic anomalies that we encountered.

The US Geological Survey topographic maps were a big help. A quality compass and dead reckoning were the rules of the day, as well as proper training.

We can definitely say that we truly tested our skills while navigating through Woodland Caribou. And I am pleased to report on our scores—when our abilities were measured at the end of this twelve-day High Adventure we had successfully arrived at our rendezvous with the outfitters right on time, and a half hour before Ojibway Joe!

As difficult as this Adventure was at times, I did not want it to end. I always look back to this trip as the time I learned for real that I could use every challenge to make myself stronger and smarter.

The Daily Routine

We had a mandatory morning meeting at breakfast each day to go over the morning trek. We'd also review the overall goals for that day which we had planned out and agreed upon at our evening meeting the night before.

We had twelve canoes total, and each morning we assessed the weather conditions. We purposely split up the canoes by assigning slightly separated routes for each canoe just for the morning treks, using a modified version of the buddy system.

We employed a system of three canoes per "flex Canoe Buddy" System group. We could cover more ground for counting wildlife by spreading the twelve canoes out. The canoes needed to keep one canoe, either the one to the left or the one to the right, in sight at all times. Both canoes in sight at once would be ideal.

This was both safe and practical, considering we might be spread out over a couple of miles as we all proceeded through a maze of islands toward the vicinity of the agreed upon meeting location for lunch. I did say "the vicinity"—believe me, this proved to be a real-life test of all of our best orienting and navigating skills.

We moved out every morning together, singing the song "Rise and Shine" as we broke down camp. We often finished breaking camp just as the song was ending. We were that good!

No slackers—everyone had to have their own compass, their own maps, and the required navigation skills.

We had practiced for three months, and everyone had approved of everyone else's skills. If everyone navigated correctly, we should reconnect at lunch. *Should!*

A clue to the ancient Ojibway shelter locations was found in the Ojibway rock paintings we saw in the caves and in the photo below.

We found evidence of natural caves used in the past for thousands of years as winter shelters by the native Ojibway Indian tribes.

Two dark gray wolves appear to chase the small red caribou towards the edge of a cliff? Or what does it look like to you?

What do I see? Just to the left of Ray's head in the photo an enlarged spike antlered caribou head followed by its body emerges from the rock in tones of gray. (Hint: The darker gray area near Ray's nose becomes the large gray caribou's snout.)

I had read about the Ojibway artists' paintings being formed of pieces that are parts of several different paintings simultaneously.

But it wasn't until I was photo editing for this book that the reality of what I had read just appeared before my eyes. I was adjusting the contrast for the photos and the paintings literally took on a new life as action photos!

Read more about the stories behind the Ojibway pictographs and cliff paintings in a separate publication by the author.

For the afternoon treks we stayed together as a group so we would all have a say in selecting a place to set up camp for the night as we approached our goal for the day.

There was always a lot of discussion about the camp location for the overnight. Would we end up setting camp in a place like this?

Or would we be lucky and find a site like this one?

I remember how difficult it was to find any real soil that would hold a stake. Most of the land area was covered in rock and exposed bedrock which made erecting tents and tarp shelters a real challenge.

We also tried to find trees large enough to haul up bear bags—no small task. We even caught a glimpse of a brown bear running away from us (we were still in our canoes), on what otherwise might have been a great island to set up camp! Since he liked it so well there, we figured we'd better leave that island for him.

This was one of the nicer beaches that we found. But it was still just mid-day. Too bad we couldn't stay!

We'd usually be done paddling by 4:00 p.m. which allowed us a little time for shedding our wet clothing, pulling leeches, tent site decisions and individual tent setup, setting clotheslines and hanging our gear out to dry, etc.

Then it was time for our group commitments. We would gather to set up camp under the direction of the Quartermaster.

We employed a three patrol system. Patrols consisted of five or six scouts each and had been selected during the practice sessions. Patrol units remained the same for the duration of the High Adventure. Patrol leaders answered to the Quartermaster.

Patrol #1 was to gather together the portion of the troop gear that had been carried in each canoe. The Quartermaster reviewed the inventory, organized the gear, and distributed each Patrol's equipment and the food for each scout.

Patrol #1 set up the overnight shelter as a base camp and headquarters for the Quartermaster and the gear, to serve as the location for the evening and morning meetings, and as a location for food and gear distribution.

Patrol #2 was to cut and collect all of the firewood for the overnight fires and kept all of the fires going through the night as required.

Patrol #2 also set up the group campfire areas for cooking, the logs for seating, and placed rock rings to contain the fires.

An overhead structure of some sort would be lashed together from which we hung large pots of water for heating.

Patrol #3 was in charge of the troop water supply and water procurement including the water purification. They pumped water through approved bacteria filters directly into storage containers. They also hung up the canvas bag gravity-fed filters that were suspended from tree limbs and dripped into collection vessels, including the personal water containers of the entire group.

The water patrol kept the water running until all necessary containers had been filled for the next day.

Stephen Sable selects his MRE and fills the burnable packaging with boiling water to prepare his dinner.

The three patrols rotated duties daily. The Senior Patrol Leader chosen for the Adventure acted as Quartermaster and assigned any other special duties to the three patrols as required.

Sunsets at these latitudes were late, leaving time after setting up camp to relax, have dinner, explore, or even do a little fishing.

Pickerel were the first fish that we encountered as we paddled through the lakes at the lower elevations.

Walleye were abundant in the lakes of the middle altitudes.

Lake trout populated the lakes at the higher elevations.

We documented two new lakes on this two-week adventure that weren't even on the maps. They'd been created by beavers and natural events like flooding and erosion in the 150 years since humans had been there.

It took us a few hours to figure out the lake we were paddling on was in fact uncharted!

After perusing the shoreline of the lake we discovered that this lake stood in the center of what should have been a swampy lowland portage leading to Mexican Hat Lake, where we intended to paddle next. In fact we had *not* lost our way! But how and why had we lucked out and paddled across a couple of miles of lake that should have been a long, difficult, swampy portage?

A busy beaver hard at work.

Look closely for the lineup of the beaver dams that had formed this new uncharted lake that we happened upon!

The symmetry in the construction style of each beaver hut in the dam was truly extraordinary! These creatures inherited the knowledge of how to create this lake that nourished them and provided for their habitat. The line of dams at its outlet that formed this lake was a good quarter mile long.

The animals we encountered on this High Adventure didn't know what we were. The two huge brown bears we saw were clearly puzzled by our presence and avoided us, as did the wolves. We never even saw them—they'd just circle our campsite each night howling their wild calls, their tracks plainly visible in the mud around our campsite each morning. That wolfpack dogged us for the entire adventure!

Nor did we ever have a sighting of that shy herd of endangered woodland caribou we had gone there to see. We did have two scouts observe moose on the outskirts of our camping areas. And yet there was still so much more to marvel at that we did see! All we needed to do was to open up our eyes to the gifts in plain sight throughout this journey.

This photo shows the stunted growth of the evergreen trees that is common in the rocky substrate at these harsh latitudes.

The wildflowers emerging from the swamps were varieties we never see back in West New York!

Even the birds were unique to this latitude and climate!

So we never saw anything of that herd of endangered woodland caribou to photograph. Or had they simply eluded our cameras? Low and behold! It was nearly seventeen years later. As I was editing my photographs from Woodland Caribou for this book, I learned one reason why this herd of caribou are described as shy and elusive.

They have great camouflage!

The proof was right there in front of us, probably more times than we even know. I first noticed a large lump of brown color behind the trees in a photo I was editing that looked out of place. I thought it was a boulder at first. Except most of the boulders near the lake shorelines there have a gray color, not brown.

(Enlargement) When I enlarged that area of the photo it was a woodland caribou emerged from the forested background!

The identification was unmistakable. The unique antlers, white face markings, and white cape were a dead giveaway.

The irony in this story is that I took that photo after the entire group had just finished silently paddling the shoreline of a sheltered cove one morning. This was after LaRue McAfee believed he'd heard a "blat" sound that may have been a call from an animal. We'd spent an hour peering into the wooded shoreline hoping to catch a glimpse of a woodland caribou, but to no avail. Or so we thought.

In fact the animal we were looking for was right there, concealed in the brush the whole time! He stood hidden amongst the standing deadwood and the new foliage now returning to an area that had burned several years before. Which reminds me of another miracle of Mother Nature revealed through that morning's photographs.

Woodland caribou (file photo)

We had heard about a rather unconventional practice being followed by the Canadian wildlife authorities regarding dealing with wildfires. They have discovered that the natural occurrence of forest fires in this wilderness habitat is a critical cycle in this established and well-balanced ecosystem. When the fires begin in many of these wilderness areas, they will close the affected zones to human activities and allow the fires to burn without intervention until they are extinguished by natural forces.

They have learned that the unique characteristic of the initial growth of vegetation in the forest after a burn is itself an important factor in the return of the natural cycles of this habitat. The burn is also critical for the health of the mosses that play such an important role in the winter diet of many species, including the woodland caribou.

With that enlightenment I went ahead and took the following photos of the regrowth of forest vegetation after a fire, or burn as they called it up there.

Natural regeneration of the forest vegetation attracts the animals back to feed on specific varieties of flora vital to the animals' health.

The return of the brush to the waters' edge follows the ferns and the grasses, helping prevent erosion.

Many of these varieties only appear in the cycle of growth following a burn, hence the official adherence to the natural "Let It Burn" policy.

The surviving fir and spruce replenish their needles and new trees emerge from the enriched new layer of soils. The young mosses and lichens return to carpet the floor of this miracle, and the forest is renewed! The burn of the fires is but a single sunset in the cycle of life in the forest.

The "Big Storm," stirred by the heat and the light of the day, followed later this evening.

Left to rest peacefully through the night, the light returns once again, blessing the sky with its dawn, a new day!

Those late evenings when the sun was just disappearing at 10:00 p.m. in August, the light left me breathless every time.

And the forests rise up once again!

Chapter 9

Listening to the wolves howling, a sense of peace came over me as I turned in each night. Pondering the challenges that would undoubtedly be awaiting us tomorrow, I drifted off to sleep. My dreams left me feeling blessed just to have been able to appreciate this High Adventure!

The pink and greenish hues of the Northern Lights lit up the sky for many of the nights.

These moments, each moment, became part of my soul, part of my dreams, and my source of inspiration for telling the stories of some of the best adventures of my life.

Passion Five:
Chef Mike

Our Homegrown Tomato Sauce

The beginnings of our fresh home-grown tomato sauce: slice up the tomatoes and put them in a large, thick-bottomed pot after first adding a few tablespoons of olive oil. Don't use a thin-bottomed stock pot, or the tomatoes will stick to the pot and the flavor will be ruined! We add a handful of fresh basil leaves at this time, but that of course is optional.

And Maria fills the cupboard!

Tomatoes simmering on low heat

After cooking and continually stirring for a short time on low heat to break down the tomatoes, the seeds and skins will begin to separate. They can be completely separated and removed now using a crank style mill or food mill/strainer. This will give your sauce a smooth consistency.

Hint: I usually leave the warm broken down tomatoes—juice, skins, seeds and all—covered on the stove with the burner OFF for a couple of hours, even overnight. I believe this allows the natural pectic enzymes in the fruit to extract more of the flavors from the skins of the tomatoes. Then we put the room temperature sauce through the mill.

If you desire a chunkier, more rustic style sauce you can skip the milling step altogether, but beware! The chunkier style sauce is much more prone to sticking to the bottom of the pot when reducing.

Sylvia turns the mill at home!

The smooth milled sauce simmers for several hours on low and is stirred regularly until it reduces to almost half its volume, as you prefer it. Your home will smell fantastic!

For those making a chunky style sauce, the tomatoes can be reduced as much as desired, stirring frequently.

The next step is balancing the sauce with sugar and salt. Allow time when balancing the sauce. Add only small amounts of sugar at a time, stirring and tasting after each addition. This brings out the tomato flavors.

You will know when you have added enough. This will vary from season to season depending on the ripening of the tomatoes.

Follow the same instructions with the salt, a little at a time.

Add seasoning to taste. Follow the same instructions as with the balancing. A little at a time!

If seasoning is to include fresh garlic, onions, celery, carrots, or mushrooms, we suggest a short sauté in olive oil first for these raw ingredients.

Remember that dry seasonings such as basil, parsley, thyme, and oregano are much more potent than their fresh counterparts and should be added to the sauce like the sugar and the salt—a little at a time, stirring and tasting as you go until you get just the right flavor.

There really isn't an exact recipe for seasoning our sauce. We make several styles during the course of the tomato harvest, always keeping in mind that the basic ingredient, the fresh tomatoes, will vary in ripeness and flavor from year to year. We think this is part of what makes creating our fresh tomato sauce such a pleasure.

Enjoy!

Our finished homegrown fresh tomato sauce, milled and ready for seasoning!

Sauce Recipes

Sauce Recipe #1
Sauce Seasoning 101

A General Italian Style Tomato Sauce "Large Batch" Seasoning Guide

Guidelines are based on using a 12 quart thick bottom pot or Dutch oven and using 28 ounce cans of your favorite purée. For larger batches, and for canned or home-grown purée, you can increase or decrease the quantity as desired.

Start with a half cup of quality olive oil, add ten cans (280 ounces) of purée and reduce if necessary to your preferred texture by simmering slowly, stirring regularly. (Optional: add tomato paste in lieu of reducing.) Don't let the sauce stick!

Then balance the tomato sauce with sugar and salt.

Quick Guide for Balancing

The purpose of balancing is to highlight the tomato flavor so that it stands up to the seasoning regimen. The amount of balancing required depends a lot on the product that you start with, and how much seasoning that you plan to add later.

Start the sauce by balancing about 256 ounces (eight quarts) of tomato sauce with two tablespoons of salt. Then adjust the salt after tasting, in several steps, using smaller amounts each time you add.

Once you are satisfied with the salt, then add the sugar, again starting with two tablespoons. Then adjust to taste in several steps, adding only a little at a time.

Now add any optional fresh flavors or vegetable ingredients to the balanced tomato sauce as desired.

Garlic should be finely chopped or even minced, and sautéed ever so lightly in olive oil before adding to the sauce. Do NOT let the garlic brown. The idea is to have the garlic melt into the tomato sauce as it slowly simmers.

Fresh basil leaves cut into fine strips add an extra layer of flavor and complexity when added at this stage. An especially complex flavor profile can be achieved when dry basil is used along with fresh basil, adding the dry seasoning later.

For any other fresh flavors or vegetable additions, I recommend a light sauté in olive oil to soften them to al dente texture and to mellow out the flavors before adding them to the sauce. Some options are: zucchini, eggplant, yellow squash, onion, carrots, green beans, celery, sweet peppers, Italian peppers, roasted garlic (add as a paste), shallots, and leeks.

Next, add the dry seasonings. For an eight-quart batch of sauce, here are some good starting points for various dry seasonings options:

- Basil 1/2 cup
- Parsley 1/4 cup
- Oregano 1/4 cup
- "Italian" 1/2 cup
- Thyme 1/4 cup
- Dried garlic 2 tablespoons
- Dried onion 3 tablespoons
- Rosemary 2 teaspoons
- Sage 2 teaspoons
- Lavender 2 teaspoons
- Red pepper 3 teaspoons
- Whole bay leaves 8

The above amounts are just my suggestions. I suggest starting with half the amounts shown above and adjusting to taste. Just as with the salt and sugar balancing amounts, work with the dry seasoning a little at a time. Be sure to stir well and allow the seasoning to release its flavor before tasting and adding more.

Simmer and stir, simmer and stir... Give it some time.

Enjoy!

P.S. If you make a small "mistake" when balancing or seasoning and add too much of an ingredient, don't despair—add more purée to the sauce and see how much that helps. It happens to the best of us!

Sauce Recipe #2
Rosa's Style Tomato Sauce

You can use store bought canned purée or your own homegrown tomato purée for large or small batches of my ever-popular Rosa's Style sauce that we make every year. I'll share with you the ratio of seasonings and a few chef's tips.

Just as with Sauce Recipe #1, be sure to use a thick-bottomed pot, and use high-quality olive oil. For a 112-ounce batch using four 28-ounce cans of purée, add 1/3 cup olive oil to the pan, and as it heats up add the purée and stir. Never let the sauce stick to the pot. Stir often. When in doubt, stir!

Rosa's sauce is a milled style (smooth) well-seasoned sauce that begins with a good size handful of fresh basil leaves, rinsed and finely chopped. Add the fresh basil to the tomato purée while it is simmering gently and reducing to the desired texture and thickness.

Next after reducing comes balancing the sauce with salt and sugar, as described in Sauce Recipe #1. This step will also remove any bitterness from the use of the fresh basil. The amount of salt and sugar added varies with the character of the tomato purée used—fresh or canned, the brand, etc., and by your own preference. The balancing enhances the tomato flavor so that it holds up with the seasoning and is not overpowered.

Balancing tip

Try setting aside a small sample of the heated and reduced purée in a separate container. Add salt a little at a time, stir, and taste to see what I mean. Then do the same thing with the sugar. Repeat until you taste the pronounced flavor of *tomatoes*! This will give you an insight into how to proceed with the full batch in terms of quantities.

When adding salt and sugar, add a little and taste, repeating until the desired level is reached. Remember, you can always add more, but you can't remove what you have already added!

Another technique we use is to sauté a considerable amount of finely chopped garlic in olive oil. This *must not* be allowed to brown, only to soften. We want the garlic to melt into the sauce shortly after it is added. The garlic is added after the milled sauce is done reducing and after it has been balanced with the desired amount of salt and sugar.

So, now we have the reduced basil tomato sauce, balanced with the salt and sugar, with the sautéed fresh chopped garlic added and brought to cooking temperature while stirring.

The ratio of dried seasonings that we add to Rosa's Sauce are as follows: 4 parts basil, 2 parts parsley, 2 parts oregano, 1 part thyme, 1/4 part rosemary. So if I start with 112 ounces of purée, I would use 1/4 cup of the dry basil, 1/8 cup parsley, and so on.

After adding the seasonings continue to simmer on low. Once the seasoning has been stirred in well and allowed time to give the sauce its flavors, then we taste it.

Add more seasoning (by the same ratio) *a little at a time* until you reach the desired flavor level. You can always add more, but you can't remove what you've already added! For me, the "desired level" means the tomato flavor still plays the leading role.

If you have had Rosa's Sauce then you know it has a little kick to it! Now is when we kick it up a notch with crushed red pepper to taste. Go back and add up the amount of rosemary that you actually used in total. Divide that amount in half, and that's a good starting point for the crushed red pepper. Remember—add, stir, wait, sample, add more as desired.

Enjoy!

Paprikas Recipes

My versions of these paprikas recipes are based upon the "five and five" style Paprikas recipes, popular with both my dad's family, the Bruzdowski branch of the Sable family tree, and the Krivanek family—the family of Karen Krivanek, the mother of my children, Stephen and Sylvia Sable.

The "five and five" style Paprikas uses five pounds of sweet onions and five pounds of the chosen meat being served. My two favorites are based on chicken and pork.

Over the years I have had the opportunity to sample many different and very good Paprikas recipes. But I've always returned to using that "five and five" ratio for the starting point, fine-tuning my own recipes and preparations along the way.

Paprikas Recipe #1
Chicken Paprikas with Tarhana (My Way)

Begin by peeling and chopping pounds five of quality sweet onions. Whatever you can find in season is of course preferred over those that have been stored for extended periods. Set aside.

Add four tablespoons of olive oil and a half stick of unsalted butter to a large Dutch oven (one that you have a cover for), heat up but don't let the oil smoke.

Season five pounds of bone-in, skin-on chicken thighs with salt and pepper. Brown well on medium heat in single layer batches, browning on both sides. Remove and set aside.

Add two more tablespoons of olive oil and the other half stick of butter to the Dutch oven, and then add the onions, stirring to coat them with the oil and butter as you add them. Continue stirring the onions until they begin to soften and become translucent. Cover, reduce heat to low and cook for fifteen or twenty minutes or so.

Remove the cover and stir the onions. They should have reduced enough to add the chicken back to the pot. First stir the reduced onions well to deglaze the inside of the pot.

Add the chicken thighs skin side up in layers and cover. Cook over low heat for two hours covered.

Carefully remove the chicken thighs and set aside in a clean bowl. Try to keep the chicken thighs intact with the bones and skins.

Slowly add sixteen ounces of chicken *stock,* not broth. Stir and increase the heat to medium high. When the onion and the chicken stock sauce begin to bubble continue stirring and allow the liquid to reduce and thicken slightly.

Add one quart of sour cream slowly while stirring and reduce heat to medium low. Add one half pint of heavy cream to sweeten and thicken the sauce.

Add one teaspoon of salt and three tablespoons of quality Hungarian paprika. Stir. The sauce should be a light orange color. Add more paprika to taste if you'd like.

Carefully add the chicken and simmer covered on low while preparing the Tarhana (an egg-based, pellet-shaped Hungarian noodle). For half of the liquid in the Tarhana preparation I like to substitute chicken stock.

Carefully remove the chicken thighs and serve each thigh with a side of Tarhana, adding additional sauce on top as desired.

Enjoy!

Paprikas Recipe #2
Recipe For Pork Shoulder Paprikas With Egg Noodles
Also Known As "New World" Paprikas)

Early Eastern European settlers coming to America prepared this meal with the wild boar that was prolific in the "New World" in the 18th and 19th centuries.

Begin by peeling and chopping five pounds of quality sweet onions. Whatever you can find in season is of course preferred over those that have been stored for extended periods. Set aside.

Add four tablespoons of olive oil and a half stick of unsalted butter to a large Dutch oven (one that you have a cover for), heat up but do not let the oil smoke.

Thoroughly season a boneless five-pound tied pork shoulder (butt) roast with salt and pepper. These roasts are usually purchased tied for even cooking and should remain that way during cooking and until ready to serve. Brown the roast well on all sides on medium heat. Remove from the pot and set aside.

Add two more tablespoons of olive oil and the other half stick of butter to the Dutch oven, and then add the onions, stirring to coat them with the oil and butter as you add them. Continue stirring the onions until they begin to soften and become translucent. Cover, reduce heat to low and cook for fifteen or twenty minutes or so.

Remove the cover and stir the onions. By this point, they should have reduced enough to add the pork shoulder back to the pot. First stir the reduced onions well to deglaze the inside of the pot.

Add the pork and cover. Continue to cook on low heat for three hours.

Carefully remove the pork shoulder and set aside in a clean bowl. Try to keep the tied pork shoulder intact.

Slowly add sixteen ounces of apple cider to the onion sauce while stirring and increase the heat to medium high. When the onion and cider sauce begins to bubble continue stirring and allow the liquid to reduce and thicken slightly.

Add one quart of sour cream slowly while stirring and reduce heat to medium low. Add one half pint of heavy cream to sweeten and thicken the sauce.

Add one teaspoon of salt and three tablespoons of quality Hungarian paprika and stir. The sauce should be a light orange color. Add more paprika to taste if you'd like.

Carefully return the pork to the pot and simmer covered on low while preparing the egg noodles.

Carefully remove the pork shoulder. Slice thick single slice servings and serve each slice over egg noodles, adding additional sauce on top as desired.

Enjoy!

Crockpot Paprikas

With a little bit of creativity both of these Paprikas recipes can be prepared in a Crockpot.

- The meat should be well browned prior to placing over the onions.

- You will need to use a larger size Crockpot.

- You must wait until the meat is finished cooking and remove it from the Crockpot before adding the sour cream, cream, and the seasoning to finish preparing the sauce.

Venison Recipes

Venison Recipe #1
Crockpot Recipe for Venison Roast Braised in Apple Juice
with Pear and Wild Mushroom Salsa

We prefer the hind quarter roast that's shaped like a football. Back strip loin works well also. About two or three pounds.

Set the Crockpot to high, adding a quart of apple juice and warming it through with the lid closed. Then with the lid partly open continue cooking on high until it begins to reduce. This may take some time. If you'd like, you can speed up the reduction process by starting it on the stovetop before moving it to the Crockpot.

We add one teaspoon salt, one sliced large, sweet onion, six cloves of garlic chopped, and let that reduce partly uncovered on high for an hour or so.

While that is reducing, thoroughly salt and pepper and then brown the roast on all sides on the stove top in a tablespoon of olive oil and a quarter stick of unsalted butter. Then set the roast aside.

Then slice the mushroom combo (about a pound of assorted wild mushrooms) and six ripe pears. Set aside.

When the reduction is ready, add the roast to the reduction and cook until it reaches 125 degrees Fahrenheit internal temperature. Be sure to check the temperature with a thermometer about a half hour to an hour after it begins cooking. You don't want this venison overdone!

Remove the roast. Set aside.

Add the sliced pears and the mushrooms. Add 1/2 stick of unsalted butter. Continue cooking the remaining ingredients on high, covered, for fifteen minutes or until the pears begin to soften slightly.

Turn off the Crockpot, slice the roast, and serve over wild rice, covering the roast with the pear and mushroom salsa.

Enjoy!

Venison Recipe #2
Recipe for Venison Liver Snacks (Like Fries)

You might remember that I used to cut the liver into French fry sized strips.

You must remove the tough outer membrane from the liver after cutting the strips or the liver will curl up when cooking.

Take the raw liver strips and marinate them for several days in a quality whole grain mustard with a significant amount of horseradish (prepared with vinegar) added to taste. However spicy you prefer!

Remove the liver strips from the mustard marinade and let them drain through a colander.

Then toss the strips in a good flour.

Fry them up in a high heat oil (like canola) but don't put too many in the pan at once. Fry until golden. Do not overcook.

Put them on a wire rack to drip dry.

You can eat them hot, but I used to keep them in a bowl in the fridge for snacks. It's really good! (Great chew, venison flavor, and seasoning!)

Enjoy!

Venison Recipe #3
Venison Heart Tartare

We start with a whole venison heart, uncooked, fresh or frozen.

Cut the heart in half from top to bottom.

Cut each half in half again from top to bottom.

Trim away all of the string-like attachments that operate the heart valves, including the hardened areas where the strings attach to the heart muscle tissue.

Trim off the fatty white portions, arteries, and veins attached to the tender red muscle tissue from the top area of the heart muscle.

Cut the good tender red heart muscle tissue that remains into strips roughly the thickness of a French fry.

Cut these strips into one-inch lengths approximately.

Marinate these one-inch strips in your favorite vinegar-based salad dressing. (I prefer the Italian balsamic varieties with the venison heart.) About an hour is fine. There's no need to heat or cook the strips—the venison actually cooks itself in the salad dressing!

Spear each piece with a toothpick and serve skewered with a slice of apple or pear and a small slice of cheese, like a mini kabob.

Enjoy!

Chapter 10

Going to School in the 60s and 70s

I'd like to share a few memories from my years spent going to school, from kindergarten all the way through high school. My grandchildren and great-grandchildren might be amazed at how different their world is from the one I grew up in.

While on the one hand I wish I could be more upbeat about my entire experience in the public schools, I nevertheless am satisfied with the person that I have become. We are all formed by the sum of our life lessons.

So even though some of my experiences were not entirely positive, they are a part of the process that made me who I am. And I have come to appreciate that.

I have decided to arrange this story both chronologically and by the school I was attending. So here it goes...

PS 23 Avenel, New Jersey

The first school I attended was Public School 23, from kindergarten, starting in September 1964, through most of second grade. I walked to school and back home each day starting with the first day of kindergarten. It was just over a mile and a half *each way*. I remember how tired I would be on the walk home. And realizing, even at that age, that if I was going to get home I would have to keep walking until I got there. There just wasn't any other way. Mom was home with my three younger siblings and Dad was at work. I guess I learned right then that I had to depend on myself. I also recall looking out of my kindergarten windows and watching the guards with automatic weapons walking atop the walls of what was then the Rahway State Penitentiary. I knew I didn't want to end up there!

Oak Tree Elementary School, Edison, New Jersey

I attended Oak Tree Elementary School for third, fourth, and fifth grades. Another long walk—though at least it was downhill for the 1.9-mile trek home each day. (I just missed the two-mile minimum distance requirement to qualify for a school bus ride.) I remember the odor rising from the floor in the school basement smelled like a sewer. We had to go down there for our air raid drills every week to reach the bomb shelters below. The highlight for me was fifth grade and my teacher, Miss Learni. (What a perfect name!) She was a young single woman and liked to push her boundaries. She encouraged our class, without any assistance from any other class in the school, to raise funds independently as a class to take a field trip by train to Washington DC, which we did! She also had a new 1969 Pontiac Firebird convertible—a very cool and liberated woman for the time. (Even though that Firebird was a dark green!)

Woodbrook Elementary School, Edison, New Jersey

For sixth grade I attended Woodbrook Elementary School in Edison—a brand new school just a half mile from our home. I made new friends, and I was the undefeated pitcher for our sixth grade baseball team! I was also a member of the Safety Patrol. We each wore a badge as we safely directed our younger schoolmates across the busy streets. I was responsible for the busy corner at the base of the street where we lived.

I was also allowed to ride my bike to school which was a very cool perk. Unfortunately, not all of my siblings were as fortunate as I was in winning a spot in the lottery to attend this school in our own neighborhood. I will address that at the end of this section.

John Adams Junior High School, Edison, New Jersey

I attended seventh and eighth grades at John Adams Junior High School during the period of racial integration by school busing. It was rough for my sister Julie and me, and I can only imagine what it must have been like for black students. We didn't use our names on our written assignments—that might lead to prejudice. We were assigned a number to use instead of our name. I remember that my number was 009—how dehumanizing. Athletics too was racially fraught. While this was a painful experience for all, I am thankful for the progress our society has made since those days.

Hammondsport Central School, Hammondsport, New York

I attended Hammondsport Central School for my freshman through senior years of high school. It was like I had died and gone to heaven! I was finally given credit for what I could do in the classroom, on the field, on the stage, and even in gym class. I was actually invited to play on the varsity baseball team as a *freshman!* What a boost for my self-esteem. This school, and moving to Keuka, changed my life forever!

Chapter 11

Commentary for These Times

Caring for Our Planet Earth

While growing up in the 60s our dad taught us how bad the pollution was in our home state of New Jersey.

The four of us children used to literally gag and sometimes even vomit when driving near the Esso/Humble Oil refineries, built upon the precious wetlands, and whenever we drove by the Sherwin Williams Paint factory on Route 287, with their slogan "We Cover The Earth" emblazoned on their water tower.

And there were places Dad used to take us fishing in 1965 that became too polluted for fishing by 1968, for example Lawrence Brook, near New Brunswick, New Jersey.

Thinking we were too young to understand what had caused such widespread pollution, Dad had a story he'd tell us to explain how pollution happens. He said that bad men had "taken their oil tanker trucks down to the rivers and cleaned them out with a hose." A simple way of saying it, but I must admit that I understood! And apparently that story made us all think about pollution a bit.

As a postscript to this, in November 2020 my siblings and I took Mom and Dad up into the mountains near Naples, New York for a drive across the rural mountain-tops. We got a rather dramatic and closeup view of the colossal windmills of the nearby wind farm. Mom and Dad were both impressed and talked about it for days after. We all shared a great view of the future that afternoon.

As I write this in 2020, we have never been as aware of how humans have negatively affected our planet as we are now. And we have never been more capable of doing something about it.

Clean Energy

We are at the advent of the elimination of the use of fossil fuels and replacing them with sustainable energy sources. According to scientists, the United States must end its reliance on fossil fuels and complete the transition to sustainable energy no later than 2040. We need to begin making the necessary changes ourselves today if the planet and the human race are to survive.

Renewable energy sources like wind power, solar power, and hydropower must re-place fossil fuels.

I believe it wise that we begin, right now, to reduce and then eliminate the huge sub-sidies our government gives to the oil, gas, and coal industries.

These funds should be redirected to building new infrastructure for the wind, solar and hydropower industries, creating new jobs and new training for the displaced fossil fuel industry working class.

The automobile manufacturing industries are already poised for the transfer from internal combustion power to electrically powered zero emission vehicles. Several manufacturers already have electrically powered vehicles on the market.

Here we see additional opportunities for repurposing the existing fossil fuel indus-try subsidies. These funds can also be used to retrain displaced auto industry work-ers.

These two examples help us understand how the future can, and should, be better than the present. These ideas represent just a small fraction of what we can do to save our planet.

We should also study how our diets affect our health, and how our food choices affect both global health and the health of our planet.

In both cases, the result of continuing the status quo will lead us to dire consequences for our own health and the health of the planet.

Common principles employed in shifting the direction of government investments to include Earth's health can be used moving forward to solve a multitude of worldwide planetary health issues. The human race is destroying planet Earth—our home, the very habitat that allows our existence.

We must forge ahead with confidence and courage.

We, as Americans, possess the qualities and the resources required to lead the rest of the world in global health and to saving our planet.

Preserving Our Unique Democracy

Unity vs. division in governing poses the single greatest threat to the unique form of democracy we cherish and which has thus far endured in our country.

Nearly 250 years have passed since our founding fathers first conceived these United States of America. They achieved this union by uniting diverse groups of people under a common principle: "Life, liberty, and the pursuit of happiness."

On the opposite end of the spectrum we find nations ruled by autocrats, dictators, and demagogues. Their power comes from dividing diverse groups of people by arousing suspicion and distrust based on their differences (ethnicity, religion, race, wealth, aspirations, etc).

The disaster associated with divided nations starts when a new so-called "leader" emerges, rallying a chosen group of people to usurp the power, wealth, and liberties of the other groups.

This wealth and power then gets transferred exclusively to that leader and to that individual's chosen supporters. This process can, and has, occurred in countless democracies around the world. Many of these countries can no longer identify themselves as democracies.

Where does the United States fit into the world of democracy? Our government has evolved into what today is primarily a two-party system.

On its best days the two parties debate one another, then vote to decide the outcome of the debate, and come back together with mutual respect at the end of the day. This is key to our unique democracy—another debate will surely follow, and our democratic process endures.

On its worst days the two parties approach one another with suspicion and distrust. Accusations ensue and blame is assigned. At the end of a day of finger pointing, one party may go home with all of the spoils. The other party may leave the table with nothing, sowing seeds of suspicion and distrust on both sides of the divide.

At that point democracy is at its weakest. This is where the United States finds itself today—a nation divided.

We have not found ourselves in such a precarious position since the middle of the nineteenth century, and it took a civil war to preserve our democracy back then.

The divisions in our Union today are a product of partisan politics. The customary levels of respect between the parties have been publicly eroded.

As the current lack of respect between the parties has grown, some politicians and overzealous citizens fuel the divide. Both groups insist on labeling some of our cities and states as red or blue, identifying them with one of the two parties.

For God's sake, there are no red or blue states. We are the *United States!*

Until we accept that, we will never resolve the serious issues facing our nation today.

Both red and blue need to see themselves as partners in our democracy. Together they maintain a balance of power. They may be opponents in debate, but they are not enemies!

Politicians and government officials who seek to divide us and refuse to respect and to accept responsibility for the whole of their electorate need to be removed from office.

The Balance of Power

I am not now, nor have I ever been registered with a particular political party. I have always preferred feeling free to vote for candidates of my own choice and not feeling bound by any political ideology or party platform.

I do expect political parties to at least have a platform; one that is debated and clearly presented to voters before any given election.

I prefer to examine the parties, their platforms, and the candidates, for how their plans will impact—or not impact—the political climate at the time of the election. I base my vote on the exercise of that privilege.

I don't fret or worry if the candidate I voted for loses an election. That's been a part of our democracy for nearly 250 years and a key strength of the design of our Constitution.

The balance of power and the swing of the pendulum is why our democracy has survived. It is a steady system, and painfully slow to change at times.

What concerns me the most is any blur of the roles between the three branches of our government. The separation of those roles and powers is prescribed by our Constitution. Maintaining the separate roles and powers of the executive, legislative, and the judicial branches is as sacred to our democracy as the document, our Constitution, is of itself.

Balancing power between the parties, maintaining a balance of power between the branches of our government, and letting the process play out, is exactly why our unique system of democracy has survived. Allowing these critical balances to blur into one another is an open invitation to autocratic rule.

For example, if the executive branch were to use its position in appointing key members of the judicial or the legislative branch exclusively to further the agenda of the executive branch, that would represent a clear violation of the system of checks and balances and the balance of power as prescribed in our Constitution. This would be akin to autocratic rule.

Don't hate the other party. Respectfully debate the other party and expect the same thing from them. That is the way that consensus is reached, one that both sides can, and will, live with.

It doesn't matter how many people voted for the winning candidate and the losing candidate in any election as long as debating with respect leads to a consensus at the end of the governing day. Neither side should expect to hold the upper hand in any debate, or even a percentage of the spoils of that debate, based upon the results of the previous election!

In other words, the upper hand in debate goes to the side that presents the best arguments during that debate, measured debate by debate!

The respectful acceptance of the will of the people, not the will of the party, is at the heart of the success of our unique democracy.

We all must respect those that we disagree with. They are not our enemies. They are our partners in our democracy.

The Media and Disinformation

The pervasive disinformation campaign clouding productive debate in American politics today threatens our effective approach to creating policy to deal with the issues facing us.

- Why must Americans learn to avoid seeking information related to government and politics through traditional media and social media?
- How did the spread of disinformation get its start in the media?
- How are our own citizens and politicians complicit in the spread of disinformation?
- What kind of damage can the acceptance of disinformation cause to our nation?

Disinformation likely began in written journalism when once dependable news sources abandoned their journalistic ethics and added their editorial opinions to their publications.

As for the television news: disinformation may have had its beginning when the first twenty-four hour news channels appeared. Seemingly, when there wasn't enough news to fill their programming needs for twenty-four hours seven days a week, the news channels added the pundits, along with their opinions, to their program lineups.

I believe in both of these cases unwary readers and audiences were caught off guard and began accepting opinions as genuine facts. Substituting opinions for facts is not a good starting point for productive debate, and a terrible starting point for selecting leadership in our democracy.

Social media is the least dependable media source for obtaining accurate and factual information.

It seems that everyone who posts on social media has an agenda. Even the individuals doing the posting don't always realize they are actually promoting their own agendas, not passing along facts. As a result we see components of personal and political agendas seemingly displacing the facts and the truth.

Sadly, even sources within our government can no longer be trusted to tell the truth. Government officials, some occupying the highest offices in our nation, have recently been caught lying to the public.

Government officials have also admitted to forwarding posts that support their own political and personal agendas. We must not allow these government officials to shield themselves behind the excuse that they were "just forwarding posts" when they are confronted and asked to explain the often outrageous content of these posts.

The media, our citizens, and our politicians need to be admonished for intentionally passing along disinformation. The damage this behavior causes is immeasurable for citizens who buy into what these people have to say.

Debate is one of the most important tools we employ in formulating policy in our nation today. Productive debate tests both the popularity and the validity of ideas from both sides of the aisle. This invariably leads to creating more effective policies which also reflect more of the wishes of the whole of the electorate.

Productive debate depends upon our ability to obtain accurate information based on fact. Unfortunately, our pervasive consumption of disinformation is eroding our ability to participate in productive debate.

Moving Forward

People need to be educated about the pervasive amounts of disinformation they are consuming. And we need to learn how to validate our fact-checking. Through accurate fact-checking, we will no longer be completely dependent on the media and public officials for our information.

Do yourselves and our nation a big favor—either be awake and be aware, or denounce social media and cancel your accounts. Cancel them today.

The immutable foray of lies and misinformation being spread on social media today are potent enough to destroy our nation's unity and our democracy. And then our freedoms will disappear at the hands of a dictator.

Fact-Checking 101

Life in the United States today revolves around our constant interaction with the media, and our affinity for media in general. We are also distracted by the media, whether it be by televised, journalistic media, social media, the internet, truly any type of media. The media has the ability to distract us because all forms of media are designed to grab our attention and focus it somewhere else.

Sadly, and ironically, today we find our way of life under an attack being waged through all forms of media.

This attack is being led by big technology in order to strip us of independent thinking. They use our attachment and comfort with media to gain control over us. Simply put: big technology wants to control our lives in order to further its own agenda—$$$. Big tech has been developing the media for years to do just that.

People have knowingly and unknowingly passed along disinformation to further their own agendas since the advent of communication. I believe big tech has engaged this seemingly immutable foray of disinformation as a weapon, using it to addict us to defaulting to the media as our primary source of facts and the truth.

The same disinformation we are addicted to is being filtered for content by big tech using algorithms, reintroduced back through the media, then fed right back to us. It's a cycle of continuous consumption. The more we choose to depend upon the media for facts and truths the more control big tech has over our lives.

This attack of disinformation has also had a crippling impact on our ability to unite as a people against our common enemy. We must find a way to come together to ward off this attempt to strip us of our independent thinking and to control our lives.

Our nation is composed of free-thinking people. We govern ourselves through independent thinking based upon truth and facts, not with disinformation.

Remove the disinformation from our lives and then we can stop big tech.

Fact-check everything! And then verify your own fact-checking. Be sure of the facts before acting upon anything that you see, hear, or learn through the media.

Challenge and verify all details and evidence offered through the media associated with "newsworthy" events, including any details regarding issues surrounding these events.

Refuse to pass along disinformation and that will go a long way to hindering big tech in their attempt to control our lives. Disengage from social media!

> I am the eye in the sky, looking at you
> I can read your mind
> I am the maker of rules, dealing with fools
> I can cheat you blind
>
> *Big Technology*
> *(Actually the Moody Blues)*

Confidence in Our Election Process

Any discussion regarding confidence in our election process must begin with a discussion of how our election process relates to confidence and respect within our unique democracy.

Confidence

Why is confidence in our election process considered to be of paramount importance in preserving our democracy?

We are committed to a unique system of democratic rule in our nation. We decided nearly 250 years ago that our government would be of the people, by the people, and for the people—ALL of the people—no matter their party affiliation.

With that in mind our citizens rely with confidence on holding regularly scheduled fair elections to select our government officials and representatives. Those elected officials will then take an oath to faithfully execute the duties of their office.

Every vote cast in any election, whether local a national, must be cast with the confidence that each vote will become part of the total number of votes compiled for each candidate. Federal, state, and local election laws have historically insured that this has been the case.

We must maintain confidence in our election process and its components. Our systems ensure that our election results will always result in majority rule.

Have confidence in our election process and our election laws! They have flawlessly delivered the required accuracy in our election results for nearly 250 years. The accuracy of our election process is the envy of the free world. Challenges, lawsuits, and recounts are continually pursued in nearly all contests, even today. History has proven no reason to doubt the results.

Confidence in the results of our elections is more than historically justified. Compiling our election results lies in the hands of our duly elected bipartisan officials.

They and their dedicated bipartisan appointees oversee the election processes and observe the tally of the ballots—exactly as our election laws specify.

The dependability and integrity of our election process is one of the reasons our democracy has endured. And, just as important, that integrity has kept the autocrats and dictators at bay. (At least for now.) As long as we maintain confidence in the integrity of our elections those wannabe autocrats and dictators cannot threaten our democracy.

A great deal of confidence is required on the part of the voters. They need to remain confident that the elected officials will govern according to the will of the people.

Those who hold government office must be able to maintain confidence that they will be free of encumbrance to faithfully execute the duties of the office to which they have been elected. Freedom from encumbrance requires that the necessary system of checks and balances separating the legislative, judicial, and executive branches of government remain intact.

Any politician or government official who attempts to blur the lines between these branches of government for any purpose represents a threat to our democracy and needs to be removed from office.

Respect

Additionally, in order to properly serve its citizens, our unique democracy relies upon respect in several areas:

The winning candidates in our elections must respect the role of the citizens in granting them the opportunity to govern at the will of the voters.

Mutual respect is necessary amongst the citizens of our democracy, especially when we disagree. Feeling secure when expressing our opinion and while casting our vote is then guaranteed.

Mutual respect is required between the parties as well as between the candidates while campaigning, transferring power, and later when governing. This allows for meaningful and productive debate throughout the process. Debating with respect is the hallmark and the foundation of our healthy democracy.

Respect for the will of the voters allows for a peaceful transfer of power between parties when the result of an election requires such. Lack of adherence to this concept represents a national security threat and must be dealt with immediately!

Conclusion

Confidence in our election process and mutual respect across the parties are two cornerstones of our democracy. Candidates and government officials whose words and actions do not reflect these values are dangerous for our democracy and dangerous for the unity of the United States of America. When we identify these individuals we must seek to remove them from the process.

The True Patriots?

I have a question for the American people: *what if* what happened at the Capitol Building on January 6, 2021, which was painfully visible to all—what if it was proven to be the work of an international terrorist group like ISIS and not homegrown domestic terrorists?

We'd have no problem seeking out the offenders and prosecuting them to the fullest extent of the law. In fact we'd also seek out the individuals who organized, initiated, and provoked the insurrection and hold them equally responsible.

Why is it, then, that Congress finds it so difficult to walk over to their colleagues (Cruz, Gosar, Hawley, McConnell, McCarthy, Paul, Greene, Lee, Johnson, Roy, Hice, Clyde, etc. to name a few), call them out and hold them accountable for the same heinous actions? How about our deposed President himself? It was their culture of lies and disinformation that provoked these domestic terrorists, calling on them to assemble and take action!

Furthermore, what do we make of:

- Those members of the House and the Senate who, with absolutely no evidence whatsoever, continue to perpetuate "The Big Lie" that the election was somehow "stolen" from Donald Trump?
- Those members of Congress attempting to cause the public to doubt the integrity of our election process?
- Those members of Congress who are presently organizing to restrict access to voting in selected areas in order to influence the outcome of elections to favor their own party?
- Those members of Congress who assist in spreading of disinformation about our election simply because their candidate did not prevail?
- Those members of our Congress and government who are turning their heads, standing there quiet and Idle, and who will not call out their own colleagues as promoters of this culture of lies and disinformation?

These individuals are all members of our government currently busy at work for us, undermining our democracy! Allowed to continue without abatement the influence of this culture will not only persist, it will grow.

Don't be fooled. The enemy of our cherished democracy is often found among our most educated, wealthy, and powerful citizens and government officials. (Rich and smart people can also be associated with the ranks of the very selfish and narcissistic!) And now we can say for sure that these enemies of democracy certainly include white supremacists in their ranks.

This culture of lies and disinformation is currently at war with our cherished democracy. They have been known to recruit people from all walks of life, preying upon those who are most ignorant of how to conduct a valid fact-check. Face it, America: if it's not something that will benefit them, then this culture of lies and disinformation would rather not even know what the TRUTH is, much less inform anyone else!

There is often a wide range of reasoning reflected in the arguments made on the floors of the House and the Senate by both sides that needs to be called out for the voters to base their judgments upon.

We all should be actually listening to or reading the entire unabridged text of debates on the floors in the Houses of Congress. This information is readily accessible for those who seek to make sound judgments. It takes the public's commitment and attention to fight this war against the culture of lies and disinformation. And then it requires everyone's vote.

It further requires that everyone who has the right to vote have equal access to voting. As I write this, access to voting and the restriction of that access is another battle that will be fought in this war very soon. And this is a war—for our freedom from autocrats, and to preserve our cherished democracy.

The Autocrats

I listened to several young citizens of voting age express their opinions about democracy recently, people I consider intelligent and influential amongst their peers. They basically expressed frustration with both the efficacy of and the speed at which our present form of democracy operates.

As a result of that frustration they are tempted to seek an alteration of the unique balance of power that the Constitution of the United States of America affords us.

They believe that furthering the influence of the executive branch of our government would empower our president to more quickly advance the agenda he or she was elected to support. But I believe that such a change would come at great expense.

Such a prospect leaves the door wide open for those voted into power to favor only their own personal and party agendas, while ignoring the wishes of significant portions of the electorate that they also have been sworn to serve.

Former President Donald J. Trump was one autocrat who really tested the resolve of our elected leadership to uphold our constitutionally granted balance of power. He was a dictator in the making if we hadn't voted him out after one term.

Thank God that the Supreme Court came forward with the statement that they made in rejecting the recent arguments put forth by the Texas attorney general in a lawsuit. (The Texas AG brought a lawsuit in December of 2020 against several other states related to those states' election laws, including how the electoral college casts its ballots.)

The result of that lawsuit, had it been successful? The electoral college would have been free to deny the vote of the electorate and cast their ballots as they saw fit to choose our president.

With the ability to affect the appointment of electors, that leaves our presidents with the ability to re-elect themselves, regardless of the will of the voters! (This was exactly Trump's end game once it became apparent that he had lost the 2020 election by 7 million votes!)

Arguments like those from the Texas AG are most dangerous when they challenge the independence of states. That very independence indirectly protects the balance of power between the three branches of our government.

How? Cases like the one described above force the decision making process out from under the potential influence of the legislative and executive branches of government. When required the Supreme Court interprets the constitutionality of the issue in question. This is our system of checks and balances in action!

What is the solution? We've got to impress upon our young leaders and citizens the critical importance of patience in working within our democracy. Give Democracy the time to reach a consensus, employing all three branches of government when required. Then the policies of our government will best reflect the will of the entire electorate.

Postscript

Shortly after completing this manuscript, Mike's health further deteriorated as his ALS progressed and he became no longer able to write. It might be observed that it was no coincidence this occurred only after he had accomplished his goal of recording his Legacy in this book. He passed away peacefully in his home on May 23, 2022, surrounded by the family that he loved, to the sound of his guitar.

He lived a long and storied life.

Printed in the USA
CPSIA information can be obtained
at www.ICGtesting.com
LVHW070742161023
761152LV00029B/29

9 781087 963693